STRAIGHT
FROM
THE TOP

———

THE TRUTH ABOUT

AIR CANADA

ROBERT MILTON

with JOHN LAWRENCE REYNOLDS

STRAIGHT

FROM THE

TOP

GREYSTONE BOOKS

Douglas & McIntyre Publishing Group

Vancouver/Toronto

Greystone Books
A division of Douglas & McIntyre Ltd.
2323 Quebec Street, Suite 201
Vancouver, British Columbia
Canada V5T 4S7
www.greystonebooks.com

National Library of Canada Cataloguing in Publication Data
Milton, Robert, 1960–
Straight from the top : the truth about Air Canada /
Robert Milton ; with John Lawrence Reynolds.

Includes index.

ISBN 1-55365-051-4

1. Milton, Robert, 1960–. 2. Air Canada—History.
3. Airlines—Canada—History. I. Reynolds, John Lawrence. II. Title.
HE9815.A93M54 2004   387.7'06'571   C2004-902542-2

Editing by Nancy Flight
Copy editing by John Eerkes-Medrano
Jacket and text design by Peter Cocking
Jacket photograph by Brian Losito
Printed and bound in Canada by Friesens
Printed on acid-free paper that is forest friendly (100% post-
consumer recycled paper) and has been processed chlorine free.

We gratefully acknowledge the financial support of the Canada
Council for the Arts, the British Columbia Arts Council, and
the Government of Canada through the Book Publishing Industry
Development Program (BPIDP) for our publishing activities.

In this book, I talk about how much I admire Dreams Take Flight, a non-profit organization made up of volunteers from the Air Canada family in Canada and the United States. Teams in Vancouver, Calgary, Edmonton, Winnipeg, Toronto, Ottawa, Montreal, Halifax, Los Angeles, and Tampa each organize the trip of a lifetime for physically, mentally, or socially challenged children. The destination—Walt Disney World, Florida, or Disneyland, California—for a day. Air Canada donates the aircraft, and the employees do the rest. The adventure is supported through fundraising efforts, corporate sponsorships, and public donations. All royalties I receive from the sale of this book will be donated to Dreams Take Flight.

ROBERT MILTON

CONTENTS

PREFACE

IT IS hard for me to believe that I am in my thirteenth year at Air Canada and have entered my sixth year as CEO of what is truly one of the world's great airlines. I have read that the average tenure of a CEO at a major corporation is three years, and for a major airline today, it is perhaps half that—so I guess I'm helping to average the numbers up. In my years as CEO, we have had to deal with a hostile takeover attempt, the high-tech meltdown, September 11, the Iraq war, SARS, and, most recently, oil prices approaching $50 a barrel. When I was growing up, I used to dream of running an airline one day. I had no idea that my dream might become a nightmare.

There has been much to keep me going, however, in the face of a total lack of support from Ottawa, unrelenting media criticism, and generally intransigent unions. The first was that I knew I had called the sea change correctly. In employee messages, press interviews, and any forum in which I could get my voice heard, I warned that the threat of the low-cost carriers was real and that we had to adapt quickly. Our North

American competitors were in denial, the then minister of transport advised us to remain a full-service carrier, and our unions screamed that I was just trying to hurt them and our employees. Change is tough, and although events like September 11 and SARS made it impossible to adapt smoothly, I am pleased that we have led so much of the world's airline industry in the drive to transform.

While I am not one to quote Machiavelli, I feel that the following words, which were forwarded to me, appropriately describe the events through which I have lived over the past few years: "There is nothing more difficult to execute nor more dubious of success nor more dangerous to administer than to introduce a new system of things. For he who introduces it has all those who profited from the old system as his enemies and only lukewarm allies from those who may profit from the new system."

The people I have worked with have also been critical in enabling me to get up again and again to go another round. You always get into trouble when you start listing names, if only because you upset those you don't mention. But I'll do it anyway.

I'd like to thank a group of true troopers, the Air Canada Board of Directors. My goodness, we've all been through a lot. But through it all, they were wonderful, supportive, and dedicated. I wish I could have presented them with more good news, but you just had to watch the nightly news to know it wouldn't happen.

In particular, I'd like to thank the two chairmen I've worked with: Jack Fraser and Bob Brown. Jack was the chairman who gave me the CEO job and was beside me through the Onex episode and in the aftermath of September 11. Bob and I had been friends long before he joined the Air Canada Board. He took over in the midst of SARS and just before we filed for CCAA. At first, things were strained; he was pulled in so many directions. Some directors wanted him to try to get a government bail-out, an idea to which I was violently opposed. But once things began to settle down, he was fantastic throughout the restructuring process. I cannot thank Jack and Bob enough.

I want to thank Calin Rovinescu, the lawyer I hired away from Stikeman Elliott after the Onex takeover battle. I have never dealt with a smarter, faster business mind. No matter what the mission, no matter how impossible the situation sounded, Calin was always there and we figured out a way to handle it. The tales of bringing this carrier back from the brink that I will never be able to tell bring a smile of satisfaction to my face. He was, and is, an amazing friend, a fellow I would do anything for.

Duncan Dee, senior vice-president, corporate affairs, is in the same category. Everyone loves Duncan. As his wife, Mary, once suggested, and I agreed, he is my Radar O'Reilly. He has a sense of people and how they are feeling, and an uncanny instinct for the media and government and where they are heading. He also has an IQ that is matched, I suspect, by few on the planet. He, too, has become as good a friend as anyone could hope for in life. Calin, Duncan, and I fought tirelessly, always protecting each other, and, in the end, I believe, took Air Canada through to the other side as a re-defined legacy carrier able to compete effectively. Together we made a lot happen, and I suppose that camaraderie is what it is really all about.

I would also like to thank my parents. They are remarkably different people, but they both gave me so much. Their love was limitless and obvious. My mom, now "Granny," is a sweetheart and instilled in me deep values of what is right and wrong and what family and love are all about. Whenever I see her interacting with my own children I am always reminded how she used to tell us that she loved her children more than life itself. Only now that I have my own children do I truly understand what she meant.

My dad encouraged my interests and honed my instincts every step of the way. I remember as a child his bringing me home *Wall Street Journal* articles on the airline industry. He travelled frequently, and he would give me thorough debriefings on every flight he would take for each trip. I would practically shine the interrogation light into his eyes: "What was the landing like? The food? Was the plane clean?" It went on and on and he rolled with it. I remember his travelling on crazy routings with me so I could fly exotic aircraft, stopping in far-flung places and taking hours more than necessary to get to our destination. But he also taught me lessons in business that are with me to this day. I remember standing in our driveway in Brussels in front of our blue vw 1600 at no more than ten years old and asking my dad if he'd prefer his vw or a Porsche. He answered: "I'd prefer the Porsche. I'd sell it, buy a vw 1600, and pocket the cash." I liked his logic. As I grew older I often came across situations where one of his truisms came to life, such as: "Banks will lend you all the money they don't think you need."

But through all the misery and strain of the nightmare years, my only truly happy moments were at home. No matter how difficult things were, no matter what anyone was saying, my Emily and Nicholas simply had to say the most wonderful word I have ever known, "Daddy," and I would melt. As I worked through obstacle after obstacle at work, with few understanding the difficult conditions we were trying to overcome, I would come home to my children and to my wonderful wife, Lizanne, and they would make the problems go away. On too many occasions over the years to mention, Lizanne would come up with the most pragmatic responses to problems at work, always going to the heart of some matter that a group of us were whipping ourselves into a lather over.

I never would have kept at it were it not for my family, whether it was getting a 5 AM wake-up visit from Nicholas saying "Daddy, let's play Lego," or, once I was up, playing dolls with Emily. After that, I was ready to do battle another day.

Perhaps, though, what made the battle worth fighting was a desire to prove the naysayers wrong and, for that matter, to simply outlast them. I think back over the years and can't help but notice how many of our detractors have vanished. Perhaps they just became exhausted, but whether they were politicians, reporters, or competitors, many seem to have simply gone away.

As for myself, I realize that Air Canada is a never-ending story and that I am just part of a moment in its history. Others will come after me, and my hope for them and all the truly wonderful people who work at Air Canada is that our effort through these early years of the new millennium will give them a true opportunity to soar.

ROBERT MILTON
September 2004

ACKNOWLEDGEMENTS

PEOPLE often say, "If I had a dollar for every time someone asked me to _____, I could retire." In my case, I could probably fill in the blank with "write a book." Ever since American Airlines and Onex attempted their hostile takeover, it's a refrain I have frequently heard. Later, after September 11, during the SARS crisis, and as we restructured under CCAA, people would raise the idea over and over. I just laughed it off, until one day I was approached by Greystone publisher Rob Sanders to actually do it.

Rob didn't come at me too hard, but he was persuasive in his pitch that I had a story to tell. I thought it might be cathartic to write a book, but I still wasn't completely convinced I should do it. Rob kept coming back, however, occasionally flying in to Montreal or phoning to try to convince me. Eventually, he did, and I would like to thank him for his persistence and for making this book a reality. I would also like to thank John Lawrence Reynolds, who co-wrote the book, and Nancy Flight, who edited it, for their efforts.

More than anything, I wanted this book to be written for the employees and retirees of Air Canada. This collection of individuals comprises some of the most wonderful people you could ever hope to meet, and I want them to know more of what was going on behind the scenes and what we were collectively up against, whether it was takeover artists, terrorism, war, viruses, or the government of Canada.

I hope that this book helps to provide clarity and comfort about the way things were ultimately handled and that it instills confidence in Air Canada's future.

ROBERT MILTON
September 2004

$$\equiv \; 1 \; \equiv$$

GETTING STARTED

M ANY people vividly recall the first time they attended a music concert, saw a theatrical production, or read a book that opened up a whole new world to them. For me, that life-changing experience occurred the first time I saw a Boeing 747. I was about ten years old and was living with my family in Belgium. I had always loved airplanes and could easily identify them before I was ten. But I really loved the 747, even though I had never seen one. I remember returning to the International School in Brussels after summer break and finding that many of my friends had flown on 747s to the United States that summer. I was crushed. Unfortunately, we flew back to the States for home leave only every other year, and that year we went to Spain. I flew on Iberia DC-9s, and my friends were on 747s—how depressing.

One misty morning I squinted into the distance to see a Pan Am 747 above a nearby village on its final approach for landing. It was a huge, beautiful piece of machinery, just hanging in the air with total control and grace, floating almost silently through the mist. It seemed just to hang motionless. I held my breath, afraid to blink. The vision of that aircraft remains as fresh in my memory as if I had seen it yesterday. From that moment forward, more than wanting to know everything I could about the 747 and about other aircraft that soared so high above the earth—where they were going, how they worked, and what their features and specifications were—I wanted some of my own.

Many years after seeing that 747, when I was the COO of Air Canada, I met the man responsible for the design of the 747, Joe Sutter. Along with thousands of engineers and their slide rules, he created the entire concept of the aircraft—its shape, size, and features. Some men have been thrilled to meet athlete heroes from their boyhood like Mickey Mantle, Joe Montana, or Bobby Orr, and they remember the encounter as a highlight of their life. A similar experience for me was meeting Joe Sutter and being awed in his presence.

I was at the Boeing wide-body manufacturing facility in Everett, Washington, to take part in the ceremonial delivery of a Boeing 767-300 and enjoy a test ride on the prototype of the company's new 777. My first conversation with him began as I knelt looking out one of the 777's windows at its magnificent wing. I commented that I was surprised to see vortex generators (small fences on the surface that improve airflow over the wing). Joe chuckled and said, "Yeah, these kids with all their fancy CAD [computer-aided design] systems still couldn't do it without them." There was nothing wrong with the new aircraft, Joe said; but the implication was that he could have done it better. Years later I was seated next to Joe during dinner at an airline industry function at the Smithsonian in Washington, D.C. He was engaging and surprisingly modest, considering how much the entire industry admires him.

The 747 remains my favourite aircraft, and Joe Sutter remains a hero. He lives and breathes large passenger aircraft—endlessly fascinated by their performance, magic, and practical beauty—and so do I.

AT SOME POINT, all children are asked: "What do you want to be when you grow up?"

My answer from the day I saw that 747 in Belgium was, "I want to run an airline." Not be a cowboy or a fireman. Not an astronaut or an athlete. Not even a pilot or a navigator. It was the idea of *running* an airline that appealed to me—choosing the aircraft, selecting the destinations, scheduling the flights, and overseeing the operation. I guess I did have a short spurt where I wanted to be a pilot, but my dad told me that the job of the pilot was increasingly like that of a bus driver, who operates a machine where the company wants, when it wants, over and over. "If you want to be a pilot," he said, "just make a lot of money and buy yourself a Learjet." I didn't agree with my dad, but I listened. It really didn't matter anyway—deep down I just wanted to run an airline.

My fascination was strengthened by the amount of travelling I did as a child. I was born in Boston, where my father was completing his MBA at Harvard. Within weeks of my arrival we moved to New Jersey, where my sister Andrea was born a year later. There was a short stay in Virginia, and then we moved to Hong Kong when my father accepted a position with a start-up electronics firm. It was there, four years later, that my little sister Elizabeth was born.

Hong Kong in the 1960s was far different from the hectic metropolis you see today. Just as bustling, it was much smaller and very British, proudly identifying itself as a colony. To a young boy, Hong Kong was endlessly exotic and exciting. I remember taking the Star Ferry to get across what was then a much wider harbour. The only reason to go across to Kowloon was to get to Kai Tak airport, where the runway jetted out into the water. We would drive there in a green 1960s-vintage VW beetle. I also recall typhoons so destructive that they closed roads and transportation facilities. Following one especially powerful typhoon, families like ours living atop "the Peak" had to depend on helicopters to bring food and supplies until the roads down to town reopened. I have a deep love for Asia, its culture, and its people, a love born during those early years in Hong Kong.

When I was seven years old, we left Hong Kong for Beirut, but the outbreak of war in the Middle East diverted us to Brussels. I learned French while in Belgium, where we lived for about five years before moving to England. There I attended the Wallop School in Weybridge, Surrey, for about a year and a half. We were constantly challenged to achieve great things, and I loved the school. But it was run-down and

3

the food was disgusting—the fish often arrived complete with gyrating maggots. Somehow the cooks could never get the storage and preparation of food right. My grades were decent, or "gentlemanly," as the headmaster said. Despite the bad food and austere conditions, I enjoyed being at Wallop and the time there went by quickly. Soon we were on the move yet again, back to Asia, where my father had secured a new position in Singapore.

Singapore in the early 1970s was everything that Hong Kong had been ten years earlier. Today it is glittering and pulsating, crammed with chrome and glass high-rise buildings, but when we arrived it was still a somewhat sleepy ex-colony that had yet to emerge as the commercial and manufacturing power it is today. Singapore's old Paya Lebar airport, for example, was tiny and lacked comforts such as air conditioning. (Today its Changi airport, in my opinion, is the world's best, developed over the years as the city-state of Singapore responded to its rapid expansion with legendary foresight and efficiency.)

I can describe Paya Lebar down to the last detail because a classmate, Doug Green, and I spent much of our spare time standing outside its rusty wire fence in the blazing tropical sun watching aircraft arrive and depart. We grew familiar with the airlines and their origins, and we learned the distinctive features of various aircraft. In a nanosecond, we could tell a 707 from a DC-8, a BAC-111 from a Caravelle, and a Lockheed TriStar from a DC-10 while they were still miles away. Even at night we could recognize approaching aircraft by the location of their landing lights—we were obsessed with aircraft.

Doug and I would spend about ten cents and forty-five minutes riding to the airport on a public bus if we couldn't get Mom's Toyota Crown "taxi," which was invariably taking her along for the ride to my sister Andrea's ballet class or Lizzy's horse-riding lesson. These activities were naturally on the other side of town, which in Singapore meant the opposite end of the country, all of 19 by 42 kilometres (12 by 26 miles). When Doug and I got there, we would walk about half an hour around to the back of the airport, through a kampong, a small village with structures made of corrugated iron. We would buy ourselves cold drinks, usually Fanta Grape, which would come in a plastic bag with a chunk of ice in it that the vendor would chip off a big block of ice with a screwdriver. That was Singapore in 1973. Today, people there go to Starbucks for Frappuccinos.

For generations, kids have had this fascination with aircraft. I differed from most other kids around the world who hung out at airports because I was even more engrossed by the airline business than by the aircraft as machines. When I wasn't watching planes arrive and depart, I was poring over airline schedules, deciphering their logic. I would trace the airlines and flights I might take to travel around the world exclusively on 747s, landing with one airline and taking off with another, making optimal connections, always on a 747. I was determined to travel at least once aboard a 747 operated by every airline in the world, and I almost succeeded, flying a 747 on over fifty different airlines. (This was my equivalent of collecting stamps, I suppose.) I missed only about half a dozen airlines, including the likes of Iraqi Airways, Iran Air, Syrian Arab Airlines, and Cameroon Airlines. By the time the list was whittled down that far, I was married and had serious responsibilities beyond boyhood dreams, so I was forced to abandon the idea.

My obsession with airplanes led to a spot of trouble from time to time. While visiting family friends in Thailand, I walked through a gate on the military side of the field directly onto the runway at Bangkok's Don Muang airport, carrying a camera and notebook. I took several pictures of aircraft before the authorities arrived and carted me off to the police station. While armed cops guarded me, they checked my bag and discovered my book of aircraft registrations, which made them pretty excited. Assuming I was a dangerous spy, one was about to open my camera and expose the film in it, over my protestations, when another checked my passport and burst into laughter. The passport revealed I was thirteen years old, although at about 1.65 metres (five-foot six) I was tall for my age, certainly taller than any of the Thais in the room. After all the officers had a chuckle over suspecting that a thirteen-year-old kid was a spy, I was released with a pat on the back and a warning to stay off the runway.

Another time I was picked up while prowling the Singapore airport. The police in Singapore have a more no-nonsense attitude than the

Thais do, and they held me in security until my father arrived to explain things and take me home. By this time my parents were resigned to my fascination with aircraft and airlines, even if they didn't fully understand it, and although rescuing a teenage son from a police station is never pleasant, they took my adventures in stride.

I devoured every monthly edition of the travel agent's ABC flight guide, the source of global airline timetables before the Internet made the data available to everyone. The ABC guide was like a bible to me. I could hardly wait for each new edition so that I could see what changes the airlines had made and how they had adjusted or expanded their schedules. I became so familiar with the schedules that I could anticipate how an airline might change its schedule to improve efficiency, and it was always a kick to see a company make the moves I had predicted.

In time, I memorized the flight schedules for whole regions of the world, a feat not quite as difficult as it sounds, because there were far fewer international flights back then. My parents' friends even began calling my mother and father to ask questions like: "We're off to France next month. Can Robert suggest the best route to take?"

Those were good times, and they still resonate with me. My closest friends in Singapore, Doug Green and Mario Rosario, shared my love of aircraft from a different perspective. Doug is a smart and funny guy and remains a lifelong friend. Unlike me, he not only loved aircraft but wanted to fly them. Doug lacked the cash to pay for flight training, so he chose the next best thing by accepting a job with an aircraft ground-handling company at Gatwick airport, near London. One of the most personally fulfilling things I've done in my life was to lend Doug the money in the early 1980s to achieve his dream. Doug obtained his commercial pilot's licence in the States and returned to the U.K., where he is now a captain with British Airways. To this day, he prefers flying 737s on short-haul routes over the more prestigious and better-paying international flights, taking off and landing as many times during the day as he can because it's more fun to him than spending eight or ten unbroken hours on the flight deck—the man just loves to fly. When I gave Doug the money I told him that I didn't expect to be paid back, but being Doug he returned every penny.

Mario obtained a pilot's licence as well, and I joined him on a few flights in a Cessna 150 (including one on a day when I snuck out of school just to go flying). He eventually gave up flying but not the aviation industry, and he now manages some of Air Canada's Asian operations out of Singapore.

Mario is one of the great characters I've known, possessing a wonderful wit and tremendous street smarts. He is terrific at building relationships and more than once has built up a strong sales presence in Southeast Asia for a large North American company, which is what I asked him to do for Air Canada. He also has an uncanny ability to meet important people.

For high school, my parents initially chose a private school in New Jersey for me to attend. As a mark of their confidence in my maturity—and an indication of how times have changed since then—I was permitted to make the journey from Singapore to New Jersey entirely on my own. Two times that year I boarded an overnight flight stopping in places such as Kuala Lumpur, Bahrain, Damascus, and Amsterdam on my way to London, where I would spend the day hanging out at Heathrow airport before making the final leg of the journey to New York. At JFK airport I boarded a bus to the East Side Terminal, caught a taxi from there to the Port Authority bus terminal, then hopped a commuter bus to Lawrenceville, New Jersey. These journeys were no big deal to either my parents or me, although I cannot imagine parents permitting their children to make the same trip today.

After a year at Lawrenceville, though, I wanted to be back in Singapore, so I went back to finish high school there at an amazing institution called the United World College. I was both class president and editor of the school yearbook, an activity notable for the fact that the publication actually made money for the first time in its history. UWC had kids of over forty nationalities, and we got along brilliantly. Before having my own family, it was the best time I ever had.

I have always wanted to be in charge of things, a trait that is responsible for some of my achievements as well as some of the criticism lobbed my way.

7

When I graduated from high school, I knew I wanted to study business at university—it seemed the most obvious path to operating an airline. I narrowed the list of universities to two, for official and unofficial reasons. Georgia Tech, where my father had earned his undergraduate degree, was an obvious choice, and I added the University of Chicago as another because its faculty included Milton Friedman, the most celebrated economist of his day. Those were the official reasons for applying. The unofficial reason was that these universities were located near the two busiest airports in the world.

I mailed my applications and by midsummer had heard only from Georgia Tech, so Georgia it was. I went off to work in London for about six months (foreigners were not allowed to work in Singapore without a work permit), taking a job first in the toy department at Harrods and later at a McDonald's near Victoria Station. I loved working so much that the last thing I wanted to do was go back to school. Nevertheless, I returned to the United States and had just settled into my college accommodation in Atlanta when I received a phone call from a buddy back at the boarding school in Singapore telling me that an impressive-looking package had arrived from Chicago. I asked him to open it, and he informed me that the University of Chicago was pleased to accept me as a student. Unfortunately, someone at the university must have assumed that Singapore was in Alabama, because the package had been sent at the very cheapest postal rate; it had spent several months crossing the Pacific, probably on a tramp steamer out of Seattle.

This was one of those events that appeared to mean little at the time but had a major impact on my life. That error by some geographically challenged person in the University of Chicago admissions department diverted me to Georgia, where a man named Hollis Harris had graduated about twenty years earlier. Our Georgia Tech connection later opened the door to a business relationship with Hollis that spirited me from the southern United States to Montreal and eventually deposited me in the president's office at Air Canada. Had the route started in Chicago, I doubt that it would have ended in the same place.

At Georgia Tech I tended to write every essay and design every project around aircraft and airlines. When I graduated in 1983 my heart was set on working at a major airline, but my timing was poor. As is often the case, it was a terrible time in the airline business, and I stood little hope of being hired by United, American, Delta, or any of the other large passenger carriers. I needed another option, and my father and my friend Mario provided it.

For a graduation gift, my father gave me $15,000 to buy a car. Before I could decide what to do with it I heard from Mario, who had graduated from the Florida Institute of Technology a year earlier.

"Bob," he said, "I think you and I should start our own company."

"Start a company?" I replied. "Why?"

"Because I need a job." The comment was vintage Mario, but it wasn't a bad idea—and he knew exactly the kind of business to launch.

I didn't buy a car with the $15,000 gift from my parents, and I didn't take a year to hike around Europe either. Just before finishing college, I started an airline.

SMALL-PACKAGE DELIVERY was one sector of the industry that was expanding through the early 1980s, and many of the larger companies were inviting smaller firms to pitch for contracts. A lot of people were jumping into this market, most of them running beat-up aircraft that were slow-flying and often unreliable. We thought we could kick it up a notch with better service. The secret of success in package delivery was speed and reliability, so Mario and I decided we would go with faster and newer airplanes than the other guys had.

We began searching industry trade magazines and found an ad placed by a pecan farmer in Sacramento who was looking to lease a twin-engine Piper Seneca. This wasn't exactly the faster, newer equipment we planned on, but it was a start. He had purchased the Seneca, a six-seat aircraft, primarily for tax purposes. I flew out to meet him and negotiate a deal. I must have impressed him, or perhaps he just had no clue what to do with the aircraft, because we cut a deal on the spot— $1,650 a month.

Next we located a guy about our age from the Netherlands who was living in North Carolina and who had just earned his commercial pilot's licence. He became our first pilot and was responsible for getting our

9

FAA (Federal Aviation Administration) Part 135 operator's certificate. Then Mario and I began checking out the private airports we expected to be using and identified the fuel companies located there. Airport A had Shell, so we applied for a Shell credit card; airport B had Amoco, so we went for an Amoco credit card; and so on. We increased our working capital by completing credit card applications at various gas companies and using the cards to keep us flying. When everything was in place we contacted parcel delivery giants like UPS, Purolator, DHL, Federal Express, and the rest, talking our way into getting a trial assignment or two.

That's how Midnite Express was launched. It was an audacious idea, almost insane as I look back on it, but this never entered our minds. Mario and I wanted to run an airline, and by gosh we were doing it. Since most of the capital was mine, I became president and Mario claimed the title vice-president of operations.

We began with common carrier service, getting paid about $50 a bag for whatever we transported. Once we had established ourselves as reliable guys, we were offered contracts. The contracts provided us with the resources to add new aircraft and expand our services, and soon we were flying as far north as upstate New York and covering much of the United States east of the Mississippi.

Mario and I maxed out our credit cards more than once to keep the company flying. The first few years he and I worked all day handling administrative chores, all night worrying that the deliveries were made on time, and all weekend ensuring that the planes were properly maintained.

It paid off. We added more Piper Senecas and moved up to a Beech 99, a beautiful turboprop aircraft designed for a crew of two and fifteen passengers. As business expanded we added newer and larger airplanes to the fleet, including Embraer Bandeirantes, commuter turboprops also built for a crew of two and sixteen passengers, and eventually Shorts 330s, stubby turboprops that could carry as much as a 3.2-tonne (7,000-pound) payload. Each new plane required new crews and new backup pilots, plus qualified personnel to handle more complex maintenance procedures. Soon we were as concerned about managing employees as we were about operating the aircraft. Five years after our first flight, Midnite Express was a regional feeder to several of the major couriers in the southeastern United States; it had a fleet of twenty-five aircraft, a perfect safety record, and a first-rate reputation for reliability. We were considered a success by almost everyone's measure except my own.

I would have preferred to make my mark in business as a ground-breaking entrepreneur, someone whose vision changes the nature of an industry. Starbucks and Wal-Mart are two examples of operations that altered the way things are done in their fields. No one can launch a coffee shop franchise or a department store without treading the path laid down by those firms. It would have been great to make a similar impact on the airline industry, as Fred Smith had with Federal Express and Herb Kelleher had with Southwest Airlines. Midnite Express was just a commodity supplier to the big, integrated carriers who were our customers.

I also wanted to deal directly with customers. Because Midnite Express operated under contract for larger outfits who were serving the end user, we were always under a gun held by two or three big guys. When they made demands on pricing or scheduling, we had to knuckle under. If the economy was bad and fewer people were shipping packages, or if competition put the squeeze on UPS or one of our other customers, we were told, "Cut your price by 20 per cent." We couldn't refuse. The cut might represent our profit margin, but we gave it up just to keep flying and looked for ways to reduce our expenses. Of course, when we went out of our way to see that the end customer was satisfied, the big guy got the credit. Being squeezed in the middle meant that we lost every time, and I promised that I would never again be part of a business that didn't either have a unique product or deal with the end consumer.

We picked up many lessons from those years. One was learning the practical definition of an entrepreneur, something no college education alone can teach you. An entrepreneur is someone who spends Thursday worrying about meeting Friday's payroll. I was always conscious of what that week's pay meant to an employee's family, and as a result I was something of a soft touch. My father had prophesied as much. "You need three things to be successful in business," he told me. "You need to be smart, fast, and tough, and you're only two of those. You're just not tough enough with people."

Over the years I made loans to Midnite Express employees who needed help. Some loans were to assist their kids with school, braces, or medical care; others enabled them to buy a house. One Christmas I received a greeting card from the wife of an employee to whom I had lent money as a down payment on a house. Inside the card, she had written: "I want to thank you on behalf of Marty and my son. We are in the first home we have ever owned this Christmas! Thank you for making it possible!" That card underscored the importance of remembering the family behind every employee, and that is why I have always said the toughest decision I have to make is to downsize the work force. That card also made up for a lot of the un-repaid loans.

Midnite Express proved to be a good training ground for budding commercial pilots. We gave younger pilots an opportunity to gain experience with good maintenance and training, unlike many of our "fly-by-night" competitors. Most of our pilots went on to successful careers in commercial aviation, flying much bigger and more sophisticated aircraft for companies like United and FedEx. Our original pilot, the young guy with the new licence, went home to the Netherlands and is now a captain with KLM.

Along with giving us experience in running an airline, Midnite Express provided a few lessons about human nature. The first Piper Seneca we leased, flown by the young pilot from the Netherlands, was always spotless. As we began adding other Senecas to handle the expanded business and pilots to fly them, plus backup pilots to give the other guys time off, I noticed that the aircraft were no longer as immaculate or as mechanically reliable as they had been in the beginning. Because the pilots might fly any of the planes, they lost the sense of ownership they had had when each pilot identified with his or her aircraft.

When CC Air, a commuter arm of Piedmont Airlines, made an offer to purchase Midnite Express's operations in 1988, I decided to sell. Still short of my thirtieth birthday, I had demonstrated that, at one level of the industry at least, I could manage an air services company and operate planes safely and reliably. Although I remained as committed to the airline industry as ever, I didn't feel that Midnite Express was the place to make my mark. So, with some relief and little regret, I closed the deal.

After everything was signed and the operation was CC Air's, I climbed into my car and turned on the radio. As I drove away, a local radio station began playing Eric Clapton's "After Midnight." "After midnight," Clapton sang as I pulled away from the airport, "we're gonna let it all hang down."

CONSULTING

FOR AIR CANADA

FOLLOWING my experience with Midnite Express, I was even less inclined to start working at the bottom of someone else's airline. By this time I had acquired a few contacts in the industry, and through them I began consulting for British Aerospace, developing a business plan to convert off-lease passenger aircraft into freighters. This job led to consulting work for other companies, until one day I was introduced to Hollis Harris by a family friend. Hollis had been president of Delta Airlines before joining Continental as CEO, and he and I hit it off from the very beginning.

It didn't hurt that I had graduated from Georgia Tech. People often refer to a "Georgia Tech mafia," meaning the loyalty that alumni share, not their business practices. There was much more to my relationship with Hollis than the alumni connection, however. He and I shared a similar passion for aircraft and a similar vision of what an airline should be and how it should be managed—with solid business-based decision making. Hollis liked to gather all the information he could get on a topic, make a decision, and move on.

In many ways, Hollis had groomed himself for the role of an airline CEO from the very beginning. He joined Delta when it was still a minor player in the industry, compared with rivals like American, United, Pan Am, and TWA. Hollis progressed through marketing, engineering, facilities, in-flight services, and operations at Delta, finally landing in the president's chair in 1987.

By then Delta was a major airline, and after a short time as president, Hollis surprised everyone by leaving the company to join Continental, which was once again stumbling towards bankruptcy. Hollis wasn't the kind of guy to play a caretaker's role if it meant maintaining a plan set by someone else, which had been his situation at Delta. He wanted a challenge, and he certainly found one at Continental. "I learned more about people and crisis management in one year at Continental than I did in thirty-six years at Delta," Hollis has said. Unfortunately, he came aboard Continental too late in the game to turn the airline around, and when he found himself at odds with the board over a personal commitment he had made to Continental employees—Hollis argued that the commitment had to be respected, whereas others argued it should be broken in the name of expediency—Hollis left the airline, as did Lamar Durrett, a lifelong friend of Hollis's whom he had brought with him to Continental.

Returning to Atlanta, Hollis began planning a low-cost airline that would use Atlanta as a hub and fly DC-9s exclusively. DC-9s were plentiful and reliable, and their range matched the needs of the planned operation. By flying only DC-9s, the airline would also be able to cut maintenance costs significantly. Hollis asked me to write the plan for the company, which he planned to call Air Eagle. The concept was great, but the airline business is cyclical, and once again the timing was terrible. It was 1991, and the economic climate was forcing investors to keep their chequebooks shut. Ironically, although our timing was awful, the business plan subsequently proved to be perfect for the folks at ValuJet, who essentially built the airline we had hoped to.

During a trip to Frankfurt to meet with Lufthansa officials in our search of financing for the new airline, Hollis received a phone call inviting him to an interview with Air Canada for the position of vice-chairman, president, and CEO. He told me about the call over breakfast the next day, explaining that Air Canada had been privatized a few years earlier with a weak balance sheet and was headed for trouble. Launching a new airline was exciting, but the prospect of directing a major international carrier like Air Canada, a company that commanded respect around the world, was something else, and Hollis was eager to take the job. He also wanted me on board with him. "Give me your thoughts on what we might do for the company," Hollis said.

Back then I saw Canada as a kind of oversized Switzerland, maintaining a low visibility on the world's radar screen while displaying positive attributes like politeness, cleanliness, and a safe environment, which also happen to be appealing qualities for an airline. But it was curious that the country appeared intent on maintaining two flag-carrying airlines when the size of its market could justify only one.

The paper I submitted to Hollis in 1992 was based on merging Air Canada and Canadian Airlines, a move I believed was essential to ensuring Air Canada's success. Combining the international routes into one operation and eliminating the inefficient duplication of domestic routes seemed like a lesson right out of Airline Management 101. The changes would also eliminate the need for the federal government to continue trying to play King Solomon in supposedly balancing route rights between the two airlines. Whenever one airline obtained approval to serve a new international destination, Ottawa would decide that the other had to receive some sort of consolation prize in the form of similar rights. This simply perpetuated underachievement by both carriers as Canadian charter carriers and foreign scheduled carriers poured more capacity and new routes into international markets to and from Canada.

Over time, this kind of gerrymandering of destinations led to nonsensical divisions of the world. I discovered, for example, that Air Canada could serve all of Germany except Munich from eastern Canada and Frankfurt from western Canada, and that Canadian could fly from western Canada to Frankfurt but not to the rest of Germany. The policy was insane. On the other side of the globe, Canadian could fly virtually anywhere it chose in the Asia Pacific region, but Air Canada's only potentially viable market was Korea. India was to be served across the Atlantic by Air Canada and across the Pacific by Canadian. The list went on and on. Bringing logic to this situation would require either merging the two operations or keeping the federal government's hands off things that should have been determined by market realities. Time would reveal the second option to be a fantasy.

When Hollis moved into the CEO chair at Air Canada, Lamar joined him as his Number Two man. I was not given a salaried position initially. As the first U.S. citizen to run Air Canada, and with another American southerner in the co-pilot seat, Hollis realized that Canadians might be concerned that one of their business icons was being run by a troika from south of the border. The three of us had established a good working relationship in assembling the Air Eagle plan, and in an effort to keep the team together Hollis offered me a contract to work as a consultant for Air Canada's freight operation. There would be no salary and no security; I would be paid a fixed daily fee, and when my task was completed, I risked finding myself unemployed and back in Georgia.

The chance to work alongside an industry leader as highly regarded as Hollis Harris, at an airline with the status of Air Canada, was too good to resist. On May 25, 1992, I flew into Dorval airport, and during our final approach I received my first lesson regarding commercial aviation in Canada.

Although I had never visited Montreal, I knew that the city was served by two airports, Dorval and Mirabel, and that Mirabel was the newer of the two. I knew of Mirabel's size and design and in fact had passed through there on KLM on the way from Amsterdam to Toronto. On the basis of that knowledge, I assumed that Dorval would look like Washington National or LaGuardia airport, older facilities hemmed in by a community that had enveloped the location over the years, stifling expansion. Otherwise, why build a second airport at Mirabel? Looking out the window during our approach to Dorval, I was surprised to see vast areas of land adjacent to the airport available for expansion. So why build Mirabel? Why not just make Dorval larger?

Mirabel's creation could only have been motivated by political strategy rather than by any practical necessity. When construction began in 1970, Mirabel was touted as "the airport of the year 2000," with

17

projections that it would handle twenty million or more passengers annually. International visitors would arrive and depart via Mirabel, and domestic passengers would route through Dorval. Or so the plan went. Unfortunately, only a few of the largest cities in the world can support two airports, and Montreal isn't one of them.

Mirabel proved a failure from the beginning, and everyone has a pet explanation why, including a promised high-speed link with Dorval that was never completed, the replacement of Montreal by Toronto as Canada's gateway city, and an inability to foresee changes in technology and travel patterns. But there is a much simpler explanation for Mirabel's failure: *it just wasn't necessary.* Had the decision been made free of political overtones, it would have been abundantly clear that the best alternative was to expand Dorval—the space was available, the infrastructure already existed, and the very idea of having international passengers arrive at one airport and be trucked for an hour or so to a second airport in order to continue their journey would have been seen as the absurdity it proved to be.

Many indirect costs were associated with Mirabel, beyond the cost of constructing the site. To build the airport, a huge amount of land in a picturesque part of the province was covered in tarmac, three historic villages were destroyed, and thousands of residents were uprooted. The city of Montreal also paid a price—I am convinced Mirabel set Montreal back twenty years in the development of its air transportation services, and perhaps in its economic development as well. Business tends to seek out the most efficient option, and Pearson International airport, though hardly a world-class facility, provided a simpler, more convenient, and more attractive means of arrival in Canada than Mirabel. As a result of this and other factors, Pearson and Toronto thrived while Mirabel and Montreal declined. Things have finally begun to shift, however. As I write this, Montreal and the province of Quebec are thriving economically and culturally, and Montreal has resumed its growth as one of the most exciting and attractive cities in North America. But this has taken much too long and comes at a very high price.

In spite of the airport situation, I learned to appreciate Montreal as a great city. It was not difficult to adapt to its cosmopolitanism, its festivals, the many good restaurants, the abundance of parkland to wander through, and a European atmosphere that was both intriguing and easy to love. Of course, I happened to arrive in May; had it been a grey, sleet-ridden day in February, I might have reboarded the plane and flown back to Georgia.

I was happy to be working with Hollis and Lamar and happy to be associated with Air Canada. It took me only a few days to realize the scope of the changes needed. Privatization had taken place just five years earlier, and much of the company's culture remained entrenched in a Crown corporation mode. The closest I had come to an organization with a similar working environment was when I lived in Britain during the pre-Thatcher years; the same inertia exists anywhere service efficiency comes second to job security. This is not a criticism of the people I encountered in those first few months or of the way the airline functioned, for the most part. Air Canada knew how to safely operate and maintain aircraft and take care of passenger needs. It had a great heritage and many wonderful people who just wanted to be led. Corporate culture, not personnel quality, was the problem. The culture was a holdover from the Crown corporation days and was also related to the airline's function as one of Canada's flag carriers.

Flag carrier airlines were not unusual during the 1960s and 1970s, the prime expansion years of the industry. As the industry matured, however, the drawbacks of government-owned airlines became apparent, and the advantages of privatization, including the opportunity to deliver operating efficiency and flexibility, became compelling. To the federal government's credit, Canada was one of the first countries to convert a state-owned airline to private ownership. I just wish, more than fifteen years after the fact, that Ottawa had lived up to the promise that the deputy prime minister and president of the Queen's Privy Council, Don Mazankowski, made to Claude Taylor, chairman of the board of Air Canada. In his letter dated August 24, 1988, Mazankowski wrote: "I wish to confirm that the position of the Government of Canada will be that it will deal with its shares as an investor and not as a manager."

It is not my intention to lay all of the blame for Air Canada's problems at the doorstep of privatization; too many other factors have played a role over the years. Still, if the company's critics are going to assess our progress—or our lack of it, in their estimation—it is only fair that they acknowledge the airline's situation when it supposedly emerged from the cocoon of a Crown corporation into the reality of a competitive environment.

At the time of privatization, Air Canada was saddled with weight that wholly independent airlines would never encounter, and the company has been unable to eliminate this handicap in the years since. I wish those people who ask, "Why can't you be more like _____?" [fill in the blank with some new non-union, high-quality, low-cost service company] would keep this in mind.

Calin Rovinescu, our former executive vice-president of corporate development and strategy, played a significant role in the privatization process when he was practising law at Stikeman Elliott. In a paper delivered to IATA (the International Air Transport Association) in 1998 he identified elements of the privatization agreement that have hamstrung the organization to one degree or another:

1. Air Canada was handed a directive by Ottawa to maintain its head office in Montreal, plus operational and overhaul centres in Montreal, Mississauga, and Winnipeg. On the surface these are not onerous, but they exemplify the difference between private and publicly owned corporations. A private company makes decisions concerning the location of a head office and major maintenance centres on the basis of economic realities; a publicly owned company makes them on the basis of political expedience and advantage.

2. Shares in the company were distributed in two stages. Revenue from the first stage flowed into the newly privatized company, but revenue from the second stage of issued shares, representing 55 per cent of the total, flowed directly into the coffers of the federal government. Fifteen years later, the impact of Ottawa directing this $460 million into its own pockets instead of into capitalization for the airline still resonates. It is, however, indicative of the government's long-term attitude towards Air Canada as an extension of federal policies and federal treasury requirements.

20

3. Despite raising $460 million in the second share offering, the federal government did not use the proceeds to retire any of the debt Air Canada had accumulated while it was a Crown corporation. As a result, Air Canada was saddled with a debt-to-equity ratio that was much higher than it should have been.

4. Air Canada was made subject to the provisions of the Official Languages Act—a requirement that applied to no other company in the Canadian transportation industry.

Air Canada will always serve its customers in their language of choice. It makes good business sense to do so, especially when a full quarter of your potential customer base is French speaking. But attaching an act of Parliament to this business practice only adds to bureaucracy and administration, taking up scarce resources that would otherwise go towards improving the very services the Act is supposed to protect.

More crippling to the company's potential success than the constraints identified by Calin was the cultural baggage that remained in place for some time. It's fine to tell the management of a state-owned corporation to operate, starting tomorrow, in the same manner as a private corporation, but that's like telling a dog to walk on its hind legs from now on. It can be done, but it takes a long time for the dog to get used to the idea.

State-owned enterprises and Crown corporations are always aware that they can rely on the financial backing, direct or indirect, of the government. What's more, lenders know they will be repaid if the company encounters financial difficulties, so management is not faced with the same hard questions posed by private lending institutions when dealing with private borrowers. Inevitably, Crown corporations learn to conduct business in a less formal manner than that imposed on private companies, and the managers rarely, if ever, feel the performance pressure that is de rigueur in companies that must answer to shareholders and financial analysts. In this atmosphere, business decisions, when taken at all, are often made for reasons that managers of a private enterprise would find mysterious or laughable.

Bob Perrault, a terrific guy who now runs our Jetz division, tells a story that illustrates this point perfectly. Before privatization, Bob managed our Texas base of operations, running DC-9 flights in and out of Dallas and Houston. Economically, this route made no sense because the passenger revenue on virtually every flight was not enough to cover the cost of putting the plane in the air. Yet the route continued to be flown. Why? Because Air Canada had a right to go in and out of Dallas and Houston under Canada's bilateral agreement with the United States, and Air Canada was going to exercise that right.

One of the elements in the Air Canada mission statement, however, was an assurance that the company would never be a burden to the Canadian taxpayer while it was a Crown corporation. The company did not have to show a profit, but it was to be operated in "anticipation" of showing one and was instructed to avoid year-to-year deficits. One day, an order arrived from Montreal for Bob to close shop—Air Canada was suspending its service to Texas. Bob had been proposing the idea for some time without any luck, so he wondered why the company had suddenly decided to withdraw after all those years of losses on the routes.

Because, the answer came back, we are nearing the end of the fiscal year and a loss has been projected. Rather than declare a deficit, even a relatively small one, management chose to sell one of the DC-9s, thereby generating enough profit to move the bottom line into the black. With one fewer aircraft, not enough DC-9s would be available to service the Texas routes, so the company was pulling up stakes.

That's how financial and scheduling decisions had been made for many years at Air Canada. Never mind eliminating inefficiency, reducing costs, improving service, or expanding markets. Sell an airplane! Pocket the cash! And we'll keep the bureaucrats off our backs until next year.

Even when I felt I had a handle on how things worked, there were still discoveries to be made. One of them concerned our fleet of international Boeing 767s, which featured a midship galley along the starboard wall, something not found on other airlines' 767s.

"Why do we have these extra galleys on the 767s?" I asked.

"Because the company specified it in the original order to Boeing," came the reply. "In-flight service said they needed them when the planes were originally spec'ed."

I asked if the galleys were used.

"Well, no," was the answer. "See, the aircraft are never used on flights long enough to make the extra galleys practical."

The galleys had sat unused for years, occupying valuable space on a very expensive aircraft. I raised the issue with Hollis, suggesting they be removed and their space be filled with six extra seats. It took Hollis about two seconds to agree, and the order went out. No one missed the galleys, but every 767 flight from that day forward had capacity for six more paying passengers, representing an immediate increase of 3 per cent in the aircraft's potential passenger load.

When work to remove the galleys began, I received a call from George Reeleder, one of the most talented and funniest people in the organization and currently one of our senior directors. George was astonished. "I've been trying for two years to have those galleys replaced with seats," he said, "and nobody listened to me. Then you show up, make a couple of phone calls, and it's done."

I got it done because I wasn't part of the old system, the one that tended to accept things the way they were—and of course I was Hollis's boy. This was more evidence that Air Canada's employees were not the source of its problems. The problems were the product of an organization ill-equipped to improve service and efficiency.

AS AN OUTSIDE CONSULTANT closely associated with Hollis and Lamar, I expected resistance whenever I proposed a change in procedures. Most of the people I encountered were terrific, especially the hands-on men and women. They knew where the inefficiencies were and how much they were costing the company, and they recognized that their future earnings and job security depended on doing a better job than they had in the past. The middle-management level was where change had to begin, and that's where I came up against resistance. Rod Eddington, the CEO of British Airways, came up with a line at one of our IATA board of governors meetings that produced a lot of laughs when talking about middle management's resistance to change: "As they say when it comes to cuts, turkeys never voted for Christmas."

Air Canada had a contract with Purolator to provide overnight cargo service. This kind of stuff was my bread and butter. My background with Midnite Express involved dealing with topnotch shippers like FedEx and UPS, and neither tolerated anything less than total reliability and on-time performance. Using their standard as the one Air Canada should emulate, I took a look at the schedule and modified it to provide Purolator with a win-win situation—the changes enabled us to both improve customer service and greatly reduce operating costs.

Yet unacceptable flight delays continued to occur, so I began probing the reasons behind them. Most of the delays proved to be the result not of an equipment fault or a glitch in the system but of a lack of focus on service. Once I noted a serious delay in takeoff of a DC-8 71-Series freighter, the only freighter-type plane in the fleet. The weather had been good, the plane was loaded, the crew was aboard, and clearance had been granted. What had prevented it from leaving for so many hours?

The answer, I discovered, was that the lavatory hadn't been working and the crew chose to delay the flight until a mechanic could be found to repair it. There were only three people in the flight crew, all of them men. "Next time this happens," I suggested, "somebody hand the captain an empty bottle and arrange to have the toilet repaired at the other end of the flight. Then get moving." There is no doubt that a FedEx or UPS crew would have taken off without a question; nor was there any doubt in my mind that our own crews could and would do the right thing if asked. They needed only to appreciate the critical nature of the flight and the need for those packages to make cross-country connections as a means of ensuring the company's success.

This was not a unique situation. On another occasion the captain refused to go because a meal other than the steak he had requested had been ordered. Somewhere along the line, it would be necessary to understand that eating a tuna sandwich instead of an anticipated steak dinner might be unfortunate, but it was no reason to hold up a flight and disappoint our customer and the hundreds of shippers whose packages were on board. Reliable overnight service was the basis of our operation, or it should have been. If we failed to provide customer satisfaction, someone else would. We needed to realize this fact of life and run the business accordingly.

Sometimes the problem was rooted both inside and outside the company. We had subcontracted a portion of our freight business to Kelowna Flightcraft, which was operated by a shrewd businessman who scored a number of successes by pitching for government contracts. He also proved very adept at using other people's money to finance his ventures.

When I began examining our freight performance records in detail, I noted that certain flights operated by Kelowna always arrived substantially later than scheduled. The reason for these repeated flight delays became evident when I looked into Kelowna's operation. It was using converted Convair 580 prop-jet aircraft on these routes, plus two Boeing 727s for jet service. Convairs are rugged aircraft, although the original design was nearly forty years old at the time, in 1992. The delays weren't the fault of the aircraft but were caused by the bulk-loading method Kelowna used to get cargo on and off the planes.

With a cargo capacity of 7 tonnes (15,000 pounds), the Convairs were suited for conversion to containerized loading, the most efficient way of loading and unloading freight. Kelowna had converted only one of its Convairs for containers, and it was not assigned to our contract. Instead, our shipments were bulk-loaded onto unconverted models, meaning that every item on every flight was individually loaded at the departure city and unloaded at the destination. With all the extra time needed for bulk loading, there was no way Kelowna could meet our schedules.

I asked Air Canada's freight managers to instruct Kelowna to convert the aircraft on our routes for containerized loading. The company refused because, I assume, the conversion would have required an investment that it didn't want to make. Kelowna would have preferred to keep its healthy profit margins, no matter how much damage this did to our shipping schedule. In that case, I said, insist that Kelowna's lone containerized Convair be assigned to our routes. Once everyone saw the time saved through containerized handling, I believed, the solution would become apparent. I even had our manager contact operations personnel at DHL and UPS to confirm that this was the best way to go. They confirmed that this was the only basis on which they would employ Convair 580s.

But the first flight on the containerized aircraft arrived over an hour late. The next flight was an hour and a half late. There were plenty of excuses and explanations, but the most efficient system in the world will not work unless the people using it want it to work. And no one seemed to want this one to work at all. This was a classic Air Canada NIH—Not Invented Here—situation, which crops up in all organizations as a means of resisting change.

I decided a meeting with the top man at Kelowna was in order, and I arranged a session at the Air Canada offices with all the key cargo managers in attendance. The Kelowna president proved to be an affable guy, but he resisted every idea proposed for improving our freight operations. What's more, our own people supported him with nods of approval whenever he objected to the suggestions. When I realized nothing was going to be achieved, I ended the meeting and asked the Air Canada people to remain behind.

"Do you realize how much money that guy is making from us?" I said to the managers when the Kelowna president was gone. "Did you see the watch he was wearing? It's a gold Rolex with diamonds around the face. It's worth thousands of dollars. I can't afford a watch like that. Do any of you guys have one?"

"He's got a really nice boat, too," one of the managers said. "He takes us out cruising on it." Our own staff was being schmoozed to death, and it was costing the airline millions of dollars a year, not to mention damaging our reputation with customers.

Things had to change, but as a consultant I knew that the orders would have to come from Hollis. Before approaching him, I took a close look at some of the prices we were paying Kelowna and compared them with the cost of operating our own aircraft.

We used six jet aircraft for long-distance freight services—four of our own DC-8-71s and two 727-100s operated for us by Kelowna.

"What are the operating costs for these aircraft?" I asked. The answer came back: $6,500 per hour for our DC-8s and $4,500 for the 727s. That didn't sound right, so I dug a little deeper and discovered that these figures incorporated both ownership and operating costs for both the DC-8s and the 727s. But we *owned* the DC-8s—they were ours free and clear. When I subtracted the ownership costs applied against the DC-8s, the hourly cash costs for the two aircraft were virtually equal, yet the DC-8s had a capacity of eighteen containers per plane versus just eight for Kelowna's 727s. The contracted aircraft were costing more than twice as much per container as our own planes. This was disturbing enough, but the schedule revealed that one of our DC-8s had been sitting on the tarmac totally unused while the Kelowna 727s were in the air at high levels of utilization.

Things had to change, and they did. We pressed the fifth DC-8 back into service, gave priority to our own freighters, and reduced our reliance on Kelowna to an absolute minimum. Within a few months, I could measure the accrued savings for the freight division in millions of dollars a year, without making any new capital investments to speak of. It was all a matter of recognizing and eliminating various roadblocks in an organization that still retained many vestiges of a "just break even" Crown corporation.

With just a few months' experience under my belt, I totalled all the confirmed and projected savings in freight operations based on the changes I had made and came up with an impressive multi-million dollar figure. I was being paid a decent fee for my consulting services, but I figured I deserved more. One night, Hollis and I had dinner at a restaurant in Old Montreal, and I reviewed the savings I had generated. Then I sprang the idea on him. "Hollis," I said, "I would really like to go on commission."

Hollis peered over the top of his glasses at me and said with a cheesy grin, "When I go on commission, you go on commission." Well, no one can blame me for trying.

For some time I had been bombarding Hollis with scheduling ideas for passenger service, and he agreed that they made sense. So, instead of commissions, I received a new position with the company and a new title: senior director, scheduling.

RESCHEDULING
FOR PROFIT

I HAD two strikes against me when I started work at Air Canada: Most people suspected I was some sort of hatchet man for Hollis, and I was much younger than many of the old-line Air Canada people I had been brought in to manage. No one believed that I had won the job strictly on my ability. I had been awarded my position, the rumours said, for some other reason. Like nepotism, perhaps.

On a flight out of Seoul, a flight attendant approached me with a sly expression on her face and said, "By the way, Mr. Milton, we all know you are Mr. Harris's son-in-law."

"Actually, I'm not," I replied.

"Well," she said, "I have it on good authority that you are."

When it comes to knowing my wife's family, I don't know any authority that would be better than me, but rumours of that kind are difficult to refute when someone has it "on good authority."

The notion that I had obtained my job by being married to Hollis's daughter took on a life of its own, and though I treated it lightly, others were much more serious about it. At an Air Canada sales team meeting someone asked, right up front, if I was Hollis's son-in-law. I laughed it off by saying, "Hollis is a fine man, but my wife was born in Hong Kong and grew up in Singapore while Hollis was in Atlanta, working at Delta. So if Hollis is Lizanne's dad, he's sure one lousy father!"

I thought this said it all. Apparently it did not. Sometime later, our vice-president of sales, Marc Rosenberg, told me he was getting feedback from a number of people that I hadn't been clear enough in my answer.

"Hey," I said, "I thought I settled things when I told that story about my wife being born in Hong Kong and raised in Singapore while Hollis was in Atlanta. Wasn't that enough?"

Marc shook his head. "You didn't come right out and say he *wasn't* your father-in-law," he said.

For the record: I am married to the former Lizanne Lietzan, who admires Hollis Harris as much as I do. She most definitely is not his daughter, however, and has no blood connection with his family. Lizanne lived in Singapore at the same time I did. We met and began dating when she visited Atlanta with her mom and sister some years later. Mario's dad had worked for Lizanne's dad in Singapore. Although we went to the same high school at the same time, we had never met. I am five years older than Lizanne, and an 18-year-old hanging with a 13-year-old just wouldn't have been cool. It was one of those "had to be" coincidences, or maybe it was fate, if you believe in it.

SOON AFTER stepping into my new role, I found myself at odds with a new group of middle managers. Despite the prevailing view among them that the airline had to shrink to become successful, I believed it had to expand. The infrastructure of the company was overblown and there appeared to be insufficient discipline to reduce overhead costs, so the only way to improve our profit picture was to expand our services.

I hoped that Hollis would change his mind about deferring delivery on some Boeing 767-300s the company had planned to acquire, but he stuck to his guns, focusing on three Lockheed L-1011 TriStars, mothballed in the Arizona desert, that had been sent there by previous

29

management. Hollis loved the TriStars, and bringing them back into service would provide almost a thousand new seats we could sell.

The first response from Air Canada managers was negative. "TriStars are unreliable," they said. "Require too much maintenance. Too expensive to fly. You can't turn a profit with them."

I had heard similar comments about the TriStar in the past, and most of these comments were based more on fiction than on fact. A certain prejudice existed against the aircraft in some quarters, perhaps because both Lockheed, the builder, and Rolls-Royce, the engine supplier, encountered serious difficulties during the aircraft's development. It was also seen as a Johnny-come-lately, entering service after the revolutionary 747 but with shorter range and fewer passenger seats. In addition, I suspected that the old guard—those whose roots extended back to the Crown corporation days—resisted using the TriStars because none of them had come up with the idea. This was that familiar NIH phenomenon, which I frequently confronted in my early days at Air Canada. Unfortunately, some of the middle-management personnel at Air Canada treated it as a mantra. To complicate matters further, Air Canada was traditionally a McDonnell Douglas airline, having built its jet fleet with DC-8s and DC-9s. As a result, the Lockheed aircraft had few champions in Montreal.

I was appointed to a team assigned to conduct detailed evaluations on bringing the TriStars back into service. Each time we had a justification for the idea, somebody would find a way of loading enough costs into it to kill the idea. Eventually I dropped the group approach and worked out a simplified evaluation based on configuring the aircraft for 58 business class seats (which would be refurbished first-class seats we had just taken off our long-haul aircraft) and 180 economy class seats, and flying them on three high-volume routes: Montreal/Toronto, Toronto/Vancouver, and Toronto/Los Angeles. "It won't work," the Air Canada marketing people told me. "We'll lose our shirts running the planes on those routes." Nothing I said could shake their opinion, so I decided to take the idea directly to Hollis.

Hollis was an enthusiastic fan of the L-1011. During his years at Delta, he had operated over fifty TriStars and made money doing it. "Let's see what everybody else thinks," he said.

I remember all of the Air Canada vice-presidents plus me sitting around the boardroom table later that day, waiting for Hollis to get the meeting started. "I have a proposal here," Hollis said, holding up a single sheet of paper, "that says it makes sense to put the TriStars back into service. How many people support me on this?" When there was no response, he said, "All right, let's count those against me." Hollis started counting heads—"One, two, three, four"—and so on, skipping me. "Fifteen, sixteen, seventeen." He pointed to himself. "One. Seventeen to one. Well, I've faced worse odds than that in my time. The TriStars are coming back."

Then he turned to me and said, "The TriStars can only fly to four cities. I don't care what four cities they are, but four it is. Except for a diversion I never want to hear about those aircraft flying anywhere else but those four cities. So, Robert, what are they going to be?"

I immediately answered, "Vancouver, Los Angeles, Montreal, and Toronto." And those were the destinations we used.

Hollis insisted on fixed destinations for the aircraft because he recognized that many of Air Canada's operational problems in the past had been the result of inefficient management of our fleet, especially the TriStars. In the past, the aircraft were hopping all over Florida one day, somewhere in Europe the next, the Caribbean the following day, and so on. Considering our widespread network, there just wasn't enough support at many of these destinations to get the aircraft turned around and operating reliably. That's one reason the previous administration had pulled the TriStars out of service. Limiting them to four cities meant they could become money makers instead of money losers.

And they did. For the year and a half they flew before being replaced by those new 767-300s that I wanted, they were the most profitable aircraft in the fleet.

31

THROUGH 1993, Hollis and Lamar Durrett began shaping Air Canada into a more efficient operation, one that could finally put its Crown corporation mentality behind it. The two functioned as a team, and like many successful teams, this one was composed of contrasting personalities. Hollis was up-front and in-your-face about everything. If he had a problem with you, you learned about it immediately and directly. And though Hollis loves a good debate, he retains the right to shut you down if you fail to convert him to your point of view. During my first executive meeting, where at age thirty-four I was the youngest vice-president in Air Canada's history, Hollis made a point about some aspect of the company's operations and concluded by asking: "Anybody want to add anything to that?"

I had a contrary view, and I stated it as emphatically as I could.

Hollis heard me out, then said with a smile, "Robert, there is something you should know about newly appointed vice-presidents. They are intended to be seen and not heard." Everyone, including me, burst into laughter.

Where Hollis laid down the law, Lamar looked for consensus, choosing a less direct and confrontational approach. I like and admire Lamar very much. He and his wife are godparents to our daughter, and I will always be thankful for the assistance and guidance he provided me.

Even easygoing Lamar had his breaking point, and I encountered it one winter's day after something had gone awry in the maintenance department. I was so frustrated by this particular screwup that I wrote a scathing memo complaining about the overall inefficiency and excessive turnaround times we were having to deal with. I poured all my anger and irritation into the memo, but instead of sending it to Lamar and asking him to deal with the situation in his position as executive vice-president, operations, I shot it directly to the Tech Ops manager responsible for the error, where it landed like a scud missile.

Within a couple of hours, I looked up from my desk to see Lamar enter my office wearing his winter coat and hat. He calmly closed the door, then began to shake. His face turned red as he launched into something between a tantrum and a tirade, spewing venom at me for sending the memo to Tech Ops instead of through him. It was totally inappropriate, Lamar said—actually, he shouted—for me to send a letter like that to staff in an area for which I was not responsible. It made Lamar look bad. Worse, it made him look foolish. He grew so angry that he threw his hat on the floor, pounded on my desk with his fist, and generally expressed more rage than I had seen from anyone, least of all calm, laid-back Lamar. When he finished, he retrieved his hat, slapped it on his head, and left for home.

32

Lamar was right, of course. I should not have by-passed him with my complaints. I should have alerted him to the problem and relied on him to fix things. He was also Hollis's right-hand man, someone whose counsel Hollis sought and respected. If my angry memo could generate a response like that from Lamar, how would Hollis react when he heard about it? My job might very well be on the line. I decided to bite the bullet. I called Hollis and asked if I could come upstairs and see him for a few minutes.

In Hollis's office, I explained the situation. "I want you to hear it from me first," I said. "I did something I should not have done. I sent a memo directly to Tech Ops about a screwup over there without going through Lamar, and I didn't hold anything back. Here it is," and I handed a copy of the memo to him.

Hollis took the letter, scanned the contents, read it again, and looked at me over the top of his glasses. I was prepared for the worst. He chuckled, handed me back the letter, and said, "What's wrong with that?"

BY MID-1993, we were $250 million off our business plan and something was needed to put us back on track. To this point, our strategy had been to pull flights out of the schedule, meaning fewer aircraft and employees were working (although they were still on the payroll), and fewer customers could be accommodated. This had the effect of handing passengers over to Canadian Airlines.

"This is madness," I said to Hollis. "We don't need fewer flights. We need to make better use of our current fleet and our current employees." I pointed out the proven correlations between flight frequency and market share and between market share and profitability. By pulling back capacity on profitable runs, we weren't saving money—we were practically forcing people to switch to Canadian Airlines, even though we offered more destinations, newer aircraft, and a better frequent flyer plan.

I located points in our schedule where both crew and aircraft sat idle for extended periods. By redesigning the schedule, I showed that we could produce the equivalent of seven A-320 aircraft each day, adding over nine hundred seats to our inventory without bringing in any additional personnel or aircraft. It made perfect sense to me, so I circulated my proposal among the executive group, asking for their opinion.

The response was tepid, to say the least. Paul Brotto, a VP in our finance department, sent a note to Hollis calling the idea suicidal. According to Paul, the idea was flawed and the timing was wrong. "We need to contract, not expand," Paul said.

When Hollis passed Paul's comments on to me, I countered that no airline in history had successfully downsized unless it was restructuring under court supervision. "You can't shrink an airline to profitability," I argued, "without doing something unnatural to the cost structure, like a restructuring through bankruptcy. We have the aircraft, we have the people, and we have the opportunity—let's use them."

Hollis was in a spot. I had scored some significant victories, but Paul is a bright guy and is respected within the company. In addition to weighing our arguments, Hollis was wrestling with the banks, who were concerned about our bottom line, and with politicians in Ottawa, who were concerned about everything. Finally, he turned to me and said, "Robert, do what you have to do."

He had given me carte blanche to rework the entire schedule. I can't remember tackling anything with more enthusiasm or with more certainty that it was going to pay off in a big way.

Years earlier, the previous administration at Air Canada had ordered three brand-new Boeing 747-400 combis, a combination passenger/cargo aircraft. When the aircraft were ready for delivery, management chose not to introduce them into the fleet. Instead, they went directly from the Boeing plant to storage in Arizona, where they sat baking in the sun at a cost to the company of about US$4.5 million every month. I remembered reading about this decision to store the aircraft and not operate them before I joined Air Canada and thinking at the time that it was an insane move. Like the TriStars, the 747s were both an asset and an opportunity, and with my encouragement Hollis pressed them into service before I took over the scheduling responsibilities. One of the 747s flew Toronto/Los Angeles/Toronto a few days each week, not an efficient way to use a 747. The other two aircraft flew Toronto/London/Toronto and Montreal/Paris/Montreal. These were logical routes for the planes, but the Montreal/Paris aircraft was isolated and so didn't connect to the rest of the schedule efficiently. This was costly and, with no backup, it had to be ferried back and forth to Toronto for maintenance, another waste of money.

These were virtually brand-new aircraft, which were being under-utilized. I proposed a schedule that would get them into the air more often, carrying more passengers and cargo. The new schedule had them flying daily Toronto to Vancouver, Los Angeles, and London, but also flying five nights a week between Toronto and Paris. Essentially, this schedule produced the equivalent of an extra 747 at no additional cost. To achieve this would require turnaround times of 120 minutes at Toronto, Los Angeles, and Vancouver, something most people at Air Canada claimed could not be achieved with 747 combis. I knew it could, and I issued the challenge to Air Canada's operational people by showing the tight turn times being achieved by other world airlines with their 400 combis. But I couldn't seem to convince many people that we could do it. To his credit, one of our airport operational managers, Bob MacCallum, went out and studied every aspect of these schedules and how we turned our 400s, using a stopwatch to show that 120 minutes would be enough time if we got it right.

We eventually proved the new schedule would work, but I kept encountering resistance to change—people from almost every corner of the company kept coming up with new excuses. Our marketing department had been pleading for more premium-seating capacity to Los Angeles, but when they saw the dramatically increased number of seats available on the revised schedule using the 747s they changed their tune—now they claimed there was too much premium capacity and muttered that they might not be able to sell all the seats. Eventually they did, but the defeatist attitude and the habit of shirking responsibility for missing objectives by lowering expectations were part of the game at Air Canada in those days.

Eventually I moved beyond revamping the 747 schedules and redesigned the company's entire flight schedule. Inevitably I encountered yet another roadblock, this one thrown up by the finance department. "Even if you can make the new schedule work," they told me, "when Operations sees an increase in seat capacity of 5 per cent, they will go out and hire 5 per cent more people for staffing and we'll be no further ahead."

"That's ridiculous," I said. "Look at the projections. We can increase capacity by 5 per cent simply by improving utilization without hiring a single new employee."

"Trust us," the guys in finance told me. "If you add 5 per cent capacity, they'll add 5 per cent in labour costs. That's the way things work around here."

I couldn't believe it, but I didn't want to waste time fighting. My solution was to prepare two schedules. One schedule would be deployed in the computer reservations system for the marketing and sales departments showing the actual new capacity, which was 5 per cent greater. The other schedule was solely for our operations people and showed no increase in capacity, so it did not add to our employee head count. By doing this, we managed to instantly net a quantum leap in financial performance, which proved to be a turning point in the company's improved financial performance through the mid-1990s. We also broke the habit of adding new personnel in direct proportion to every increase in capacity.

While working out a solution to the problem of overstaffing, I encountered a classic Air Canada response—classic for that period, anyway.

The airline was heavy with middle-management people, and no department was more overstaffed than the finance department. In my experience, overstaffed departments tend to launch the biggest resistance to change, so to get them onside for the new schedule and the fact that there would be two schedules—one for sales and the other for operational purposes—I set up a presentation explaining the concept and its benefits. We would put more seats in the air with the same number of aircraft and the same number of employees. It would strengthen our financial picture, enable us to purchase more new aircraft, redefine the airline, position it for growth (at the time we had fewer than 100 aircraft and today we have more than 200), and generate more job security.

At the end of my pitch, I waited for a response. For several seconds, there was nothing but silence. At last one guy raised his hand. I will never forget his words, because they summed up so much that was wrong with Air Canada at the time. "Mr. Milton," he said, "if we do this, it means that we will have to make a decision to take risk."

Like many in his position, he avoided making a decision and abhorred taking a risk. Yet this is something that private businesses do every day, especially when faced with a crisis. You make a decision to act. And you accept the fact that it involves risk. No one in management at the time seemed to appreciate this.

That employee wasn't with Air Canada much longer, though not because of what he said that day. Neither was a vice-president who, in spite of our obviously improved revenues, margins, share price, and staff morale, stated his unhappiness because our "hidden" growth had caused his branch to be over budget for the first time he could recollect. I was stunned, as were most of the vPs present. This guy was more worried about not meeting his budget than he was pleased about the airline's improved fortunes. When the results were announced, another vice-president who hadn't liked my approach was good enough to nod in my direction and offer his congratulations. Then he walked out the door and I suspect began looking for a new job, because he left Air Canada soon after.

The silo mentality kept popping up, though. Studying our Florida schedules, I noted we were using DC-9s heavily to fly the Toronto/Miami route and to fly to other Florida destinations. Our new Airbus A-320s appeared more suitable for that traffic, and sure enough, after asking the finance department to compare costings, I found the variable cost of operating A-320s was only about $10 more than the DC-9s on a typical Florida route, yet the A-320s offered about forty more seats.

"Wouldn't you guys rather spend an extra $10 or so and get forty more seats to sell?" I asked the Florida route managers.

They agreed they would, except that the DC-9s were paid for and the A-320s were leased. If the A-320s were used on the Florida routes, the lease costs would be charged against that manager's profitability; no such charge was applied against the DC-9s, making it easier for the managers to turn a profit and meet their personal objectives. Either it did not occur to the route managers that the lease charges existed wherever the newer aircraft were used in the company (and I'm sure it did), or they simply ignored that fact to make things easier for themselves. In any event, until we could become profitable again, I wasn't worried about aircraft ownership costs; they were sunk. I wanted the maximum revenues from the least amount of flying.

Both Air Canada and its customers would benefit from having the A-320s on the Florida routes, one from greater profits and the other from greater comfort. But the route managers resisted the idea. In spite of being capable people, these managers were so out of sync with the company's overall objectives and were so poorly directed that they emphasized individual route profitability over corporate profitability. From that point on, the silos were crushed and marketing managers were freed to look beyond their own routes and also at the impact of their actions on the whole company.

THERE WERE LESSONS to be learned on both sides during those years under Hollis Harris. Many Air Canada people discovered the satisfaction you get from succeeding in a truly competitive climate. It may be fun to hang around the water cooler, discussing last night's hockey game or next year's vacation, but ultimately it is not very fulfilling, nor does it generate any job security. We wanted to create an efficient but fair work environment at Air Canada, one that would enable the company to escape its Crown corporation identity for good. We wanted people to take some pride in their careers at Air Canada, not just earn a salary.

While aiming for that goal, I learned a few lessons myself. One was that the company employed a substantial number of people who were more than competent in their jobs but had never been given the chance to prove it in a competitive environment. This was especially true of the staff in the operations department. When handed a challenge, they rose to it, and I admitted to them and to myself whenever I underestimated them. Let me say it again: Air Canada in the mid-1990s was a great company with some lousy habits, most of them inherited from its days as a Crown corporation. Here's a perfect example:

Walking through the technical operations department one day, I glanced across to see a number of people working in cubicles set against an outside wall. Several windows lined the wall, each covered with brown paper. What's happening here? I wondered. Is the view through the windows so wretched that nobody wants to look at it—or so attractive that it might be distracting? The view, I discovered, was nothing special, neither better nor worse than any other from the building.

When I asked for an explanation, I was told that the employees along that particular wall were part of a compensation grouping level that did not qualify for a window, but for various reasons they had been located against a wall with windows. Some organization bureaucrat decided, I suppose, that breaking that rule would lead to anarchy and ordered the windows covered to correct this intolerable situation. Needless to say, the paper was gone within minutes of this explanation being offered.

A similar attitude occasionally filtered down through all employee levels. One day I walked through an aircraft undergoing maintenance in a hangar to find a mechanic sound asleep in an executive class seat. He was almost resentful when I woke him up and asked why he wasn't working, as though long mid-day snoozes were part of his job description. Of course, when I sought to have him disciplined, I was advised to simply forget about it, but I refused.

In no time at all one of the senior vice-presidents at the time called me into his office wanting to know what had happened. When I told him, he suggested that nobody handled things that way.

I responded by saying that I didn't care and that it was absurd to pay a guy to sleep. Apparently some of the Tech Ops managers were concerned that the IAM, the machinists union, would call for a walkout if we treated its members as I had.

I believe that to be hogwash. Neither the IAM nor the guy's fellow employees would condone such nonsense, and sometimes issues have to be dealt with head-on. People had to understand that change was in the air.

Any company can find itself in an environment where employees can just "get along" and not demand more of themselves than the minimum, and Air Canada was no exception. With all the challenges facing us in 1993, we couldn't afford this attitude, and when we began demanding more from everyone, we heard a little grumbling now and then. But things worked noticeably better, and when that fact became apparent, the grumbling faded. "When this place doesn't squeak, it doesn't work well," I have commented to a colleague more than once over the years.

This approach, not surprisingly, did not win me a fan club with everyone at Air Canada, and I suspect that's when certain aspects of my reputation were born. I have been referred to as Machiavellian by at least one union representative. I don't enjoy the implication that I am some kind of hatchet man who delights in slashing jobs. I dislike firing anyone, and I hate the idea of having to lay anyone off.

The culture at Air Canada when I arrived included widespread fear of being fired for making a bad decision or for alerting management to a problem. I have never fired anyone for either reason, nor could I imagine doing so. If, after weighing all sides of an issue, an employee makes an honest decision based on knowledge available at the time, and the decision proves faulty, that's unfortunate, but it is also understandable, and we should move on.

More often than not, people who glide through their careers without having to make a decision eventually find themselves in a spot where a decision cannot be avoided. At times like that, they stand like deer frozen in the glare of approaching headlights and get run over.

There is no reward in life without risk, and there are times in our lives when we all must balance risk against reward and make a decision accordingly, whether we want to or not. If I were to emphasize any single lesson I've learned in running a company, it would be this one: I will congratulate any employee who demonstrates the confidence to act like a manager and truly *manage*. I have little respect, and less use, for someone who avoids making any decision at all in a difficult situation and simply refuses to deal with the issue. Yes, I have fired a few under those circumstances.*

* In talking about "risk" in this context, I am not referring to flying. Nothing must interfere with safety when it concerns putting a plane in the air. I am never annoyed to hear that an Air Canada pilot, for example, chose to remain on the ground in bad weather when other airlines were taking off. Every Air Canada pilot knows that he or she has the absolute support of the company and should proceed only when comfortable. There will be no second-guessing about it from my office or from anyone else in the company.

4

MARKETING
THE AIRLINE

"**B**E CAREFUL what you pray for," Hollis Harris used to say to me, "because some day you just might get it."

I didn't pray to be handed responsibility for marketing at Air Canada, but in March 1995, after I had expressed my frustration with that department's efforts to reflect the changing culture, Hollis Harris handed me the job of vice-president of marketing. As long as I was able to get the job done, Hollis kept adding to my responsibilities.

AS SENIOR DIRECTOR of scheduling I had launched something of a crusade to improve our efficiency, and as vice-president of marketing and then subsequently as the senior vice-president of marketing and in-flight service, I cranked up the efforts. Air Canada needed to maintain its drive for improvement because the company faced challenges unique in its industry. The fact that Air Canada remains highly respected outside of Canada is a tribute to the things it has done well in the past and continues to do well today. It manages to achieve them even though no other airline in the world encounters the adverse environment that Air Canada deals with much of the year.

Consider the competitive climate we operate in. Other airlines may contend with U.S.-based competition, which tends to have the leanest, meanest, and most aggressive players in the game, but only Air Canada goes toe-to-toe with them on all cross-border flights and on international flights from North America to the world. Airlines such as KLM, Lufthansa, and British Airways are justifiably proud of their performance and reputation, but how well would they cope if 60 to 70 per cent of their markets were duplicated by companies like Delta, American, and Continental?

Air Canada operates shoulder-to-shoulder with these giants on most of our routes, serving a home-market population smaller than California's and spread across 5,000 kilometres (3,000 miles). To add to the challenge, no international airline—including our U.S.-based competition—flies in weather conditions as bad as those that Air Canada deals with during the long winter months. Many conditions we encounter between December and March, in high-traffic areas like Toronto and Montreal, are considered a novelty by other airlines.

This was driven home to me on a Qantas flight I made to Australia a few years ago. The flight had been oversold, so the captain kindly invited me to ride on the flight deck, my favourite place to be. During the long journey there was lots of time to chat, and at one point the first officer turned to the captain and said excitedly, "Hey, did I tell you what happened last week on my flight out of Frankfurt? We had to be de-iced!"

Like Air Canada, Qantas is one of the most highly regarded and safest airlines in the world. The cockpit crew were as competent and professional as you might expect, but a trip to the de-icing bay was a special treat for them. Of course, where else on their route map were they ever to encounter snow and ice? Los Angeles? No. Fiji? Hardly. Bangkok, Sydney, or Singapore? No, no, and no. It might occur in Japan or Europe from time to time, but that's about it.

Our people fly in lousy winter weather all season long, often being de-iced up to four times during a day's flying. This kind of weather causes frequent disruptions to our schedule and costs us tens of millions of dollars every year.

As much as I admire Qantas, I experienced one of our proudest moments at its expense in September 2000 when U.K.-based Flight-Safe Consultants conducted an exhaustive survey on airline safety. It was the first time that accident rates, aircraft fleet, management strength, and other qualities were investigated in so much detail to produce world safety ratings. The result proclaimed Air Canada the world's safest airline.

I happened to be on my way to Australia when the news broke, and when I arrived in Sydney I saw that the announcement was front-page news there. Qantas, widely considered the safest airline in the world, could no longer claim that distinction. Air Canada had dethroned it on the most important measure of all—safety.

IN LOOKING at operating conditions, Southwest Airlines is worthy of comment. It is the one most critics cite as the model of a modern, efficient air carrier. Efficient and successful it is, and I respect their leader, Herb Kelleher, and his team for their accomplishments. Herb is truly one of the nicest, funniest, and smartest people you could ever hope to meet.

Herb and his team built Southwest, against the backdrop of tremendous challenge from the established carriers, on the premise that "if you get your passengers to their destinations when they want to get there, on time and at the lowest possible fares, people will fly your airline." I agree with them. But consider the things Southwest claimed it would *not* do as it built its operation:

· It would not operate to congested airports.
· It would not fly to cities where airport fees and expenses resulted in high fares or slimmer profit margins.
· It would not fly to areas where weather conditions were not conducive to reliable operations or where frequent cancellations were encountered.
· It would not service centres with inefficient air traffic control (ATC) or airport operations.

43

Reviewing these conditions makes me chuckle because they define where Southwest will and won't fly. If the company sticks to its guidelines, I won't have to worry about Southwest coming to Canada!

In my view, the real beauty of the Southwest model is that its one-class value-based pricing has allowed the company to win in any economic climate. When times are good, American Airlines is full in first class and coach, Southwest is full, and Greyhound buses are empty. When times are tough, Greyhound is full, Southwest is full, and although American might have decent coach-class loads, first class is empty. In both pictures, only Southwest stays laughing.

The refusal of Southwest to serve cities with inadequate ATC and airport operations may surprise some people, who assume that these levels of service are standardized around the world. I wish this were so. Canada's ATC operations have made considerable progress in the past few years, but they remain inefficient in comparison with those in many countries, including the United States. Once again, the problem rests not with the individual workers, who are as capable, well trained, and dedicated as any, but with the vestiges of an old bureaucracy-dominated system that has been slow to change.

At Toronto's Pearson International airport, for example, an aircraft may receive taxi instructions from as many as three controllers, each operating on a different radio frequency, just to go from the gate to the departure runway. The same procedure is necessary on arrival. This system makes no sense. Aircrew are busy enough when preparing for takeoff or bringing passengers to the gate. They should, and usually can, be directed by the same controller on the same radio frequency all the way from exiting the runway on arrival to parking at the gate. Three hand-offs simply are not necessary—except, seemingly, at Pearson. At an efficient and busy airport controllers often give an instruction as brief as "follow the United 320 to your gate."

BEING IN CHARGE of marketing meant that I would be responsible for providing passengers with a positive experience aboard our aircraft. All of my experience to this point had centred on freight, schedules, and operations. Now I was responsible for ensuring passenger comfort and enjoyment.

I have always kept myself informed of what issues were most disappointing or irritating to our customers, and I have tried to ensure that steps were taken to address these issues. I consider the letters that come across my desk to be a terrific barometer of how we are doing, good or bad, and we use this reading to challenge our operational team to respond.

I also discovered through reading many letters that some people write to complain over and over again. At Southwest, they call them the pen pals. Letters often begin, "I fly Air Canada a lot, but on my last flight..." or claim, "I was flying on a full-fare ticket and I expect..." Every customer, whether she or he flies with us once a year or once a week, deserves the best service we can offer, irrespective of ticket price. We cannot and we will not discriminate within classes of service when it comes to overall satisfaction. I insist that we do not take the bargain-fare passenger's concerns any less seriously than the full-fare passenger's.

There are times when a screwup by Air Canada means that someone misses a wedding or a funeral or that the vacation of lifetime is ruined. When that occurs, I insist that we admit we dropped the ball and make appropriate restitution. Letters describing such problems make me cringe. We carry over 30 million people every year, and each person has on average ten employee contacts per trip. Although we begin every day striving to get everything right, realistically, we cannot expect to provide perfect service to all of those passengers over the course of 300 million customer/employee interactions a year. When our failures cause someone distress, it's no longer a statistic, of course, and wherever I can, I make an effort to see that things are corrected and that the problem is not repeated. I make it a point to apologize when an error has been made at my end of things, and I am adamant that our own people take the same attitude with customers. I fostered this attitude while in marketing, and I try to maintain it as CEO. I continue to respond to letters sent to me personally. Over the years, I have personally written letters to customers that aren't much more complicated than "We messed up. I'm sorry, and here is what we are going to do to acknowledge our regret." If we have really let the customer down, I don't hesitate to pick up the phone and personally express our concern.

WHEN ON A FLIGHT, I always walk through the entire cabin and talk with passsengers, thanking them for flying Air Canada. I genuinely want them to have a good experience on every Air Canada flight, a sentiment developed during my marketing experience.

I made an impact on marketing, I believe, by being both aggressive and responsive in ways that had never been attempted in this industry before—at least not in Canada. We were going head-to-head with Canadian Airlines, and when we were selling against each other the battle was tooth-and-nail.

The best example of this was a promotion Canadian Airlines launched in the mid-1990s, offering a flight anywhere the airline flew for $99 if you took three flights within a fixed period of time. I thought it was a dumb offer, but as Bob Crandall, a former CEO of American Airlines, once said, "The airline industry is only as smart as its dumbest competitor." They also announced it at a weird time—three o'clock in the afternoon. Within minutes of hearing the announcement, I called our marketing team together and said, "There's only one way to respond to this: We'll match them with a flight in return for three flights, but our deal will be a free flight—no ninety-nine bucks needed with us."

Everybody agreed it was a good response. Then I dropped the other shoe.

"I want banners promoting our deal in every airport in Canada and ads in every newspaper tomorrow morning."

We went to work, and when the Canadian Airlines people woke up the next morning, nobody was talking about their deal anymore. Everybody was either talking about Air Canada's offer or phoning our call centre and their travel agents to book flights. That's what aggressive marketing is all about—either you play to win, or you shouldn't be playing at all. Later I heard that the Canadian people were very upset at the way we had trumped them so fast and so solidly, negating their significant advertising expenditure. They even assumed that the newspapers had leaked word to us about their campaign. There was no leak. They just made their announcement at the wrong time of day, and we responded with all guns blazing.

OUR EFFORTS began to be noticed. We started winning awards for customer service, and Hollis won strong support from the board of directors, especially when our profitability improved and our share of the market began expanding. What's more, it became clear that the most lucrative segment of travellers, the business travellers, preferred to fly Air Canada if seats were available.

We also began addressing facets of our service that were not directly related to the mechanics of moving customers from point A to point B. In-flight entertainment, for example, remains an important element in the travel experience, and we sought ways to make it as enjoyable as possible.

Air Canada had cut back on most aspects of cabin service—for example, by finding sponsors for in-flight entertainment, we eliminated the expense of producing it ourselves. We saved money on our in-flight audio service by permitting record companies to supply the tracks, which included obscure artists whom they were trying to promote on their own label, but as a result many of the most popular performers were missing. Beyond enjoyable audio entertainment like music, investment companies offered to provide financial advice on our audio channels, again emphasizing their own products. These measures had reduced our audio programming costs, but cutting costs alone does not guarantee success. As Gordon Bethune, the CEO of Continental Airlines, once quipped, "You can make pizza so cheap that nobody will eat it." I replaced the free programming with audio selections that I knew would have wider appeal among our passengers. By spending a little more money, we created a lot more customer satisfaction.

Movies were another area where costs were being cut without regard to customer satisfaction. We would have a John Candy Month and then a Tom Cruise Month, each month's movies featuring one star. It was a silly attempt to conceal the fact that we were trying to save money by running movies that had been out for years instead of current releases, and I moved us back to showing new ones. Then we looked for better ways to improve the whole in-flight entertainment package.

I was especially impressed with British Airways' strategy at the time. In the early 1990s, it moved away from the traditional mould of showing one movie per flight and introduced the idea of wall-to-wall video programming. Fly British Airways and you never need to take your eyes from the video screen, where there is always something to keep you occupied. Or, to put it another way, you are so busy being entertained that you rarely find anything to complain about.

Everyone praises pioneers in business, and the successful ones deserve all the compliments they earn, but from a practical standpoint it's often better to be a fast follower than a leader. British Airways had led the way in this wall-to-wall programming idea, and I looked for ways to capitalize on it. George Reeleder took on the task of assessing things that British Airways and others were doing to elevate the appeal of their on-board entertainment packages. He was assigned to identify the best aspects, upgrade them to cutting-edge quality, and start incorporating them into our service.

As a result of this process, we began to evaluate using short programs, including TV hits, to better fulfill the objective of wall-to-wall programming. Could we replace one long movie with several short videos? Would passengers prefer newscasts and a couple of half-hour comedy features over a movie starring Richard Gere or Julia Roberts? On shorter flights we wanted to try comedies. There is nothing better in life than a good laugh. We decided to test the concept, and the answer came during a flight from Florida. I was on the flight deck, but through the closed door I could hear waves of laughter roaring through the cabin at the antics of Mr. Bean. I knew we were making progress.

There were times when I still believed the entire corporation was dedicated to resisting change. I had been trying to reduce meal costs while improving broad passenger appeal, looking for dishes that almost everyone would enjoy but that would cost us less to serve, when the idea hit me: Why not pizza? It's popular, it's filling, it's easy to serve, and it's cheaper than virtually any other meal imaginable. All told, the idea of offering pizza as an alternative dish had a lot going for it.

I began proposing the idea of pizza for in-flight meals, asking people to look into it. There would be a lot of head nodding, note writing, and promise making, followed by nothing. People would quietly forget about the idea and assume that in time I would too. But I refused to let go and kept bringing up the topic. Finally, I ordered a test project on the Toronto/Winnipeg route, where for a couple of weeks pizza was available as one of two meal alternatives. Halfway through the test period, Gordon Young, another talented Air Canada employee, who was conducting the test, walked into my office shaking his head. "The pizza idea just doesn't work," Gordon said. "Everybody turned down pizza and chose the alternative meal."

I was disappointed, of course, but curious too. Almost nobody I knew turned down pizza, unless... "What was the alternative meal?" I asked.

"Grilled salmon steaks."

Gee, who wouldn't choose grilled salmon over pizza? The test was about as sensible as Avis asking car renters which vehicle they'd like to drive for the same price—a Chevy Cavalier or a Cadillac Coupe de Ville.

For what it's worth, I would have chosen neither salmon steaks nor pepperoni pizza. About twenty years ago, Lizanne and I visited a sheep farm while vacationing in New Zealand. I still vividly recollect Lizanne seated in the shade of a tree, bottle-feeding a lamb cuddled in her arms. The mood was broken, however, when the farmer invited us to his home for dinner and served us grilled lamb. I never got over the impact of that event, and I returned home determined not to eat an animal again. I still don't, but I don't impose my decision to become a vegetarian on others. Our children, for example, look forward to visits to McDonald's just like other kids their age, unquestionably more for the toys than for the burgers. Actually, I want the kids to eat meat, not just because I worked at McDonald's as a kid, but because I think meat is critical for growth during their early years and because they are too young to decide to be vegetarians. After that day in New Zealand, however, my rule is: If it had a mother, I won't eat it. Lizanne was not affected the same way; she still likes a good steak.

This made me attentive, I suppose, to the vegetarian meals we were offering our passengers. I know that vegetarians are a minority of the population in North America, and thus a minority of Air Canada passengers, but I maintain that every customer deserves a travel experience of a quality equal to that of everyone else in the same cabin, and this includes those who request special meal services. Once again, the effort to reduce costs went too far; I noticed that on every flight of any length, in both economy and business class, we served the same boring vegetarian meal—a veggie loaf with corn and peas. Economy class passengers got it on plastic plates and business class passengers ate it on china plates, but it was the same monotonous meal over and over again. To minimize costs, both the variety and the quality of the food had been reduced beyond the point where any appeal remained. You can't do that to customers, and I insisted that we raise the quality and selection of our vegetarian entrées and rotate those entrées regularly.

Somewhat later, Gordon Young, who had been doing a good job of re-introducing quality while keeping costs down, approached me with a money-saving idea. "I can cut another $50,000 out of our meal costs," Gordon said, "by changing the cut of beef we serve in our meat entrées." When I asked what kind of beef we would be using and how it would be served, he explained that it was basically just a slab of beef with sauce on it.

"But what's the cut?" I said.

"I don't know what it's called," Gordon said. Then he lifted his arm and said, "It comes from under here someplace."

I laughed, then told him we would definitely not go to some unidentifiable mystery meat to save fifty thousand bucks a year, and we moved on.

After the incidents with pizza and underarm beef cuts, I began searching for ways to improve the appeal of our desserts. It seemed that every meal we served included variations on sponge cake for dessert— sponge cake with raspberry sauce, sponge cake with chocolate sauce, sponge cake with mango sauce, and so on. Sponge cake is cheap and light, but it is also boring. "Who eats sponge cake for a dessert at home?" I asked. Nobody did. "What's the most popular dessert at home?" This was easy—ice cream. So why weren't we serving it?

We began serving fresh-baked cookies and ice cream on transatlantic flights thereafter, but the initial flavour selection was so strange that I suspected sabotage again. On a Day-Tripper flight (our popular

9:00 AM departure from Toronto, which arrives in London at 9 PM, just in time for bed), my wife and I were served dessert in the form of three scoops of ice cream—one scoop of white, one scoop of brown, and one scoop of green. The white and the brown I confirmed as vanilla and chocolate, but I had no idea what the green stuff was. It looked like pistachio, but it certainly didn't taste like it, and neither my wife nor any of the flight attendants could identify the flavour.

Back in Montreal I called for a meeting with our caterers to review the dessert selection. It was actually a fabulous scene, with desserts spread out as far as the eye could see. I wanted to devour them all, but there were too many people watching, so I asked about the mysterious-tasting ice cream. "What is that green stuff?" I said. "Does anybody know what flavour the green ice cream is?"

Someone in the back row mumbled something.

"I beg your pardon?" I said.

He mumbled again.

"I still can't hear you," I answered.

"Green tea," he said. "It's green tea ice cream."

"Thank you very much," I said. "Now, who goes to the supermarket to buy green tea ice cream?" Nobody did. "We have to start serving what people want," I said, and eventually we did—strawberry, chocolate, and vanilla ice cream, but no green tea.

5

NEW ROLES

***

THE YEAR 1996 marked the beginning of the most wonderful thing that has ever happened to me—parenthood. Before we knew Lizanne was pregnant, we took a trip to Hong Kong in December 1995, arriving on Air Canada's inaugural flight. A great, long-sought victory. It was wonderful, as always, to be in Hong Kong, and to have arrived on Air Canada made it even sweeter. But Lizanne wasn't feeling very good. I took her to the doctor, who thought she had the flu and prescribed some antibiotics. Somehow, intuitively, Lizanne didn't feel the doctor was right and didn't take them. We were in Hong Kong for a few days and then went to a great vacation spot, Phuket, Thailand, for Christmas, when Lizanne developed this insatiable thirst for, of all things, v-8 juice. I emptied the shelves of grocery and convenience stores all over the island in my effort to quench her thirst. Hearts were probably racing back at Campbell Soup Company headquarters at the exploding revenue numbers in Phuket. Because Lizanne wasn't normally a v-8 juice drinker, we wondered and looked at each other knowingly but refused to speculate. My Irish heritage made me far too superstitious to say anything, but when we got back to Montreal it was confirmed—we were going to have a baby.

Lizanne had an eventful pregnancy, featuring a case of adult chicken pox (imagine no scratching or hot baths) and gestational diabetes. Her pregnancy also brought home to me, in the most intimate way possible, the flaws of Canada's national health care system. Politicians keep promising to throw money at it, but money itself will not resolve the fatal defects in the system. Private enterprise must be permitted to play a role.

Right now, despite the protests, there are most definitely two systems: one for the haves, who can go anywhere they want to get needed health care or have the contacts necessary to get immediate care, and one for the have-nots, who are forced to put up with the unacceptable waits and the substandard facilities provided by the current system. I am not advocating the U.S. approach, in which only money talks; I'm simply saying that some element of privatization needs to be introduced, perhaps a model similar to the one used in France or Singapore today. There is nothing substandard about the doctors and nurses in Canada—they are fantastic. It is simply a question of the system, the facilities, and the equipment these professionals are forced to work with and the reality that the system does not work.

When it comes to events involving my family, I easily turn into Jell-O with worry and concern, and I was a nervous wreck during the first ultrasound testing Lizanne underwent before our first child was due. The technician studied the ultrasound image obtained from the examination and said, "I don't like the look of this. I'm going to need to see the doctor." My heart stopped, and I probably looked like Jerry Lewis in one of his movies, white-faced and gyrating, on the verge of passing out, as I also tried to smile for Lizanne. The technician went to find a doctor, but she couldn't find one because they were all busy.

Lizanne and I were left waiting and wondering for about forty-five minutes: I started to get pushy because nobody seemed able or willing to tell us what was so worrisome. Finally, I cornered the technician and demanded to know what it was that she didn't like and what it might mean about our baby. It served me right for pushing.

"Well," she replied, "based on what I'm looking at, I'm concerned about Down's syndrome." My knees buckled.

When the doctor arrived, she looked at the image and, after a split-second analysis, said, "No, this is fine. Everything looks great."

At eight months, Lizanne's water broke while I was heading for the airport to pick up my father, who was coming to town for a visit. Lamar and Barbara Durrett (Barbara treated Lizanne like her own daughter) raced to our house and drove Lizanne to the Jewish General Hospital, with Barbara screaming at Lamar all the way that he was driving too slowly. Lamar might have been, because I was almost at the terminal when I got the call. I left my dad to fend for himself and zoomed back downtown, arriving at the hospital around the same time as Lamar, Barbara, and Lizanne.

In the delivery room, the staff was busy trying to keep the baby in. The staff was phenomenal—well-trained, caring, and empathetic—but the room was a decrepit facility with equipment that looked like it had been rescued from Bosnia. Two hours went by with nothing much happening except that a wall-mounted speaker spewed white noise into the room. I finally ripped if off the wall to shut it up.

After what seemed like an eternity, at just after 3 AM, our baby arrived. She was healthy, and she was the most beautiful thing I had ever seen. I'll never forget Lizanne's smile when the doctor handed her our newborn, and the words that came from her mouth: "My Emily." Then the doctors said they wanted to take Emily away to do blood tests. In an instant, as in a nature documentary on TV, Lizanne looked at me, her face snarled as her maternal instincts came to the fore. With a voice worthy of a person possessed in a horror movie, she said to me: "Follow my baby; don't you take your eyes off my baby; don't leave my baby." I'm sure I drove the doctors and nurses crazy shadowing them, but I didn't leave Emily.

I could never have imagined how one could be so instantaneously and overwhelmingly consumed by love. At the moment I first saw Emily, as would be the case with the birth of our Nicholas, I felt as though I had been hit by a bolt from the heavens.

The birth of my son, Nicholas, two years later, was also complicated. During his birth, Nicholas's heart rate began to drop, which created concern among two young interns who were attending Lizanne. After not doing much except make me nervous for what seemed like an eternity, one of them said to the other, "You'd better go get the doctor." The baby's heart rate might have been dropping, but mine went into orbit. What was going wrong, and why were these two kids in charge?

A moment later Dr. Shore cruised into the room. It was as if he had arrived from Hollywood central casting. He sported the same grey hair and calm demeanour that passengers like to see in the left seat of the cockpit when they board an aircraft. The doctor looked at me, examined Lizanne, then looked back at me and said, "You'll have your baby in two minutes." And he was absolutely right. I now had a beautiful baby boy too.

WELL BEFORE RETIRING as CEO in 1997 and handing over the reins to Lamar, Hollis had made me chief operating officer. Things were on the upswing, and we were making a little money and winning awards. That year I took a group of employees to Washington, D.C., to receive Air Transport World's Passenger Service Airline of the Year award. The climate was upbeat, and so was I. As COO, I was in charge of a group that was now viewed as offering the best and most innovative passenger service. I handled all the areas that I had previously, including the commercial world and in-flight service, as well as everything else that interested me, like flight operations, maintenance, and airports.

The year 1997 also saw the launch of Star Alliance, a network of international airlines that began in late 1992, when we reached a marketing agreement with United Airlines. This agreement occurred under Hollis's direction, with the negotiating skills of Ross MacCormack, one of Air Canada's vice-presidents and one of the nicest and smartest people you would ever want to meet. He was like a professor, incessantly compelled to scribble things on the blackboard, but he could really make people, airlines, and even former rivals come together. He is one of the Air Canada vice-presidents who were there when I arrived that I genuinely miss.

Within a year, the agreement had grown to include United, Thai Airways, SAS, and Lufthansa in a loose code-sharing agreement, in which airlines providing service between the same destinations sell seats on their flights to other partners and share the revenue. The deal proved beneficial to everyone, but we needed to assure passengers that all airlines in the pact would provide a consistently high level of service, and that's how Star Alliance was born. The alliance attracted other members seeking to cash in on its benefits, and within the next few years Air New Zealand, Singapore Airlines, Austrian Airlines, and others signed on.

Today fifteen of the world's biggest and best airlines are members of Star Alliance. The alliance rules are flexible. In some instances, we operate a joint venture, sharing revenues and costs with another airline for the same flight. In others, we function as a travel agent for a partner, earning commissions by booking passengers on an alliance partner's flight.

We all benefit by offering passengers advantages they cannot enjoy by choosing airlines not associated with the alliance. First and foremost is our global quilt of networks. Also, our most frequent passengers can use lounges operated by any alliance partner anywhere in the world and accumulate frequent flyer points from multiple airlines. All alliance partners provide high standards of safety and comfort, offering equal or near-equal seat pitch. Then there are advantages such as our Round The World fares. Passengers choose the total mileage to travel in first, business, or economy class and link flights from various alliance members to circle the globe. The trip can be as short as ten days or as long as a year and can include as many as fifteen stopovers. Star Alliance has proven a major success for everyone associated with it, and our company's role as a founding member is, in my view, one of Air Canada's proudest achievements.

In 1997 we tightened Air Canada's reins and added a number of innovations, including electronic ticketing for travel agents and e-mail sell-offs via our AC Websaver. I was also acquiring a reputation for having near-encyclopedic knowledge of the company, and I did my best to maintain that perception. Occasionally I was a bit devious. Once when

I checked in at the counter in Calgary, an agent asked if it was true that I knew every fin number—the numerical designation painted on an aircraft's vertical tail fin—and the flights that each aircraft was assigned for that day.

"Well," I replied, "I believe I'm going back on fin number 212 today."

When the agent checked her computer screen to confirm this number, her eyes grew wide and she shook her head. "Wow," she said, and then called over a couple of colleagues to tell them.

What she didn't know was that I had been chatting with our operations guys a few minutes earlier and had asked the fin number of the aircraft I was about to board. I'm sure the check-in person spread her story among other agents, and if it strengthened the rumour that Milton knew every aspect of the company's operation, right down to the fin number on each flight, that was fine with me. I wanted everyone in the company to understand that I took a keen interest in the kinds of information they dealt with as employees every day. In fact, I did have a good grasp of where all of our aircraft, especially our wide-bodies, were every day.

This reputation probably started at WOR, our weekly operations review meeting. This meeting, which took place on Wednesday mornings, was generally a regurgitation of the previous week's operational performance. Unless I challenged people, the meetings just burned up time. I usually questioned people about repeat issues, like a particular aircraft with a broken movie projector that simply wouldn't get fixed or baggage delivery problems at an airport where things just didn't get better.

As I pushed the maintenance organization to focus on seemingly small details like ensuring that all reading lights worked, carpets weren't frayed, and aircraft exteriors were spotless, I raised the spectre of implementing a maintenance approach employed by Japan Airlines, which I have always admired. At JAL, maintenance crews are dedicated to particular aircraft fins. So a crew headed by, say, Mr. Hashimoto (I use the name Hashimoto because Mr. Naoki Hashimoto is, in fact, Air Canada's operations manager in Japan who, through his actions, personifies the notion of "ownership" inherent in the JAL maintenance

57

approach), might be in charge of aircraft JA8079. By giving such responsibility and ownership to a specific crew, JAL maintains standards of aircraft appearance and maintenance as high as any that exist. The ownership detail is engrained to the point that by door L1 on JAL aircraft, there are small signs that designate both the captain for that flight and the chief of that specific aircraft's maintenance crew—in this case Mr. Hashimoto.

As I broached the subject at Air Canada, the pushback that it couldn't work here was strong. The argument was that Air Canada's aircraft are constantly coming back "home" to a different city. One day, an aircraft would be in Vancouver, the next in Toronto and the next in Montreal. At first, I thought it might be more NIH, but I soon came to agree. As much as I love the concept, it wouldn't work at Air Canada.

In fact, the multiple-hub layout of Air Canada's network, which reflects Canada's geography, provides an added challenge to both the company's operations and its profitability. For JAL, those aircraft come home to Narita (or perhaps occasionally Kansai) every day and an individual crew can own the plane. The same applies for British Airways at London, Cathay Pacific at Hong Kong, KLM at Amsterdam, Air France at Paris, and so on. One hub to connect at, one hub to maintain at; wouldn't that be nice?

As Hollis's eyes and ears at WOR, Laurie Lincoln, his executive assistant, would report to him the intensity with which I was challenging people at the meeting to do better. I suppose this was one of the key reasons that eventually Hollis replaced the then COO with me.

At my first meeting I remember getting some lip (the usual sort of mumbo-jumbo about why an aircraft wasn't 100 per cent serviceable) from the vice-president of technical operations, and I barked back from memory all the deviations (items that needed to be fixed) by fin number. He was shocked and blurted back, "I guess things are going to be different if the COO carries all the fleet deviations in his head."

I did, and I wanted him to know that I wouldn't back off until things got better. And they did.

I have no tolerance for aircraft that are not clean, on time, and 100 per cent serviceable, and neither should anyone else at Air Canada.

THE MAJOR CALAMITY during this period was a two-week pilot strike in 1998. The role of airline unions in determining the fate of individual companies as well as the industry changed dramatically with deregulation in 1978. Until then, airlines the world over were regulated by their respective governments, essentially limiting competition and preventing major changes in passenger fares and income. Labour was in a comfortable zone—wages increased steadily, if not dramatically, and productivity measures were seemingly irrelevant in the good old days. Increasing wage costs could always be covered by fare increases approved by the regulators.

With deregulation, first in the United States and then throughout most of the world, everything was turned upside down. Now only the fittest—or perhaps the smartest—of the airlines would survive. The industry began seeking a "lowest common denominator" approach to service and pricing and focused on ways to increase revenue and reduce costs. This was long before the Internet enabled smaller airlines to sidestep the travel agents, and, as a result, new carriers as a group did not survive. In essence, the industry was deregulated, but labour was not and continued to behave the way it always had.

More aggressive pricing generated higher traffic volume, and higher demands on employee productivity generated a hostile response among many of the unions. They began to push back, and the arrival of the 1980s saw waves of strikes through the industry. Some airlines refused to give in to union demands—Northwest Airlines became almost notorious for accepting the role of strike target to establish new wage and productivity levels. For a time there appeared to be an informal agreement among the major U.S. airlines in which a chosen carrier would endure that year's strike in an effort to rein in union demands and thereby benefit the whole industry.

As time passed, however, it became clear to the unions that some airlines were more susceptible than others to union demands. When unions targeted these companies, the negotiations began to look more like extortion. Too often, reasonable arguments by management were spun into outrageous and untenable positions when passed on to union members, often by leaders who retained their position through

59

acclamation and were disconnected from the concerns of both management and employees.

Pilots knew they had tremendous leverage, and they applied it to the airline industry throughout the 1980s and 1990s, winning substantial pay increases from one airline after another. The pilots' strike at Air Canada in 1998 proved disastrous, costing the company an estimated $250 million. I cannot think of many companies or industries that would take a hit like that in fourteen days. The loss was measured not only in hard dollars but in lost opportunities as well. Most companies can stockpile inventory before an anticipated strike, selling product while their factories are shut, and buyers can put off purchasing until the work stoppage is over. In this way, the impact of a strike at most companies can be softened at both ends. Seats lost on scheduled airline flights, however, are gone forever, and meetings, family events, and critical travel plans are disrupted. Although every labour dispute proves disruptive and costly to an airline, no group swings greater weight than the pilots. You cannot easily replace striking airline pilots with anyone else, including pilots from another airline.

At the time, our pilots were being represented by their newly formed union, ACPA (Air Canada Pilots Association). ACPA was formed by our pilots for all the right reasons, including improving the relationship with the company and being more of a grassroots organization that better listened to and represented its members. Looking back on that period, I think the relative "newness" and inexperience of the leaders of the new union worked against us all. ACPA, to this day, continues the process of maturing, and I hope that as it does, it will attain the ideals its founders set for it.

Many people, especially our pilots, believe to this day that I was at the negotiating table during that strike period, urging the company to maintain a hard line against the unions. In fact, Lamar felt my views were too pointed and would not let me near the negotiations. My input was restricted to how to run our operational contingency plan during the strike. I happen to believe that the strike was avoidable. Since I have assumed the CEO position, we have not had a strike, or even a work disruption, and I will try to ensure that there never is one.

The strike revealed the manner in which union leaders can and often do employ their own personal agenda to sway the operations of an entire company.

An Air Canada pilot who was a senior union rep and key negotiator at the time for the Air Canada Pilots Association (ACPA) and, quite frankly, was not a very strong flyer, let his personal issues affect tens of thousands of passengers and employees. Pilots are required to undergo periodic testing, known as a check ride, to ensure that they meet standards. Any pilot who fails a check ride undergoes retraining and another check ride. This pilot, who, I assume, feared failing future check rides and thus losing his job, proposed a new policy called Training To Standard, which meant that the company could not release pilots who failed to meet our performance levels but must continue training them and keep them on the payroll until they achieved the necessary standard of proficiency. I know that the overwhelming majority of Air Canada pilots would not be driven by this issue because they are completely competent and want equally competent co-pilots sitting in the cockpit with them. But in the midst of a costly strike this guy led this charge, all for the sake, I believe, of better preserving his own job.

In another instance the then union president, a 767 captain, was scheduled to handle an Ottawa-to-London flight just before the strike deadline. Our crew scheduling people, knowing that this guy wanted to exert as much pressure as possible on the company, confirmed and reconfirmed with him that he would show up for the flight. He said he would but he did not, delaying the takeoff for several hours while a replacement pilot was located and brought to the airport, inconveniencing a couple of hundred Air Canada customers.

I find the kind of behaviour demonstrated by these two men totally unacceptable and unrepresentative of the thousands of good people who work for Air Canada, and, in particular, our pilots. But it is representative of the tactics many union leaders are all too often willing to employ. I often wish that employees could see how some of their representatives act and hear what they say. They would be mortified.

Recently I suggested that contract negotiations be held in an open forum, perhaps in an auditorium, and that they should be Webcast so that employees could be privy to how their interests were being represented. The unions went wild in their opposition. I guess we will have to wait, but I remain open to 100 per cent transparency for our employees. The company has nothing to hide.

It is unfair to lump all union leaders in the same category, however. Many are terrific; they genuinely care about the company and its employees and would give their right arm for them. But those who hurt them really do damage.

Despite setbacks resulting from the strike, things were generally going well at the airline and we recovered surprisingly quickly in 1998, largely as a result of a booming economy. The international airline industry is relatively small, and every senior executive stays clued in to achievements and crises among the competition. Word of the new climate and attitude at Air Canada began to spread, and in early 1999 I was offered a key leadership position at Bombardier Aerospace. As much as I was enjoying my work at Air Canada, I was not the top dog. The Bombardier offer would be an opportunity to prove I could handle that challenge, and it would provide a substantial increase in salary. It also met Lizanne's number one rule for any job I was offered at the time: "You can go for a job of your liking anywhere in the world, so long as it is in Montreal." The job was incredibly tempting, but I wasn't certain I wanted it.

I didn't want to leave Air Canada. We were making progress against tough domestic and international competition, we were winning back passengers we had given to Canadian Airlines, the charter carriers were booming and failing as usual (but doing a lot of damage as they failed), and we were earning awards and recognition within the industry. I wanted to be the guy taking it to the next level, but I could only do that from the ceo's chair.

I told Lamar about the job offer at Bombardier and said I would turn it down if I were assured that his job would be mine when he stepped down. I told him it was 100 per cent about succession and 0 per cent about money. There was no rush, but I wanted that assurance. Lamar understood and asked that I not make a final decision to accept the offer until I heard back from him.

The next day I took off for a Star Alliance meeting in Sydney and arrived back in Canada several days later in Calgary, where our AGM was scheduled to take place. I had just checked into the Palliser hotel when I encountered Lamar in the hallway. "I talked to Jack Fraser [the Air Canada chairman of the board] and some key board members," Lamar said, "and I think we have something to make you happy." The "something" was $100,000 in cash and another $100,000 in stock options.

I was stunned. Lamar had totally misread me. I again explained that cash was not the issue. I deeply desired to remain at Air Canada and continue the program of changes. I simply wanted the board's assurance that I would succeed him at Air Canada, that I was the guy who would replace Lamar as CEO. Either the board members could give me their support or I would go elsewhere. If someone else stepped into Lamar's shoes when he left, I would be leaving Air Canada anyway. New CEOs prefer to place their own stamp on an organization, and I had no illusions about retaining the COO job under Lamar's replacement. If I were to leave Air Canada, I wanted to choose the timing. I had a major position waiting for me now, but who knew what the situation might be in a year or more?

Jack Fraser called to discuss the matter with me directly. Jack is a fine man and has developed into a good friend over the years. He boasted as broad a corporate background as anybody in the country, with directorships at companies such as Ford of Canada, Shell Oil, Coca-Cola, and Bank of Montreal. Like many top-level business people, his interests extended well beyond the boardroom, and he had contributed time and energy to organizations like the Royal Winnipeg Ballet and the Faculty of Management at the University of Manitoba.

I reviewed my position with Jack, who replied with excellent non-committal warm and fuzzy talk—I was highly valued and respected at Air Canada, I had achieved much, the company owed me a lot, etc. He ended by saying that the board could not make the kind of assurance I was looking for.

This wasn't what I wanted to hear, although I understood the difficulty of Jack's position. "In that case," I said, "I'll be leaving to accept the other job offer."

This prompted a surprising response. "What if we made you president right now?" Jack asked.

I shook my head. "I want the job," I said, "but only if Lamar is happy with this. Otherwise, I'll go."

A win-win solution was developed whereby Lamar would be named vice-chairman and remain CEO. I would be named president and COO. I appreciated the board's gesture, which clearly solidified my position and added new assurance that the CEO position would eventually be mine. I accepted and informed Bombardier that I would remain at Air Canada. Lamar was sincerely pleased that things had been worked out: he retained CEO responsibilities, and I was in the position to inherit his duties when he chose to step down.

AROUND THIS TIME, in a drive to improve our annual profit by $200 million and provide attractive returns to Air Canada's shareholders, Lamar had reduced our staff by 450 and removed eighteen aircraft from the fleet. Part of his plan involved discussions with WestJet, which had become a major player on domestic routes by this time, to explore the possibility of a partnership.

On the surface, this sounded like a fine idea. WestJet's ability to attract cost-conscious customers to their shorter domestic routes could feed passengers to our longer domestic service and international routes. Digging a little deeper, however, I knew that WestJet would maintain their cost advantage on longer routes as well, going toe-to-toe with us and changing the game considerably. If they could do it, they would do it, and time has proven me correct: WestJet now flies transcontinental routes and provides charter service to Mexico and the Caribbean. I have little doubt that the company is planning to add Hawaii, and someday Europe will be a plausible addition to its schedule, using its new long-range Boeing 737-700s.

64

Co-operation with WestJet, I calculated, would simply add to our difficulties of closing the gap in operating costs that existed between us. In fact, the chief advantage I could see in such an arrangement would occur as WestJet adapted its methods to accommodate our own. In other words, the only advantage that I could see for us in a relationship was that it might screw WestJet up! On top of everything else, I did not believe our pilots would be too pleased with our ceding our short-haul airplanes and jobs to another carrier. As they caught wind of the talks, they made this view clear.

Meanwhile, we watched the continuing meltdown of Canadian Airlines, which announced a $300 million cumulative loss for the third quarter of 1998 and the first quarter of 1999. Logic dictated that a merger between Air Canada and Canadian Airlines deserved serious consideration, but all preliminary discussions between us, Canadian Airlines, and its major associate, American Airlines, had gone nowhere. The bottom line was that American wanted Canadian as its feeder from the north and didn't want any interference. Canadian Airlines was shackled with a foreign ownership limit of 25 per cent, which effectively negated a complete bailout of the airline from outside Canada. In reality, American Airlines had been circumventing the rules that governed foreign ownership of Canadian and was playing the role of sugar daddy to Canadian Airlines' damsel in distress, all the while sucking it dry with expensive service contracts for everything from computer reservations systems to code-share flights.

At one point, after several false starts at trying to bring the airlines together, American Airlines CEO Don Carty said to Lamar, "Maybe we will have to buy *you* guys!" Carty's comment provoked a "What is he smoking?" from many of those who heard about it. How could any single investor, let alone a foreign airline, even kick around the idea of buying Air Canada under the prevailing ownership rules?

I took Carty's remark more seriously than others did. "Where there's a will, there's a way," I warned several people. I suspected that, as American Airlines' president, he might go to great lengths to buy us. It made a lot of sense. American had a ton of cash on hand in 1999, and its investment in Canadian Airlines was proving to be a fiasco. What better way to cover up its losses in that airline than by merging it with Air Canada, giving it enormous clout right across North America? Strange as it may seem, American Airlines had better relations with the federal government than Air Canada did, thanks to its participation in Canadian Airlines. The federal Liberal Party was always seeking to build its strength in western Canada, where residents tended to identify more with Canadian Airlines than with Air Canada.

One solution would have been for Canadian to sell us some of its international routes, especially those to the Asia Pacific region. We had offered to purchase these routes a few years earlier, when its problems were beginning to grow serious. Airline landing slots are an intangible asset that can be bought, sold, or traded according to market value. The value of routes and landing slots generally fluctuates according to market size and airpoprt capacity constraints, which means that an airline can book significant gains when these rights are sold. Several years earlier, American Airlines paid a record $120 million for Continental's Seattle to Tokyo route. For many years, air service between the Asia Pacific and much of the rest of the world was severely limited. Even if you had the rights to fly there—and these were at best difficult to obtain—slots at places like Osaka and Hong Kong were available only in your dreams. As time passed, beautiful and efficient new airports opened in Seoul (Incheon), Osaka (Kansai), and Hong Kong (Chep Lap Kok), reducing the importance and value of slots at these cities. Nevertheless, route rights to these places were of value. At a busy airport like Tokyo's Narita, prime landing slots are especially prized. Our original offer for Canadian's Asian routes had represented fair value, we felt, and in 1998 we raised the price considerably. But that offer was rejected as well.

By January 1999, when Lamar Durrett and Rob Peterson, our CFO, began discussing the possibility of an Air Canada–Canadian Airlines merger with Canadian Airlines president Kevin Benson and American Airlines CEO Don Carty, it was already clear that international air traffic represented the only growth opportunity for the old-line airlines. Southwest and its clones in the United States, and WestJet and others in Canada, were showing the future of domestic air travel: value. Although what are increasingly referred to as the "legacy airlines" should not, I believed, give up entirely on domestic travel, I knew that too much capacity directed at going head-to-head with the cut-rate airlines for that market would be a serious mistake.

Our future rested in long-haul international travel, especially to Asia and South America. Our strategy was to acquire those routes for future growth and financial stability, because that's where we could add value and profit to the service. The federal government, however, was keeping us out of those regions, identifying them as Canadian Airlines destinations exclusively, even if they weren't operating there. They could fly to any market we operated in—the United States, Germany, the U.K., France—and we couldn't fly to their jewels, such as Brazil, Mexico, China, and Australia. The ideal solution, from our point of view, would have been for Air Canada to purchase the Asian and South American routes owned by Canadian, routes being used only on an extremely limited basis, injecting cash into the airline so that it could focus on domestic and transborder service in conjunction with American.

We were constantly aware that Ottawa might at any time funnel hundreds of millions of dollars into Canadian, perhaps to the point where the company would emerge as a de facto Crown corporation. Using taxpayers' money as the glue to bind the organization together might have won support from western voters, an attractive prospect for the Liberals. I had seen evidence of this sort of government manipulation in 1992 when the Conservative government paid $195 million to purchase three Airbus A-310 aircraft from Canadian Airlines, even though the planes were not worth more than $60 million on the open market. One of these aircraft was later nicknamed the Flying Taj Mahal because of the extravagant interior that was installed in it. This aircraft was purchased as the prime minister's private jet, though Jean Chrétien refused to fly in it. I never understood why. Canada is a G8 country and its leader should fly in a good airplane, and the A-310 is just that. In any case, the deal represented a $135 million cash gift to Canadian Airlines and western vote buying for the Conservative government.

Federal governments in Canada always seemed to be trying to win favour from Canadian Airlines because of its western identity. A few years after the Conservatives bought the three A-310s, with the Liberals in power and Canadian on the ropes again, the Liberals introduced a fuel tax rebate supposedly designed to assist the entire airline industry. If you examined the rules of the program, however, it soon became obvious that it was intended to apply only to airlines whose corporate colour was blue and whose name started with *C*.

This kind of nonsense had been going on for years. Many backers of Canadian Airlines enjoyed droning on about Air Canada's Crown corporation heritage in a disparaging manner, even though we had been privatized a decade earlier and had not received a penny of government money since then.

The January 1999 talks with Canadian Airlines faded when it became clear that its management was not interested in selling the airline's international routes. Meanwhile, the fiscal hemorrhaging continued. By the end of June, even Kevin Benson had to publicly admit that Canada could not support two international airlines. During a speech to shareholders in Calgary, Benson said: "The fact that neither of us [Canadian Airlines and Air Canada] have been able to match the performance of the major U.S. airlines in the past ten years should indicate... that other options ought to be considered..." Benson proposed that the solution was for Canadian Airlines to improve its capital base—a serious challenge for a company carrying over a billion dollars in debt—and by "co-operating on routes which are too thin to support service by both carriers, [to eliminate] both an excess in, or an absence of, service," which probably suggested that we transfer some traffic from our busy routes to help his company. This recommendation was floated as if no approval would be needed from the Competition Bureau. Management at Canadian Airlines apparently thought that somehow the bureau would allow these two carriers that controlled more than 90 per cent of the domestic market to simply carve things up for their own benefit.

Neither proposal was workable, but they indicated a change in direction. As one industry observer put it, Benson was "raising a white flag" in Canadian Airlines' battle with Air Canada.

In essence, Benson was calling for government intervention. He had been hinting for some time that he could get Ottawa to sanction such talks. Although we were skeptical about the idea, Canadian had great contacts with the federal government, including Jean Carle, Chrétien's long-time aide, who had joined Canadian Airlines' board.

More significant was the claim by Benson that sometime in June 1999, Transport Minister David Collenette had asked both Canadian

Airlines and us to hold talks about "carving up" international routes to the benefit of both airlines. As soon as the news broke, Collenette denied making such a suggestion, claiming such talks would be "contrary to policy—we have a deregulated environment. Competition means you compete, you do not collude." The very next day, the Competition Bureau announced an investigation to see if Air Canada and Canadian Airlines had been colluding. This was quickly followed by Collenette's admission that he had urged us both to discuss exchanging some international routes to our mutual advantage. He added that he had "only encouraged full-blown competition on the domestic market in the interests of the customers."

A week or so later, Collenette approached Lamar and said: "How would you feel if the competition laws were relaxed, allowing you to get into a deeper dialogue over a merger?"

Lamar refused to give him a direct response, and when he told me about Collenette's query I advised Lamar against formally acknowledging it. "It's a trap," I said. "If we agree and Collenette goes ahead, it will be with our approval and we'll be giving a green light to anybody with a hostile-takeover plan." When we didn't take the bait, Collenette began floating the idea of waiving the rule as a government proposal rather than an Air Canada concept.

It was clear that something was happening behind the scenes and that we were the only participant in his plans he wasn't confiding in.

6

"HI, IT'S GERRY"

IN EARLY August 1999, we began hearing rumours that Onex Corporation, headed by Gerry Schwartz, was considering a hostile takeover of Air Canada. Lamar Durrett was CEO at the time, and his response was understandable skepticism. Although such a deal seemed to make sense economically, it didn't realistically, because too many laws and regulations were in place to prevent such a move—chief among them, the 10 per cent limit on ownership of Air Canada.

My reaction differed from Lamar's. Schwartz, after all, had strong ties with the Liberal Party, so it would not be difficult for the government to waive any rules for a long-time supporter—if they were so motivated. Then, like an overdue avalanche, things began to happen in mid-August. Soon we were all carried along for the ride.

On August 13, in response to a request from Canadian Airlines, the federal government invoked section 47 of the Transportation Act, suspending the powers of the Competition Bureau for ninety days and "permitting" Canadian Airlines and Air Canada to discuss a merger. I considered this an outrageous abuse of power by Ottawa. Collenette was inserting himself and his ministry into the picture—and for what? To fix a problem in the airline market, which was clearly in the final throes of fixing itself? Canadian Airlines was up against the wall, American Airlines was facing a rapidly worsening situation, and we were prepared to resolve the issue in a responsible, businesslike manner. There was no industry crisis; Air Canada was fine, WestJet was fine, Air Transat was fine, and Royal Airlines was fine. Only Canadian was in crisis, and Collenette was going to fix it his way.

I had little time to reflect on the minister's actions because I was soon designated to deal with them directly. The day after his announcement about invoking section 47, I stepped into Lamar's shoes as Air Canada CEO. Just two days later, Collenette revealed that he was "considering" changing the foreign-ownership rules, raising the limit from 25 per cent to 49 per cent. The news was welcomed by the stock market, which boosted Canadian's share price by 22.6 per cent and our own shares by almost 17 per cent. Personally, I had no problem, and still don't, with allowing foreign ownership of Canada's airlines, but that's an issue for Parliament to resolve after appropriate debate.

As a proponent of free-market forces I welcomed the news, but I also considered the timing so blatantly contrived as to be almost comical. Over the years since arriving in Montreal, I had come to believe that Air Canada's biggest problem had nothing to do with its people, its service, or its image. It had everything to do, however, with the deeply entrenched notion of far too many at Transport Canada that privatizing the airline had been one of the biggest mistakes since Confederation. More than ten years after the event too many people in Ottawa were lamenting the fact that we were no longer a tool of public policy, and Collenette's hasty proposal to change the foreign-ownership rules, permitting a U.S. airline possibly to seize control of Air Canada through a Liberal-friendly intermediary, was ludicrous.

I was not surprised, however, given Collenette's supposedly off-the-cuff comment to me weeks earlier. Others, choosing speculation over fact, saw it differently. According to *Globe and Mail* columnist Hugh

Winsor, Collenette asked Canadian Airlines to formally request that section 47 be invoked, supposedly "to provide the government with political cover if it comes under attack from Western politicians, namely the Reform Party." This had the ring of truth to it, but why couldn't Collenette and the federal government simply take the initiative and waive the rule, recognizing what everyone else could see clearly—that the two-airline policy was doomed?

On the face of it, Collenette's decision provided an opportunity to seriously discuss market rationalization through a merger. We had already scoped out a concept for the resulting airline, and although it would not be an easy task to pull off, it would be a global force when it was accomplished.

But on August 19, 1999, before we could get together with Canadian, the grand plan was unveiled when Gerry Schwartz leaked plans to buy both us and Canadian Airlines, subject to changes in the ownership rules for Air Canada, and merge them into one airline. This was the hostile-takeover move I had sensed was coming and had briefed our board on. I began making plans to derail it at every level—in the public forum, through links with investment banks, and at Air Canada, by building opposition to the Onex plan among the airline's employees. First, of course, we needed the details. Instead, I received a telephone call from Schwartz himself first thing the following morning.

"Hi," he said when I answered the telephone in my office, "it's Gerry." In spite of his friendly opening, he sounded tense. "Do you know why I'm calling?"

"You want us to switch our in-flight catering from Cara to Sky Chefs, right?" I replied. Onex owned 50 per cent of Sky Chefs, an in-flight catering service.

He laughed uncomfortably and we talked for a few minutes about nothing substantial. We both knew there would be a lot of action in the coming weeks, and we ended the conversation on a friendly note, with little of substance exchanged between us.

Gerry made things official at a televised press conference immediately afterwards, and I noticed that he appeared as tense in front of the television camera as he had been on the telephone talking to me. Since then I've gotten to know Gerry, and my sense is that the tension was really rooted in the audacity of the plan he was pursuing. Although there is no way an outsider could understand the media scrutiny we live under at Air Canada, he undoubtedly had an idea that this would be national news for some time to come.

His plan consisted of paying $8.25 per share for our stock and $2.00 per share of Canadian's stock. The new company, to be named AirCo during the interim, would be owned 31 per cent by Onex, 15 per cent by AMR (the parent company of American Airlines), and the rest by public investors. He also promised to "keep fares low" and to honour the frequent flyer points earned by customers of both airlines. The entire proposal was designed to circumvent the 10 per cent limit on Air Canada stock ownership.

Gerry played up the deal's appeal to both the government and the public but avoided certain critical details, such as his plan to shift the new airline's back-office services, including accounting, to American Airlines. He also stated that the new Air Canada would drop out of the Star Alliance and join the OneWorld Alliance, of which American Airlines was a member.

Our team immediately began drafting a rejection to the Onex plan, based on the fact that the offer was unsolicited and priced below the market value of our company, and noting that the new company would clearly be dominated by American Airlines. Minutes before Gerry's television appearance began I had received a telephone call from Jürgen Weber, chairman and CEO of Lufthansa, and one of the most astute people I have met in this business. Jürgen, as usual, came right to the point. "Robert," he said, "I understand Schwartz is making an offer to buy your airline. I want you to know that we're a loyal Star Alliance member and we'll support you against him. We'll help you beat this guy."

I consider Jürgen a good friend and was naturally pleased to receive his support. I wondered, however, if there were other reasons for his call. Losing us as a Star Alliance member would represent a risk to some of Lufthansa's traffic between Germany and North America, which was a practical business concern. I also knew Jürgen had dealt with Schwartz over the years through Sky Chefs and that Schwartz had made a lot of money selling the company to Lufthansa. (It was sold in two halves—one before the Air Canada takeover attempt and one after.) Was Jürgen's familiarity with Onex part of his motivation for offering his assistance in fighting off the Onex bid?

Then David Collenette acknowledged that Kevin Benson had informed the transport minister of Schwartz's proposal *before* Collenette suspended the Competition Act, thus opening the door for Onex's plan. It can be argued, I suppose, that the creation of the Onex deal and the suspension of the Competition Act were not connected and that Collenette's action acknowledged something that the rest of Canada had foreseen for months. There is enough evidence, however, to suggest that this was absolute nonsense.

It was becoming obvious that the minister of transport was complicit in shaking down Air Canada on behalf of Onex and, of all things, American Airlines—in essence, ceding control of both Air Canada and Canadian Airlines to some office in Dallas. Couldn't anyone else see it that way? Actually, they did. I realized that the rest of Canada—at least the part outside the transport ministry—recognized the implications when the TV comedy show *This Hour Has 22 Minutes* did a hilarious send-up of the situation. I obtained a tape of the show and played it to our board of directors, who howled at the show's portrayal.

The cast made it high comedy, but other aspects of the story played more like low tragedy, given the actions of certain quarters in the federal government.

Consider the revelation that Schwartz, who apparently has an interest in things military, decided that he would like a flight in a CF-18 Hornet jet fighter. Just for the record, so would I, and so would millions of other people who love airplanes. Too bad we couldn't ask David Collenette to help us hitch a ride in one. In June 1995, when Collenette was minister of defence, he took whatever steps were necessary for civilian Gerry Schwartz to strap himself into the seat of a CF-18B, the two-seater version of the Hornet. I have no doubt that Gerry enjoyed the ride and that Collenette made it all possible. Hey, what are friends for?

When details of Schwartz's joy ride became public, and complaints about cronyism were made, Collenette began retrenching. His spokesman, Peter Gregg, admitted that the defence minister had played a role in arranging Schwartz's flight but claimed that this was part of a "military civilian outreach program" and insisted that the final decision in these matters was always left up to the military chain of command. Apparently, no one told the military about this deal, because people in the Department of Defence revealed that they had never heard of a "military civilian outreach program" and that they had never taken businesspeople on a similar flight in the past. In any case, such a program was unnecessary because, as military analyst Michel Drapeau noted, "the military would find it difficult to turn down a direct request from the Minister of Defence."

If Collenette could get Schwartz aboard a CF-18, he could almost certainly help him in other ways. I don't blame Gerry for using every potential advantage he could muster to his proposal's benefit; any businessperson would. What was objectionable was the seeming complicity of a minister of the crown in facilitating a deal to the detriment of the people at Air Canada and those who depended on them.

When suspicions arose that the connection between Schwartz and Collenette was behind the Onex bid, the transport minister began scurrying here and there to protect himself. He claimed that waiving the rules of the Competition Bureau had been necessitated by the serious financial challenges facing Air Canada and Canadian Airlines. This may be have been true for Canadian but not for Air Canada. His statement was almost syllable-for-syllable the kind of rhetoric being floated by American Airlines and Onex.

My judgement is that Collenette and others in his office knew of and provided support for Schwartz's plan, if only through tacit agreement. I suspected as much during a meeting with Collenette and some of his staff that Lamar and I attended several weeks before Schwartz's official August 24 announcement. In the midst of a discussion about the difficulties both Air Canada and Canadian Airlines were encountering, Collenette had tipped his hand when he said: "Maybe somebody is going to come along and whack you two together." He repeated the idea, in different words, several times over the next few weeks while we and Canadian Airlines danced around each other, and this is precisely what Onex and American eventually proposed. Collenette kept protesting that he had not been in contact with Onex before Schwartz's announcement, but his own people conceded that he was "aware of Onex's interest in merging the two airlines" and that he supported waiving the competition rules to save Canadian Airlines from financial ruin. Responding to charges of collusion tossed at him by the Opposition and the media, Collenette stated: "It suits some interests to make a certain declaration about the intentions of the federal government, but we have no pre-conditioned view of who the owners [of Air Canada and Canadian Airlines] should be." Some may choose to believe this. I choose to believe otherwise.

Much of this became known only later, as events unfolded. From August to mid-September, we could not have responded to these developments even if we had known about them. We were too busy implementing a strategy to keep Air Canada out of the hands of the Onex team and beyond the long-distance reach of American Airlines.

IF SOMEONE pokes me in the eye, my response is to poke him back with two fingers in both eyes, and in the first day or two following the Onex announcement, I was ready to do just that. I suppose I took Gerry Schwartz's and Don Carty's actions personally, because I had had all of about two weeks to warm the CEO chair before the takeover was launched. Many ideas I hoped to implement as CEO would be put on the back burner while we fought this attack, or abandoned entirely if we lost, and I resented seeing them disrupted in this manner. It was difficult not to respond immediately and forcefully to the Onex takeover attempt, but we simply stated that the offer was both unsolicited and below market value and that we would make no comment until we had studied the proposal in detail.

76

For almost a month we published no official reply to the Onex proposal. Our silence unnerved Onex and American Airlines, which had undoubtedly expected us to react with an immediate counterproposal, which would have launched the anticipated exchange of offers and counteroffers. Without a response from us, the Onex plan just lay there to be dissected and criticized by everyone with a point of view. Our silence prodded some people in the media to call me an enigma, but it didn't matter. We had a strategy and we stuck to it.

We were silent but not inactive. We refused to make a comment or proposal until every detail had been examined and every option tested. At the beginning, it wasn't easy. Part of me wanted to step into the ring and duke it out. As time passed, however, I recognized the benefit of taking our own good time, and I began to enjoy watching the Onex team flail around during the month it took us to respond.

There was another reason for moving slowly. I was still being viewed as a marketing guy who had managed to work his way to the top of the company, as though it had all been done by some sleight of hand perhaps. I had gained considerable experience in my three years as COO before moving into the top position. Still, at the age of thirty-nine, I was the youngest-ever CEO of any major international airline, and I suspected that some people questioned my ability to handle such a high-stress situation. Appearing almost overly methodical countered a perception that I was headstrong and impulsive, and it certainly didn't hurt to double-check every move we planned to make before revealing it to the world. Time, within reason, was on our side, and we intended to use it.

This left Onex to shadow-box, and since it was the only one in the ring, every move was scrutinized and second-guessed. Whenever Gerry was asked how he could justify creating an apparent monopoly in Canadian-based international air travel, his answers or previous statements did more harm than any comment from me could. At one point in the past he had said, "Being the biggest in Canada is like being the biggest in Kansas," a comment that did not sit well with anyone uncomfortable about the idea of a Canadian icon being acquired by a guy with heavyweight American partners. Gerry took such a pummelling over this and similar comments that almost overnight a red maple leaf magically appeared on the Onex logo to proclaim the company's nationalist identity. (It has since disappeared.)

During the four weeks following the official Onex announcement, the Onex team never laid a glove on us, but it was beaten up rather badly in the media. Even more comical than the maple leaf on the

Onex logo was a scene developed for a Don Carty press conference in Toronto. Don, who probably hadn't lived in Canada for twenty years, had a backdrop of perhaps twenty Canadian flags. He started off about how he loved to spend time in the Ottawa Valley. It was all too funny.

WHILE PREPARING our counterproposal, we discovered that Onex had virtually cornered the market on the major lobbying firms in Ottawa, contracting four of the five leading companies to act on their behalf. Onex also tied up the larger merchant banks, with the exception of the Canadian Imperial Bank of Commerce (CIBC), and began a love-in with Canadian Auto Workers (CAW) union president Buzz Hargrove. Clearly, Gerry was leaving nothing to chance. By aligning all the big guns he could muster against us, he was restricting our ability to recruit allies in the political, financial, and union arenas. If he could pull this deal off, it would be amazing. Gerry was playing for keeps, and I respected him for that.

We needed some tough tactics to battle this take-no-prisoners approach. In search of advice, I contacted Michael Tannenbaum, who had attended Harvard Business School with my father forty years earlier and who rose to become vice-chairman of the investment banking firm Bear Sterns. "Robert," he said when I finished outlining the situation to him, "the best piece of advice I can give you is to go out and hire the two best investment banking firms you can find and the two best legal firms you can find."

"Why two?" I asked.

"Because you will discover, in a situation like this, that each will keep trying to top the other in showing you who can come up with the best ideas to defend the company. You will pay twice as much for the advice, but if you win, it will be worth the money. And if you lose, Schwartz gets the bill."

I received a good deal of counsel during the next three months or so, but none was better than Michael's. We hired both Goldman Sachs and Nesbitt Burns as investment bankers and retained two top attorneys at Stikeman Elliott, one in the Montreal office and the other in Toronto. All four worked harder and developed better ideas, in my opinion, than if they had been working individually for us. We gained an extra bonus when Calin Rovinescu, the managing partner at Stikeman Elliott, began taking charge of the legal side and soon became my key adviser on all aspects of our response. This would eventually become a replay of the old TV commercials for Remington shavers, in which Victor Kiam declared that he had been so impressed with the shaver that he bought the company. I was so impressed with Calin that I later hired him as our executive vice-president of corporate development and strategy.

BUZZ HARGROVE'S CAW represented ten thousand customer service staff and cargo agents at Air Canada and Canadian Airlines, and I thought it would be beneficial for Buzz and me to meet: I could bring him up to speed on what we were trying to do and on how our plans would benefit his union members in ways that the Onex proposal would not. So far, Hargrove had heard only the Onex side of things, and I was one person he would want information from. Although we were still fine-tuning our position, I believed we could outline it to him in general terms.

Hargrove and a couple of people from his staff met me for breakfast at a club near Dorval airport. Both of us established from the outset that this would be an off-the-record chat, an opportunity for each of us to absorb the other's position, especially when it came to protecting jobs at both Air Canada and Canadian Airlines. To encourage a frank exchange of ideas and positions, we also agreed that our discussion would remain confidential.

Our conversation was wide-ranging and a little tense at times but generally respectful. Because of our agreement about confidentiality, I spoke candidly about some aspects of our position, and when we parted, I hoped we had built at least a foundation of trust between us. By the time I arrived back at my office, Buzz had called a press conference and repeated many of the candid comments I had made on a range of topics, spinning the tale to put himself and his points in the best light and treating most of my views with disdain. I was disappointed that he had done this, but I learned a valuable lesson about labour leaders, especially national ones who have a limited interest in the realities of the local employees' lives. It just made it more clear that a wide array of forces had lined up against us and they were playing rough.

Buzz's warm support of the Onex plan represented a strange alliance, to say the least. Schwartz is a corporate takeover specialist. Hargrove, the Worker's Champion, whose oft-repeated mantra was "No layoffs," claimed to hold a promise from Schwartz that every union employee would retain his or her job. Yet Onex press releases were suggesting that half the CAW members at the two airlines would be unemployed when the merger took place, and here Hargrove and Schwartz were practically strolling arm in arm together.

Because I have high regard for both Gerry's and Buzz's shrewd business sense, I am sure that any agreement between the two of them would have been mutually beneficial. I suspect, and others have suggested, that Hargrove expected the federal government to inject large quantities of cash into the Onex buy-out transaction, thanks to Schwartz's Liberal connections, and that Buzz believed a fair chunk of the money would be aimed at buying out a substantial number of CAW members at the new airline. If so, this was reason enough for Buzz to throw considerable support behind Onex.

Gerry may have known exactly what he was doing in recruiting Buzz Hargrove, but on this occasion Hargrove misread his own union members—something he rarely does. Air Canada members of the CAW expressed outrage at Hargrove's buddy-buddy act with Schwartz, and they staged a protest march on CAW headquarters. Hargrove, apparently unable to understand that a group of unionized workers could be so loyal to their employer that they would defend it against unfair actions by their own union, charged that Air Canada had managed and bankrolled the protest. This accusation was totally false, and he later withdrew it.

DURING THIS TIME, Gerry asked to meet me and discuss the deal, one on one. Our board's legal adviser almost tore his hair out arguing against the idea, but I decided to go ahead anyway. If nothing else, Gerry and I could state our positions directly instead of having them delivered in sound bites or through third parties. Neither of us, I believed, would be foolish enough to ruin his position with a misplaced word or comment or distort our point of view in the media.

We met at the Toronto office of Stikeman Elliott, and after some forced pleasantries—including my teasing him about how much media attention he was getting—Gerry made a direct pitch to me. "Robert," he said, "you're the guy who will be running things. I just want you to know that people who run companies for me make a lot of money. I can assure you that you'll be comfortable with this deal."

Gerry laid it all out on the table. I saw it for what it was—a hard-sell offer to bring me on board and short-circuit a number of difficulties he would face. I thanked him for the offer and said I'd think about it. I repeated my concerns about having to drop out of the Star Alliance and join the OneWorld Alliance and went on my way. Things ended on a conciliatory note, and they even stayed that way for a few days.

I am sure that Gerry would have been a generous controlling share-holder, as he had promised. There was, however, a more important target—to get Air Canada to become a strong and internationally rele-vant carrier.

WE WERE BOTH working behind the scenes to round up support from shareholders, the government, union leaders, financial backers, and Air Canada employees. The Onex team was somewhat successful at dealing with the first four groups, but it failed spectacularly with Air Canada employees.

I suspect that much of Onex's inability to win our people over to its side resulted from its lack of understanding of the airline industry and the attitudes of people working within it. Any misinterpretation of how the industry works soon becomes apparent, especially if accompanied by criticism of the employees' performance. Combining unfamiliarity with criticism is not a good way to win loyalty and support.

Gerry discovered this when, still functioning as a lightning rod for all the media attention, he made unflattering remarks about the pro-ductivity of Air Canada pilots to a group of financial analysts in early September. He apparently also suggested that a blanket approach to seniority would determine which pilots would retain their jobs in the new airline. Since the Canadian Airlines pilots enjoyed substantially more seniority, most of the job cuts would come at the expense of Air Canada pilots. Gerry's comments were dutifully reported in the business press, and when Gerry showed up for a meeting with the pilots, he paid the price. The meeting grew raucous, and the pilots refused to support the Onex bid.

"He [Schwartz] is crashing into the Air Canada employees' world," said Jean-Marc Bélanger, an extremely bright and articulate fellow who was at the time the chairman of ACPA, "and he's changing everything in mid-stream. How can anyone imagine [the Onex plan] working when you are punishing the workforce of the successful airline?"

Air Canada pilots were not the only ones to give Schwartz a rough time. He encountered similar opposition from flight attendants, customer service staff, maintenance crews, and others at Air Canada, partially because they were being kept more abreast of developments than Schwartz suspected. We did this via the company telephone network, where employees could access messages from me, providing as much information as we could reveal in as direct a manner as possible. The employees' jobs were at stake, and it would have been both foolish and disastrous to keep them in the dark. So we explained what was going on, acknowledged their concerns, and presented our position with no fluff. Here's what employees heard from me on August 24, the day Onex officially presented its offer:

> At a press conference this morning, Toronto-based Onex Corporation, a Canadian diversified investment company, announced that it will offer $5.7 billion to take over both Air Canada and Canadian Airlines, and then merge the two companies under the Air Canada name.
>
> Until we actually receive the offer, I can't comment on its content. However, my first reaction upon listening to Mr. Schwartz's announcement is that it is difficult to understand how a below-market offer involving the layoff of some Air Canada employees could possibly be of interest.
>
> I also feel our offer to purchase Canadian's international operations is still the best solution for the future of Canadian Airlines,

because it meets the government's desire to sustain a more viable air industry while preserving the interests of consumers.

As Mr. Schwartz pointed out in his press conference, his discussions to date have excluded Air Canada, so whatever figures or numbers he used have not been seen by us. So please don't take them to be fact.

Since the government took the unusual step of invoking Section 47, we can expect there will be aggressive action over approximately the next eighty days. Invariably, there will be takeover bids, counteroffers, and various other rumours swirling around.

I want to reassure all of you that, in evaluating the Onex offer or any other proposal that comes our way, I am committed to ensuring that the final result is acceptable to all Air Canada stakeholders—our employees, our shareholders, and our customers.

Every day throughout the takeover attempt, thousands of Air Canada employees accessed these messages and provided positive feedback on their value. They also sent dozens of e-mails a day, and I tried to respond to each one. Clearly, the employees were concerned about their jobs, but I also believe that they sensed my commitment to do the right thing for them and saw my efforts to maintain communication with them in that light. When I flew into Toronto the day after Buzz Hargrove and Gerry Schwartz expressed confidence that the Onex plan would prevail, I got off the plane to discover dozens of Air Canada employees cheering me on, all wearing pins proclaiming NO CAW! and BUZZ OFF!

It was a good moment.

There were other good moments as well, made more memorable because they occurred in the midst of so much tension and drama. Long before the Onex episode had started, I had promised my daughter, Emily, then three years old, that I would take her to Disney World to see her favourite Disney characters and her cousins, who planned to be there at the same time. Both Lizanne and I could hardly wait to see her reaction at her first sight of the characters. It was a sight I refused to miss or delay. The week we planned to go, other Onex-related events

83

threatened to ruin the experience. I was to leave for a speaking engagement in Winnipeg one evening, return to Montreal overnight, and then head right off to Orlando. With careful scheduling I might steal one weekend day with Lizanne, Emily, and six-month-old Nicholas in Florida, but I had to be back in Montreal the next morning, something that no scheduled airline could accomplish.

I asked the people at Bombardier if they could provide assistance, and they kindly provided a Lear 60 to take me to Winnipeg, where I delivered the speech on Friday night before flying home to Montreal to pick up the family and head for Orlando and Disney World, where I was thrilled to watch Emily's reaction as she saw for the first time all the characters she loved. The next morning I hopped back on the Learjet bound for Montreal, leaving Lizanne and the children behind and having fulfilled a promise to myself and my family. I had assured Emily that she would meet all her favourites characters, like Winnie the Pooh and Mickey Mouse, and she had. I guess I was pretty excited, because Lizanne later told me that after I boarded the aircraft for Canada, Emily turned to her and said, "Does Daddy know the characters aren't real?"

BY MID-SEPTEMBER 1999, we were getting a clearer picture of Onex's strategy and methods. We learned that Gerry Schwartz had started buying Air Canada shares in June, acquiring $43 million worth that month through two numbered companies (by September 9, the shares were worth over $72 million). When these purchases became public knowledge, David Collenette began floating the idea of changing the rule that prevented any single entity from owning more than 10 per cent of Air Canada, which struck me as a blatant gesture in Onex's favour. It was suggested that Onex had known in advance about Ottawa's intention to suspend the competition rules and thus enjoyed an unfair advantage. When Collenette's critics pointed this out, he began a back-pedalling act, denying that he or his staff favoured either side in the takeover bid.

Most people ignored him, including Gerry and me. To be honest, we were too busy duelling with each other to spend time on Collenette and his antics. Onex launched one skirmish when it criticized Air Canada's profit performance, claiming our shareholders "would have been better off burying their money in their backyards rather than investing it in Air Canada stock." The best way to counter this comment, I believed, was to release our financial statements immediately, for less than a full quarter instead of waiting a month until they were due to be released, and to let our shareholders make their own assessment based on the facts. The figures revealed that we had made impressive increases in our earnings and were continuing to rack up substantial cost reductions—in other words, we were doing a pretty good job of running the airline under stressful conditions.

Around that time we learned that if Canadian Airlines were sold it would be obligated to pay an "escape fee" to AMR, the parent company of American Airlines, of about $500 million, plus another $500 million to cover some preferred share debt. A billion dollars paid to AMR for Canadian Airlines? The only thing more outrageous than the price was the fact that neither Canadian nor AMR had disclosed the existence of these conditions until now.

Both of us began making our case in advertisements. In Onex's case, the ads included outlandish promises we knew it could not keep, including a freeze on ticket prices for five years and a promise to maintain service to remote communities. They were making political campaign promises that could never be kept, but if we were gone, why bother?

Meanwhile, we were kept busy lining up the funding needed to ward off the attack. With pledges of financial support from our Star Alliance partners United Airlines and Lufthansa, I began working to bring CIBC to our side as a critical third source. CIBC had a long-standing relationship with Onex, but it had also done very well with our Aeroplan program. Its VISA cardholders could earn Aeroplan points every time they used the card, making Aeroplan a powerful generator of loyalty in the cutthroat credit card market. The value of Aeroplan to CIBC was enormous, because it was exclusive to the bank and because Aeroplan points are the most desired incentive award in Canada. The Aerogold VISA card is nothing less than a cash-producing machine for CIBC, representing an estimated 20 to 25 per cent of the bank's market capitalization.

My investment banking contact at CIBC was a bright guy named David Kassie, who was CEO of CIBC World Markets at the time.

Although Kassie was always willing to lend an ear to my proposal that his bank provide financial backup to help us fight Onex, I was unable to wrest a commitment from him or from John Hunkin, CIBC's chairman and CEO. I've always liked John, and he has always kept his commitments. In this case, I suspected he was relying on the bank's long-term relationship with Onex to guarantee that it would retain Aeroplan, should they be successful. Whenever I asked Kassie and Hunkin to commit to the funding plan I was proposing, they didn't say yes and they didn't say no. They just kept being coy about it, perhaps assuming that whichever way the deal went they couldn't lose. I suspected differently.

Despite CIBC's relationship with Gerry Schwartz (who was also on the board of ScotiaBank), it was TD Bank, not CIBC, that was spearheading the financial guidance for Onex. This did not appear to disturb the people at CIBC very much. I suspect their objective was to retain and enhance the Aeroplan association with their VISA card, which represented a better long-term benefit than a one-off investment banking deal. Still, I couldn't persuade CIBC to make the move over to our side and commit the financing we needed. It was frustrating.

In the midst of this, I was at home one rainy Sunday afternoon, flipping through the *New York Times,* when I discovered manna from heaven in the form of a full-page advertisement for American Airlines' AAdvantage program. American, the ad announced, had teamed up with TD Waterhouse, the discount brokerage arm of TD Bank. American's involvement with Schwartz and Onex was well known, and everyone expected American to play a decisive role in managing Air Canada if Schwartz and his people were successful. In fact, the Onex proposal stated quite clearly that American would retain two seats on the new board of directors, and American would have much more influence on the new airline's operations than those two seats might otherwise represent.

I tore the page out of the *Times,* grabbed a pen, and wrote across the face of the ad: "Dear John—If you were unsure about which bank will be aligned with Aeroplan, now you know!" I signed it "Sincerely, Robert," and FedEx'd the page to John Hunkin. Within a week, we had a deal with CIBC.

OFFERS,
COUNTEROFFERS,
AND A
QUIET ENDING

O N SEPTEMBER 21, 1999, we announced our response to the Onex plan, noting that Onex's offer had been formulated only after Onex had received assurances that section 47 would be invoked. We added that the Onex proposal was illegal because it violated the 10 per cent ownership rule for Air Canada. Then we formally rejected the entire proposal, based on five points:

1. There would be a massive transfer of wealth from Air Canada shareholders to the Canadian Airlines/Onex/AMR group.
2. The offer failed to reflect the true market value of Air Canada.
3. Shareholders would be exposed to an excessive level of risk.
4. The future job prospects for Air Canada employees would be seriously threatened.
5. The Onex proposal was riddled with serious legal and regulatory issues.

Our counteroffer was essentially a share buy-back plan in which we would pay $12 per share to acquire 35 per cent of outstanding Air

Canada stock and pay $92 million for Canadian Airlines. We intended to obtain financial assistance from Lufthansa and United, which would obtain 7 per cent of the new company between them, and CIBC, which would own 3 per cent. We planned to operate Canadian Airlines as an entity separate from Air Canada, and we made no promise to freeze airfares or cut services. I also announced that we had signed a ten-year commitment locking us into the Star Alliance and preventing Air Canada from switching to OneWorld. Onex immediately labelled this a poison pill. To us, it was just good strategy.

Gerry continued to protest that he neither sought nor received any special favours from the Liberal government. He even claimed that his past support for Chrétien's Liberals put him at a disadvantage because it cast suspicion on the government's motives. This was too much even for some Liberal MPs to swallow, and at least one of them concluded that Onex would not have made its bid without receiving assurance that the 10 per cent ownership restriction would be lifted.

Onex won a victory when a Quebec court ruling permitted them to name the date of a special shareholders' meeting. Onex chose Monday, November 8—sooner than we preferred. In any case, the showdown day was now established. We all knew what we were working towards, and when.

THROUGHOUT THIS EXERCISE, I was obliged to travel to Ottawa numerous times, sitting in stuffy rooms through far too many bash–Air Canada sessions. I can't remember exactly how many of these trips I took, but I knew I was spending too much time away from home when Lizanne told me that Emily said, "I don't like Ottawa because Daddy does so many things with Ottawa and not with us."

On various occasions during these visits I asked David Collenette and his people if they planned to waive the 10 per cent ownership rule, but each time they refused to respond directly. I found this refusal and the constantly changing rules so outrageous that I said their approach was perhaps suitable only for a banana republic, "but certainly not the actions you would expect from the government of a G8 nation!" I may have lost my temper delivering those words so bluntly, but I wanted there to be no question of my meaning. It was clear to me, as it was clear to everyone familiar with the situation, that Collenette was playing directly into the hands of Onex and its partner, American Airlines. This lack of forthrightness, added to Collenette's lifting of the Competition Act, which had permitted the entire process to begin, suggested that an egregious abuse of the law was being carried out on behalf of a corporation headed by an individual who boasted close connections at the highest level of the ruling political party. Does that not sound like the kind of shenanigans encountered in a banana republic?

I took a little flak for this comment, but I stand by my words today. Canadians did not deserve the level of arrogance displayed by some members of the federal government during the opposition-less Chrétien years, and neither did Air Canada, a target of Ottawa's disdain for fair treatment on many occasions. When people asked why I was fighting the government, I would tell them it wasn't me, and it wasn't. By bashing Air Canada, these guys could get coverage. I tried to stand up to them, and they went after me. I have no regrets.

THE BOARD OF DIRECTORS strongly supported our strategy, but some directors became nervous now and then. Their concerns necessitated an occasional showdown between the board and me at critical points, when I had to dig my heels in a bit.

Jim Goodwin of United Airlines and Jürgen Weber of Lufthansa had offered financial assistance in our battle with Onex. Although I considered both men good friends and appreciated their backing, I knew their offer contained a measure of self-interest; as members of Star Alliance they wanted Air Canada to remain in the organization instead of moving to OneWorld, where we would wind up if Onex and American Airlines proved successful. We discussed an arrangement in which, together with CIBC, United Airlines and Lufthansa would grant access to a half-billion dollars in funding, to be provided essentially in the form of a non-repayable gift. Nothing had yet been formally signed, however, and I needed their firm commitment in my pocket.

Jim, Jürgen, and I agreed to get together at a Star Alliance meeting scheduled for October 15 in Tokyo, where we could move towards finalizing the arrangements. As it happened, an Air Canada board of directors meeting had been arranged on October 13, so my plan was to join the board meeting via telephone from Chicago's O'Hare airport before catching a United flight to Tokyo.

The board meeting would be something of a challenge. I appreciated the unease expressed by certain directors, some of whom feared that going down this route with Lufthansa and United would be tough and risky. More than a few board members, I suspected, actually might have welcomed the easier option of cutting a deal with Onex. To this day, I feel that if Gerry and American had come in the front door on a friendly basis, he would have disarmed enough board members to prevent a defence from being mounted. Instead, he decided on a hostile bid, so we had no alternative but to fight back.

Our strategy—to outbid Onex with a counteroffer that would involve re-purchasing 35 per cent of outstanding Air Canada stock—would derail his plan and provide a fair return for our shareholders. The original share price of $8.25 proposed by Onex had been so low that it was insulting. Our offer to pay $12 per share for 35 per cent of Air Canada stock, plus $92 million to purchase Canadian Airlines and operate it as a separate entity, was both more appealing and less complex. We estimated 2,500 jobs would be lost at Canadian Airlines. Along with these financial aspects of our response, we announced a plan to launch a new discount airline out of Hamilton, Ontario. I wanted to do this, because I could see how low-cost carriers were encroaching on our traditional bread-and-butter markets and because I wanted to find more ways to keep more employees gainfully employed.

The price tag for all of this hovered around $900 million. It was workable, but we couldn't announce the details until all the financing was in place, and we couldn't put the financing in place unless we wrapped up the deals with United Airlines and Lufthansa, which I planned to do at the Star Alliance meeting. That was my pitch to the board from Chicago: give me full authority to finalize things with Goodwin and Weber in Tokyo, return with a done deal, and go public with our counteroffer immediately.

I boarded our Chicago-bound flight out of Dorval on the morning of October 13, slipping into the jump seat behind the pilots as I often do. As it happened, this flight was being handled by a line indoctrination captain riding with a first officer who was on his first flight with us. (The line indoctrination captain's role is to ensure that the pilot who has just completed training is suitably prepared for his or her new position.) The young pilot, sitting in the right-hand seat, turned and smiled. "My first flight," he said, "and I'm going into the world's busiest airport with the president of the airline looking over my shoulder!"

I assured him he would do a great job, and he did. Within minutes of landing at O'Hare I was on the telephone back to Montreal and the board meeting.

I had hoped the meeting would be cut and dried. In fact, I had planned on it—my flight to Tokyo left Chicago within a couple of hours of my arrival there. I expected to review the situation, satisfy any concerns that might be raised, then grab my bag and head for the boarding gate. But some board members raised questions about the strategy we were pursuing. Soon the discussion was going around and around the table, and it continued right up to the departure time of my flight. Nothing had been settled, and it would be fruitless for me to go on to Tokyo without carrying the board's full agreement with me.

My flight had been delayed by about an hour, which gave me more time to participate, but with about ten minutes left before the aircraft was to pull away from the gate, I broke into the discussion. "I have just minutes to make my flight to Tokyo," I said. "I will not get on that plane unless this issue is totally resolved and the board gives me its unanimous support to proceed with this arrangement. I cannot look my partners in the eye and tell them that I have backing from the Air Canada board of directors if I in fact do not have 100 per cent support. If I don't get it, I will return to Montreal, we will be back to square one, and Onex will maintain the upper hand. So my question is—do I go to Tokyo? Or do I go back to Montreal?"

The chairman asked for a motion, a vote was taken, I received the unanimous support I had asked for, and I grabbed my bag and jogged to the gate. In Tokyo, I assured Jim Goodwin and Jürgen Weber that

91

the board backed our strategy completely. They delivered on their promise, we shook hands on the deal, and after a night's sleep in Tokyo I caught an evening flight to Los Angeles, completing, to that point, my shortest-ever trip to Asia.

In Los Angeles I hopped aboard a Montreal-bound Air Canada A-319 and peeked into the cockpit to say hello to the crew. Looking back at me was the same first officer who had flown me to Chicago two mornings earlier. "Oh no!" he exlaimed. "On my first flight, I'm blocked into the busiest airport in the world with you looking over my shoulder. Now I'm making my first night landing as an Air Canada pilot, and you're back watching me again!"

I did the same thing I had done when we took off for Chicago. I slapped him on the back, smiled, and told him I was sure he would do a great job. And he did.

OUR SHARE buy-back offer set Onex back on its heels, especially when we announced that we had signed ten-year extensions of our agreements with Star Alliance, CIBC's Aerogold, and Cara Operations Ltd. (to provide in-flight food services). Onex challenged the legality of our Star Alliance contract, noting that it would cost a new owner hundreds of millions of dollars to back out of the deal—a classic case of the pot calling the kettle black, considering the hidden agreements between Canadian Airlines and American Airlines that we had discovered a few weeks earlier. The contract with Cara, worth perhaps $1.5 billion over the term of the deal, was admittedly a poke in the eye at Onex, who owned half of Cara's chief competitor. It made the deal less palatable to Onex, however, and that was the whole idea. We were in this game to win, just as Onex was. And we were determined to use every weapon available to us, just as Onex was.

With the shareholders' meeting looming, we appointed proxy solicitors to obtain voting rights from Air Canada shareholders. The solicitors established a toll-free telephone number for shareholders to call and direct their votes in our favour. Not surprisingly, the proxy solicitors began receiving dozens of calls from Canadians offering their support to Air Canada management. But when the solicitors asked how many shares the callers owned, the response was often, "I don't own any shares. I just wanted to vote for Air Canada." This was just one illustration of an attitude I noticed over and over again, which Onex had misjudged: no matter how much bashing Air Canada might receive in the media or on Parliament Hill, the overwhelming majority of Canadians support the company and took steps to express that support one way or another.

With our $12 per share offer on the table, Onex began scrambling for a way of topping it. Barely ten days before the November 8 shareholders' meeting, Onex announced a rebuttal offer, consisting of an increase to $13, in cash and AMR share options, for Air Canada shares, plus a promise that American Airlines would sell its equity in the merged airline and not seek representation on the board of directors. Gerry assured everyone that no involuntary layoffs of union members would take place, up to four hundred new jobs would be created in the Montreal area, and the new airline would hold fares, maintain competition, and continue services to smaller centres. In his press release accompanying the offer, Gerry claimed he had been "listening carefully to what Canadians have told us. Today, we are responding decisively on every point."

In reality, Onex was admitting that every criticism we had made about their original offer was valid. Onex had underpriced Air Canada shares and would have made a point of handing over control of the proposed new airline to American Airlines, which would continue to drain massive quantities of money from it, as it had been doing with Canadian Airlines for years. The rest of the offer sounded like political campaign promises that could be broken if necessary. Of course, if we matched or bettered the offer and won—and this appeared to be the more likely outcome as time passed—we would be left holding the bag. We refused to up the bidding just for the sake of doing it.

I could understand Gerry Schwartz's motive. Everybody has the right to make a profit at a legal enterprise, even if this particular enterprise proved a serious distraction to me and everyone else at Air Canada. It was the attitude of his string-pulling partner American Airlines that I resented. From sources throughout the industry, I kept hearing about American's president Don Carty and his staff boasting

93

that the takeover of Air Canada was "a done deal." Confidence in reaching your goal is one thing, but these guys were smug and swaggering.

Every time I read about another American Airlines executive saying, "Air Canada won't escape us" and "The deal is in the bag," it was like someone inside my head cranking up the theme music from the movie *Rocky*, making me even more determined to win this thing. Had we failed—had Onex assumed control of Air Canada according to their original proposal and merged it with Canadian Airlines under the terms set down by American Airlines—Air Canada would have become a division of American Airlines. No matter how much others might deny or disguise it, this would have been the case—I'm sure of it.

Anyone who doubts the degree of control that American might have exerted over the new Air Canada under the Onex proposal should review American's takeover of TWA in January 2001. With its acquisition and the subsequent fallout from September 11, the airline dropped twenty thousand employees, virtually all of them former TWA staff. American would have treated Air Canada people the same way, and those who believe otherwise are deluding themselves.

American Airlines had been running circles around many in the nation's capital for some time, concealing the strings they kept pulling behind the scenes. Inevitably, the strings led to Canadian Airlines' cash accounts. These strings enabled American, even though it was a minority shareholder of Canadian, to yank money out of the airline at an enormous rate, through fees for using American Airlines' Sabre reservation account, code sharing, and other deals.

We were pressuring various provincial securities commissions to force Canadian Airlines and Onex to reveal financial obligations by either company to any third parties, if the contract or agreements were of material interest to us. Canadian and Onex stalled for weeks until, in mid-October 1999, we learned the agreement between Canadian Airlines and American Airlines required a cash payment of US$500 million to American if Canadian Airlines were to break the business relationship between them. Commonly referred to as a "lock-up" clause, this agreement was designed to prevent a new management team or owner from repudiating previous agreements.

The lock-up agreement had remained buried in the company's files like a mine prepared to explode in our face if we succeeded, and I suspected that more surprises awaited us. We resumed our demands for the Alberta, British Columbia, Ontario, and Quebec securities commissions to force total disclosure from the other side. As late as October 29, Nigel Wright, a managing director of Onex, stated that full disclosure had been made in their original offer. A court order, handed down later that same day, forced Canadian Airlines to release documents to us that revealed the entire picture.

Once we examined the documents, we determined that the total amount of penalties owed to American, should Canadian Airlines withdraw from their agreement, exceeded $1.3 billion. In addition to the US$500 million default payment, AirCo—the interim company so named by Onex—had signed an agreement with AMR to use that company's Sabre reservation services or pay a US$356 million penalty. This latter payment was especially disturbing because Onex had claimed just two days earlier that Air Canada management "would have the freedom to choose Sabre or not as its information technology supplier." It was just one more bomb in the minefield, set to blow up in the face of anyone trying to operate the new airline in the best interests of its shareholders.

Our offer to shareholders included no such hidden dangers. We increased our price from $12 to $16 per share for up to 68.7 million common and non-voting shares, representing 36.4 per cent of outstanding shares and generating a cash payment of $1.1 billion. "The cash we're offering belongs to our shareholders," I stated, "and if it is to be paid out, it should be paid 100 per cent to them and not to Onex or Canadian's stakeholders."

Within forty-eight hours Onex raised the stakes again, on paper at least, offering $17.50 per share of Air Canada—a deal we characterized as the "sticker price," not the real price. The offer was tied into the assumption that all AMR rights to shares in the new airline would be purchased by Air Canada shareholders, a dubious proposition. What's more, the offer was open for only ten days and was conditional on Onex unwinding our agreement with Star Alliance, which was even less likely—especially in the time frame being proposed—than the purchase of all those AMR rights.

The offer was so preposterous that we grew even more confident that Air Canada shareholders would reject the Onex deal at the meeting in Montreal's Queen Elizabeth Hotel, now less than three days away. On Friday, November 5, I gathered members of the team fighting the takeover to finalize our strategy. We wanted not only to win the shareholders over to the Air Canada position but to do it decisively, clearing the way for an alternative arrangement to merge Air Canada and Canadian Airlines. We met in the Raptors Room, a small boardroom, down the hall from my office, furnished with a rack of audiovisual equipment and a model of an Air Canada Airbus A-320 aircraft in the livery of the Toronto Raptors NBA team—hence its name.

We began highlighting the minefield of problems in the Onex offer and expanding on our pledge to purchase outstanding shares of Air Canada at a more attractive price than the one offered by Onex. Our presentation to shareholders would have stressed maintaining our efforts to protect the interests of Air Canada employees and acquiring Canadian Airlines in a manner that would be equitable to that company's employees, shareholders, and customers. I remained convinced that our offer would prevail, and several of us were deeply involved in tying up any loose ends, when big news came roaring in.

Justice André Wery of the Quebec Superior Court announced that Onex's proposal to temporarily convert its voting shares to non-voting shares yet retain the power to replace the Air Canada board of directors was illegal. This convoluted—some might say illogical—tactic had been an attempt to by-pass the clause that prevented any individual, corporation, or defined group from accumulating more than 10 per cent of Air Canada's outstanding shares. Onex, American, and their takeover team believed they could circumvent this rule. Their lawyers had probably invented the best possible mousetrap to get around it, but it wasn't good enough. Justice Wery said they could not by-pass the clause. We were ecstatic.

After a few high-fives, we pressed on. Within an hour of Justice Wery's decision, Gerry Schwartz called a news conference to be carried live over radio and television. As soon as we heard about it, we knew he was throwing in the towel. "Onex is disappointed in the Quebec court's conclusion that shareholders cannot accept our offer," Schwartz said as we listened. "Naturally we will respect that decision and accordingly have instructed counsel that our offers and our resolutions be immediately withdrawn."

With those few short words, the most hostile battle in Canadian corporate history was over. We did not pop champagne corks or toss confetti into the air. Our media relations people began drafting press releases announcing the judge's decision and Onex's concession, adding a statement from me that Air Canada would fulfil all the commitments we had made to shareholders. We cancelled the Monday shareholders' meeting and began dismantling the presentation equipment set up for it. I called Priscille LeBlanc, our senior director, corporate communications—and one of the nicest and most unfailingly supportive people you would want to meet—to come upstairs to discuss setting up a press briefing at the Dorval Hilton within the hour.

Priscille was as ebullient as everyone else when she arrived to find everyone celebrating with smiles, handshakes, and hugs. I suppose she expected the same mood in the boardroom, where the meeting had subsequently moved to and where she came to congratulate me. Instead, she found me leaning against the wall, staring at my shoes and trying to quell a feeling of unease.

"Robert, what's wrong?" she asked with some concern. "You should be thrilled—we won!"

"It wasn't a complete victory," I said. "I wanted a complete victory in front of the shareholders. I wanted us to make our case and persuade the shareholders to express their support for us and their rejection of Onex. They would have voted Onex down. We know it and Onex knows it. I wanted everybody else to know it too. I wanted a knockout, and instead we got a TKO." I shrugged. "It's good that we won. I just wanted more."

I did not feel that way as a result of a vindictive streak. You cannot afford to risk letting your emotions control your logic in a situation as complex and significant as this one. Nor did I dislike or resent Gerry

Schwartz for his efforts (although I would rather have spent my first three months as CEO running the airline instead of battling his take-over plan). Gerry is a smart guy and a tough businessman, and I admire him for those qualities. I simply felt a need to make a point I had hoped to establish less than three months earlier, when I had been appointed CEO. I had achieved the only career goal I had had since I was a child, but within days I had been diverted from filling that role by the challenge of a supremely competent takeover specialist operating in partnership with one of the most aggressive corporations in the airline industry, both benefiting from the backroom machinations of the federal government. We had turned the lives of so many people upside down through all those months, and for what? For an exercise, a waste of time and money, and the creation of hostile feelings.

A Quebec judge had handed us victory. I was thankful, but I had wanted us to achieve it directly, and I was disappointed.

The disappointment vanished overnight. I woke on Saturday morning with a sense of elation. We had won. We had overcome challenges and situations that were more complex than any in Canadian corporate history, and we had achieved it in the bright light of constant media coverage. What's more, we were closer to carrying out the acquisition of Canadian Airlines, something that the industry knew was inevitable and would be beneficial.

Some reports claim that Gerry Schwartz was shocked at the court decision. I suspect he was relieved. Now, with the clarity of hindsight, I often wish Gerry had won. Gerry, of course, has said many times publicly that he is glad that he didn't.

I would rather be lucky than smart, and Schwartz proved to be both lucky *and* smart. Within a few months of his decision to abandon the deal, the North American airline industry started suffering the slings and arrows of outrageous fortune, beginning with the appalling United Airlines pilot contract, the high-tech meltdown, and periodic spikes in fuel prices, and extending through September 11 and SARS.

I suspect that Gerry underestimated both the negative reaction to the news that American Airlines would be pulling so many strings if Onex won and the national obsession with Air Canada and the detailed coverage it generated. The Onex people attempted first to conceal and then to play down American's role, but any hint of U.S. domination or even serious involvement in running Canada's flag-carrying airline turned people off.

Soon after we fended off Onex Corporation and American Airlines, Herb Kelleher, head of Southwest Airlines, and I were scheduled to speak at a conference in Florida. I was standing at a bank of telephones in a hotel corridor when I saw Herb, probably the most revered personality in our business, walking towards me. I quickly put the phone down, thrust out my hand, and timidly introduced myself, assuming he wouldn't have a clue who I was. Instead he smiled, gave me the thumbs up, and said, "Way to go, getting those bastards at American!"

The next time I met Herb was at a gathering of aviation industry leaders that I belong to and that assembles twice a year. Herb came bounding up to me with a hearty "Robert, how're you doing?" I couldn't believe how sharp his recall was, given that we had met just once, briefly, in a hotel corridor. Then he raised his voice enough for everyone around us to hear, saying, "Sorry I'm late, everybody, but I came out with Carty and Baker [the number one and number two men at American at the time] on a corporate jet and I kept them waiting for a long time too. I explained to them that we had been in a critically important meeting at Southwest trying to decide what we could do to screw up American Airlines, but after a meeting that seemed to take forever we decided to give up because American was already so screwed up there was nothing we could do to make things worse!" Everyone howled.

8

MERGING WITH
CANADIAN AIRLINES

B Y N O W, Canadian's financial position was fatally weakened, and some people thought we should have let the airline fail before going in to pick up any pieces worth salvaging. The reality is that we suspected that neither Ottawa nor AMR would ever permit Canadian to fail—that despite David Collenette's denials, the federal government would, if necessary, sink hundreds of millions of dollars into Canadian Airlines and claim it had saved jobs in western Canada, a tactic it would try to convert into support for the Liberals in the next election.

We could not have salvaged routes and slots from a bankrupt Canadian Airlines even if we tried. That's not my opinion, by the way—it's the firm indication I received from the transport minister himself.

Within a few days of Justice André Wery's ruling and Gerry Schwartz's decision to abandon the field to us, Duncan Dee, our manager of government relations (now senior vice-president of corporate affairs), received a telephone call from Randy McCauley, David Collenette's chief of staff. McCauley's message was as close to a direct order as a government official can give to a supposedly private enterprise. Air Canada would not be permitted to walk away from a bankrupt Canadian Airlines, meaning the market would not be permitted to unfold as it should—not while the Liberals were in power.

McCauley covered the bases well, because he also called Warren Kinsella, who was working as a lobbyist on behalf of United Airlines. Kinsella's Liberal credentials were as broad and as deep as McCauley's, so McCauley could be as blunt as he had been with Duncan. The gist of his order to Kinsella was this: send a message to United Airlines that Air Canada had better go through with the takeover under the terms the government was handing them or they would regret it. United passed on the message to Air Canada through its government relations office. Since United was an important source of financing for us, this government threat carried a good deal of weight. No one wanted to lend a few hundred million dollars to a corporation that risked being slapped by the heavy hand of the federal government.

Those were the specifics. The generalities, which would permit Ottawa to exert its authority, were detailed in *A Policy Framework for Airline Restructuring in Canada*, tabled by the government in late October 1999. Anyone who doubts the willingness of the federal government to impose its power on business in support of the government's interests should study this document. It includes much stroking of various interest groups and assurances that Ottawa believes in healthy competition and all of that, but in Annex A the proposal addresses specific questions about an Air Canada–Canadian Airlines merger this way:

> Any merger or acquisition involving Air Canada or Canadian Airlines [must] be made subject to a special process in which the final decision to approve or disapprove a merger or acquisition proposal will be made by the Governor in Council, on the recommendation of the Minister of Transport. This recommendation may include such conditions, remedies and undertakings as may be determined by the Minister of Transport and the Commissioner of Competition. No proposal will complete this process without a decision by the Canadian

Transportation Agency that it has met the Canadian ownership and control requirements set out in the Canada Transportation Act.

You got the impression that when it came to the airline file, the government of Canada sort of made it up as it went along—this continued to be the case until Collenette left. Later, the document said, if Air Canada decided to acquire Canadian Airlines or even considered acquiring Canadian: *The Minister will then have the option of disapproving, approving or approving with modifications.*

Under these rules, Collenette and various cabinet members would determine every aspect of a Air Canada's acquisition of Canadian. Like it or not, Ottawa was exerting as much control over a supposedly privatized Air Canada as it had when the airline was a Crown corporation, with a key difference: the pressure being exerted on me was more intense than it would have been on the CEO of Air Canada, when it was "The People's Airline," because that individual would have been an Ottawa insider. I had few buddies in Ottawa, and as a result I was in no position to influence the conditions being laid down. It was a take-it-or-leave-it deal.

The true intent of the restructuring policy paper was made clear to me in private conversations, where any threats were undisguised. At one meeting in a Transport Canada office, with Canadian Airlines executives present, Collenette laid it on the line. He knew that the most valuable components of Canadian Airlines were its routes to Japan and its landing slots at Heathrow, LaGuardia, and O'Hare airports. If Canadian Airlines collapsed, we wanted to acquire those assets.

"Let me remind you," Collenette said, "that those routes and slots do not belong to Canadian Airlines. They are the property of the Canadian government, and carriers like Air Transat and Canada 3000 would like to have them as much as you."

The warning was clear: if we permitted Canadian Airlines to fail, we would not obtain either the Asia Pacific routes or the international airport slots. We would have a new and even worse version of the division of the world policy. To have any hope of obtaining the routes or the slots, we would have to accept ownership of Canadian Airlines on the government's terms, conveniently preventing the government from having to deal with a problem it had created itself. For years, pundits have been muttering that buying Canadian Airlines was a bad decision on our part and that letting it slide into oblivion would have been a wiser business move. In hindsight, after September 11 and SARS, of course, I agree. But it was always a moot issue, as Ottawa would not have permitted us to do so.

I believed that if we did not agree to absorb Canadian Airlines, the government would inject enough money in it to prop it up for an indeterminate period, damaging us as it hemorrhaged and claiming to be doing everyone a favour, winning some badly needed support in western Canada, and blocking us from access to the Asia Pacific routes and the U.K. and U.S. slots. If the airline failed anyway, I suspected Collenette would grant these routes and slots to Canada 3000, in an attempt to convert it into a valid international competitor against us and maintain the country's impractical policy of promoting two international airlines. This is not a far-fetched supposition. It would be easy to create an international airline by handing government-owned routes and slots to any group that assembled a management team, a service organization, and the financing to lease aircraft. Canada 3000 was in a position to do so and would have leaped at the opportunity, especially with promises of federal government support. Had he awarded the routes and slots to Canada 3000, Collenette could have shrugged off any criticism about treating Air Canada unfairly. Since we had not owned these routes and slots in the first place, we could not claim he was taking anything from us.

Collenette continues to deny that demands were ever made to Air Canada. In a *Canadian Business* article on me and the airline's difficulties, Collenette refuted the suggestion that we were pressured to buy Canadian, saying: "The notion that the government forced Air Canada to merge is just not in accord with the facts."

The facts prove otherwise.

YOU WORK with what's handed you, and we had been handed an indirect instruction to acquire Canadian Airlines before it folded. Buying the company had been part of our strategy from the beginning; doing so under these conditions, instead of as part of a deliberate process, proved a different matter entirely.

Speculation was rife that Canadian Airlines would fall entirely into the hands of American Airlines, because it was saddled with obligations totalling $1 billion if its agreements with American were dissolved. We believed otherwise. We put together a proposal that called for American to release its ownership and step away from the Sabre agreement—and it did. Many observers later expressed their amazement to me that we had slayed mighty American Airlines in this stage of the drama. They felt that American would fight, object, and never come to terms.

Normally you perform due diligence before making an acquisition, leaving yourself an exit if necessary. Since the exit had been effectively sealed by the order from Transport Canada, this was no longer an option for us. Instead, we dragged Canadian Airlines through the Companies' Creditors Arrangement Act (CCAA) to fix its balance sheet and eliminate its numerous onerous contracts with aircraft lessors, bond holders, and others. Many people inaccurately recollect that we had assumed a debt-laden company that added to pressures on Air Canada. In fact, Canadian was cleansed of these problems before we acquired it and the debt we assumed was primarily aircraft related. Similar to Chapter 11 in the United States, CCAA enables a corporation to make arrangments with its creditors and avoid steps that might lead to liquidation.

The degree to which Canadian Airlines had been hemorrhaging money over the previous few years, much of it through excessive fees payable to American Airlines, was staggering. When we finally had an opportunity to examine Canadian's books thoroughly and get a handle on cash flow, we discovered that the company was losing $2 million a day. That was bad enough, but Canadian's passengers were abandoning the airline in great numbers, switching over to Air Canada with the knowledge that it would keep flying for the duration of their journey. Even though we were publicly conveying that Air Canada would be back-stopping their purchases on Canadian, people still insisted on flying Air Canada. This total meltdown in the public's confidence in buying tickets on Canadian eliminated any thoughts we had of keeping the operations separate. Meanwhile, we were kept scrambling to integrate schedules, get aircraft aligned with demand by route, address personnel concerns, and deal with increasing loads on Air Canada and shrinking loads on Canadian.

Our acquisition of Canadian Airlines was logical from a practical and operational point of view, but the lack of ability to plan or prepare, combined with the restrictions imposed on the integration by Ottawa, cost us heavily. Contrast this shotgun wedding with the manner in which United Airlines planned to merge with US Airways just a few months later, in May 2000. Their merger plans worked on a timetable that included one year of planning and five years of integration. In my view, five years was an excessive length of time to merge two companies into one new entity. However, when the two companies are large international airlines faced with blending flight schedules, specialized personnel, aircraft of various types and capacity, leasing contracts, multiple union labour agreements, frequent flyer plans, and much more, the need for planning and time becomes more apparent. (In the end, the United–US Airways merger was not completed, because the U.S. Justice Department objected that the merger threatened to weaken the competitive climate.) While it is said, and I concur, that the most successful mergers generally involve rapid integration, we had only a few weeks to plan and implement the merger with Canadian Airlines, all in real time.

WE WERE doing something that I felt had needed to be done for years. During the height of the Onex takeover battle I was sent a newspaper article from forty years before, stating that there was an obvious need to amalgamate Trans-Canada Airlines and Canadian Pacific Airlines. Everyone had known for decades that Canada would not have a competitive international carrier unless we combined forces. As much as I wanted this to happen, I would have preferred to do it as part of a plan, not under the pressure of a collapsing Canadian Airlines and with all sorts of government-imposed rules about layoffs and services to communities.

In the final analysis, David Collenette had not allowed what should have happened: letting the marketplace determine the outcome. Now we had to catch a falling knife. In Australia, by contrast, when Ansett drew near to collapse after September 11, the government stood back and watched and Qantas was able to pick up the pieces. I ideally only wanted pieces—the international routes—but we got the whole thing.

By getting all of Canadian Airlines—unquestionably a great airline with an excellent safety record and a lot of terrific people—we also had to deal with an obsolete fleet. The goal would normally be to blend carriers with similar fleets—all DC-9s or 737s, for example—as well as identical engine types. But with Canadian Airlines and Air Canada, if one chose McDonnell Douglas, the other chose Boeing, and if one chose General Electric engines, the other chose Pratt & Whitney. Thus, with the exception of the A-320s, the fleets were highly incompatible. Most difficult, though, was the network.

In airline mergers, it's all about acquiring network coverage, and the geographic fits were usually evident. British Caledonian, for example, brought British Airways the Middle East, Africa, and South America; UTA brought Air France the South Pacific and Africa; Western brought Delta the west; and Canadian brought Air Canada the world. The difference in our case was near-total domestic overlap, which had to be fixed. Essentially, one could see simple integration the world over, but not at home, where every key city had red and blue employees lined up next to each other at check-in counters and in every other facet of each airline's existence from coast to coast, and we had to rationalize it. Historically, it is the domestic synergies of airline mergers that prove difficult to achieve. US Airway's acquisition of PSA and American's acquisition of Air Cal, Reno Air, and TWA left them with nothing to show for their efforts and dollars. The gold is in the international routes, and so it has been for us. In the past years of turbulence, our beneficial growth has been in markets that Air Canada had historically been locked out of: China, Japan, Australia, Hong Kong, Chile, Mexico, Colombia, and on and on.

One of my goals from the beginning was to ensure that we adopted the best of both organizations for the new airline. I wanted to avoid the temptation of imposing Air Canada systems and procedures on the Canadian Airlines organization exclusively, with a shape-up-or-ship-out attitude. I knew that Canadian had good people and many efficient methods, and I wanted to retain them if possible. I was very vocal about this—the integration of the two airlines had to be achieved with fairness to everyone and with the goal of keeping the best of both organizations. I named Rupert Duchesne chief integration officer working with Eileen McCoy, our then executive vice-president for customer service. Together they spearheaded the integration, drawing on an outside personnel consultancy to evaluate specific talents.

Unfortunately, I underestimated how loyal the people assigned to manage the integration were towards Air Canada employees. This loyalty was reflected in data from the consultants. No matter how neutral those in charge tried to be in evaluating Air Canada employees against Canadian candidates, the choice tended to fall in the Air Canada employees' favour. The Air Canada people ruled the roost, and when they were given the power to make choices, the power was not always applied with full impartiality. These things happen with every conquering culture, and while that term is a little harsh given the situation, the lesson still applies.

I made it clear that only the best employees were to be kept, irrespective of whether they were red or blue (these colour refer to paint jobs on the planes). We had an independent firm come in and interview everyone in management, but ultimately, I did not exert as much authority over these decisions as I might have, partly because I handed the responsibility over to others and depended on them to get it right and partly because there were too many other things on my plate at the time. The result was a series of unfortunate outcomes that unquestionably prevented us from benefiting from the merger as much as we might have. I recall tapping a first-rate financial person at Canadian Airlines and suggesting he come with us, only to discover later that one of our most senior people, who was equally capable and dedicated, had talked him out of it. Had I made a directive instead of a suggestion, we might have retained him. Of course, then I would have heard how I told people what to do and didn't allow them discretion—but that's another story.

Of all the challenges facing us in the merger, none was more time-consuming, frustrating, and thorny than the question of establishing seniority among employee groups. The issue of seniority among union members is tricky for anyone with less than Solomonic wisdom, and nothing a CEO can do will be seen as equally fair to everyone. The solution is to stop worrying about it and get on with the job. My attitude is that we are all simply human beings, all concerned about our families, our economic needs, our health, and so on. We all have family health issues, car payments, and home payments, and where you started your career should be insignificant. Most employees agreed with that point. It was our job to ensure that the issue of airline origin remained irrelevant through the merger process.

These two historically adversarial groups of employees had dramatically different views of the world. The Air Canada employees felt that all Canadian Airlines employees should be "tail-ended," or put at the bottom of the seniority list, whereas all the Canadian employees (who tended to be more senior, since the more junior employees had been laid off in recent years as Canadian struggled financially) believed the only valid measure was date of hire.

There was no doubt in my mind that neither of these options was appropriate under the circumstances and that the only fair and efficient way to "merge" the two employee groups was for their respective union groups to agree on an independent arbitrator who would decide the outcome through an arbitration process that would be paid for by the company. Many employees wanted me to impose a solution, but the legal advice I got over and over was that I couldn't do anything that would survive legal challenges or appeals to the Canada Industrial Relations Board (CIRB).

About the only amusing recollection I have regarding seniority integration resulted from a discussion I had with Raymond Hall, a senior ACPA official. At one of the hearings in Ottawa he came up to me during a recess in the proceedings and asked me to personally get involved in the seniority determinations for pilots of Air Canada and Canadian, as Hollis Harris had done for the Western and Delta pilots when he was president of Delta Airlines. "Hollis was involved?" I asked. "Yes, personally," said Ray. "It went well?" I asked. "Yes," said Ray. "Was there one union or two, like we have here?" I asked. "Two, just like us," said Ray. "Okay," I replied. "I'll check into it."

I don't know what people expect in situations like this, but I did what seemed obvious—I picked up the phone and called Hollis. "Hollis," I said, "did you personally get involved in the Delta/Western pilot seniority negotiations?" Hollis laughed. "Absolutely not," he replied. "Was one or two unions involved?" I asked. "As I remember, just ALPA," replied Hollis. "Did it go well?" I asked. Hollis replied: "It went so well, as I recall, that the Western pilots appealed the outcome right up to the United States Supreme Court."

We were bringing together two groups of professionals who had viewed each other as opponents in the competitive arena—and, of course, they were. Under the inevitable tension that the acquisition was likely to generate, any differences between individuals were certain to be blown out of proportion and used to justify negative attitudes or to assign guilt. Either way, the sooner both groups saw themselves as members of the same team, the better.

The first step we took was to remove any obvious distinction between the two groups of employees. In several U.S. airline mergers the employee numbering system had remained unchanged, which enabled employees of the newly merged company to identify the origin of others and generated friction between the groups. To avoid this problem, we immediately assigned randomly generated employee numbers to every Canadian Airlines employee so that no one could be identified as originally an Air Canada or a Canadian Airlines employee.

We couldn't change the wardrobe nearly as quickly, so for a time the employees were dressed in different uniforms. Some wore Canadian Airlines blue and some wore Air Canada green. It is basic human nature, I suppose, that we behave in such a tribal fashion, with our native colours evoking emotion and hostility towards each other. It was amazing to see tension among the employees diminish as soon as everyone was wearing Air Canada green. We worked hard to convince them that they were all teammates with a shared identity and common problems and a shared determination, for the most part, to perform as the consummate professionals they were. I reminded employees often that we were all human beings with children and mortgage payments and stress in our lives, whether we were "blue" or "red," and gradually we made progress. I know of only one occasion in which a serious disagreement occurred between a former Canadian Airlines employee and an Air Canada employee on board an aircraft. The argument took place between a purser and a pilot before takeoff, and it was eventually resolved with no consequences. On the flight deck itself, pilots from both airlines worked together as professionals from the very start.

Not everything went smoothly from Day One, and customers who flew with us during that period know it. Many hiccups were the direct result of integrating two vastly different computer reservation systems, and I regret the confusion and delays it caused passengers while things were worked out. If we had hoped for some respite from other problems, such as weather delays, we didn't get it. Central Canada experienced a huge number of thunderstorms in the summer of 2000. To really rub salt into the wound, the number of Canadians who decided to travel by plane reached a zenith that summer. Normally, this would be cause for celebration, but added to the problems of weather, integration, and management's attention to cutting costs and relieving the financial crisis, it just made more passengers unhappy with us. I remember at the time being quoted as saying, in response to a question about the integration and what would help us the most: "A recession." I knew this would eventually come back to haunt me, and it did.

We had made a buy-back offer for Air Canada shares that would cost us $1.1 billion, and in spite of subsequent events such as discovering the true extent of Canadian's financial situation, I could not ignore that pledge. Some quarters advised me to rescind the offer and accept the inevitable trashing in the media, letting Canadian set out once again on its merry way, obtaining who knows what support from the federal government and causing us who knows how much more harm as we tried to compete with the federal government's coffers. That's not the way to do business, in my book. We had committed to purchasing those shares, and I insisted on living up to our side of the bargain. As a result of our $1.1 billion share buy-back, thousands of Canadians earned a healthy profit from their Air Canada holdings.

Still, we needed to rationalize many aspects of the integration, such as eliminating duplication among the two airline schedules, reducing our combined workforce in an equitable manner, disposing of excess equipment and facilities, and more. This is hardly revolutionary stuff in any other industry and in almost any other country, but in May 2000 it yanked us into one of the most exasperating encounters with government that I have ever experienced.

The Standing Committee on Transport, then chaired by Stan Keyes, had been discussing Bill c-26, which amended the Canada Transportation Act, the Competition Act, and the Air Canada Public Participation Act, among others. Many of the bill's provisions were targeted solely at Air Canada and affected the airline negatively, including giving increased powers to the Canadian Transportation Agency to micromanage pricing and adding new powers to the Competition Bureau to specifically regulate the airline industry and target Air Canada. All these provisions were clearly aimed at influencing, if not directing, many of our most important management issues and decisions.

As soon as my presence at a meeting to debate Bill c-26 was confirmed, the transport committee scurried around looking for a room with full television broadcast facilities and postponed the session until they could locate one. They finally found a suitable location and set a revised date.

When I entered the room, a number of committee members greeted me warmly. "Robert, how are you doing?" they smiled, pumping my hand and slapping my back. "It's good to see you." As long as we stood around chatting, before the procedings began and the television cameras were turned on, they treated me like a fraternity brother.

Things changed once they were at the committee table: I was settled into the hot seat, the lights came on, and the videotape began rolling. I delivered Air Canada's opening statement, noting that we had just created 170 new highly paid technical jobs in Winnipeg; had developed a schedule of 2,000 daily departures; had added 32 new routes and 12 new destinations to our schedule; and had made substantial achievements, all without the support of taxpayer dollars.

As soon as I finished, venom began pouring from the mouths of various committee members, much of it directed at me personally rather than at the corporation. It was a Dr.-Jekyll-into-Mr.-Hyde performance that, if I hadn't been living it, would have reduced me to hysterics. At one point B.C. Liberal MP Lou Sekora glared at me as though he were a member of the Spanish Inquisition and I were a raving heretic instead of a guy trying to explain the steps we had taken to help make the merger work while being fair to both employees and shareholders. "I could only find a hundred yards of crying towels on my way in here," Sekora said, "and that's apparently not enough for you today." He babbled on from there, building to a climax when he almost screamed, "What kind of human being is this person Mister Milton," he said. (Thirty minutes earlier I had been "Bob.") "Mister Milton, all you do is hurt, hurt, hurt and destroy, destroy, destroy!" He knew he had scored a good line; it was on *The National* that evening and in newspapers the next day.

When he finished, I refused to give him the satisfaction of an answer. Calin Rovinescu, seated next to me, responded on my behalf in a cool, collected way, as a good corporate lawyer does. None of his words made any impact on Sekora. He got his headlines, and he was pleased—but not as pleased as I was when Sekora, who originally won his seat thanks to poor voter turnout in a by-election, was defeated in the next federal election by a talented young MP named James Moore. Sekora's long-winded, largely incoherent babbling did have one positive outcome. Afterwards, Calin suggested I should have responded with: "Could you please repeat the question?" I've used the line subsequently when faced with such questioning, and it always gets a laugh.

Nothing was achieved at that meeting. I tried to present our case for the cuts we were making and to show our concern for the communities and the employees that would be affected by them. Most of the committee members weren't interested, including Stan Keyes, who had been such a warm friend just minutes earlier. They wanted a moment of glory for the folks back in their ridings, and this was their opportunity to go after someone with a high media profile who could not or would not toss the same baloney back at them.

The degree of hypocrisy this company faces in its dealings with some in Ottawa is amazing. In 1999, when Gerry Schwartz was playing his takeover game and everyone knew that without government intervention it was only a matter of time before Canadian Airlines would fade away, Air Canada's market share broke through 60 per cent. By combining the airlines, it would grow to well over 80 per cent. That's dominant in any industry and market, but as long as Schwartz's bid appeared to have legs, few in Ottawa, especially not Collenette, complained about it.

After the Onex bid failed, our 80 per cent market share was no longer tolerable to Collenette and the people around him. In fact, it was now being described as outrageous. The galling part, the insanity of our situation in dealing with Collenette, was this: One of the rules we were instructed to follow as a result of our merger with Canadian was a guarantee that we would maintain Air Canada service to every destination on the schedules of both airlines for at least two years. The left hand was telling us that it was not happy with a share of market that had been perfectly acceptable a few months ago, and the right hand was warning us of the peril we faced if we cut back services to any existing markets—which would have been an ideal way to reduce our share if a competing airline moved in. In reality, of course, I doubt that another airline would care to service money-losing routes in our absence without offering inferior service and demanding higher fares. Perhaps someone in Ottawa might explain how this would benefit the residents of these communities, because it was clear they hadn't fully taken in the picture I had provided them, showing that many smaller communities in Canada—those they represented—would not have any service at all were it not for Air Canada's ability to funnel passengers by the twos and threes from points all over the world into a small market.

Besides being told to serve communities yet to get our market share down, we were also forced by various regulators in Ottawa to price our products as they saw fit. Unfortunately, these instructions often conflicted. Ottawa's pricing appeared to be based on the Goldilocks principle. In one ear we had the Competition Bureau telling us we had to keep prices up, and in the other ear we had the CTA telling us to reduce them. We couldn't charge too much; we couldn't charge too little; we had to get it j-u-u-s-s-t right.

Around the same time that I was trying to maintain my composure while dealing with the Standing Committee on Transport, Transport Canada launched the Office of the Air Travel Complaints Commissioner. The commissioner's duties, we were informed, would centre on "reviewing consumer complaints concerning any airline operating in Canada where the airline has not responded to the satisfaction of the complainant." We could not fail to notice that the appointed commissioner possessed little experience with, and virtually no knowledge of, the airline industry.

Our fears were confirmed when the commissioner's initial report breathlessly noted that two thirds of all complaints received during his eighteen-month posting were directly related to Air Canada, and he suggested this proved that "many Canadians are not yet convinced that Air Canada's priorities are in the right place." Whatever the location of our priorities, they were more evident than the commissioner's logic, because our market share at the time approached 80 per cent of all air passengers in the country. On that basis, generating 66 per cent of the complaints suggests that we were actually *outperforming* the rest of the industry in customer satisfaction, a point that appeared to elude him. This was just more evidence of Collenette and the folks in Ottawa building up more unnecessary and costly bureaucracy.

Whenever you invite customer complaints about a particular commodity or service, be prepared for the letters, e-mails, and telephone calls that will pour in. That is exactly what happened when Ottawa announced the formation of the office of the Air Travel Complaints Commissioner.

I do not know the cost of the commissioner's office to Canadian taxpayers; its elaborate semi-annual report contains no figures for salaries and expenses. The most recent report indicates that about six hundred passenger complaints, covering all airlines, are filed directly with the commissioner each year. Of these, almost a third concern foreign airlines. Considering that Air Canada carries over 30 million air passengers annually, this strikes me as a somewhat reassuring statistic, especially when the commissioner's own report indicates that 72 per cent of complainants were either fully or partially satisfied. I would be curious to know how much it costs to respond to each complaint filed with the office. No one appears willing to provide that statistic.

A substantial number of people in Ottawa, MPs and bureaucrats alike, resent the fact that Air Canada is no longer a Crown corporation. When Air Canada was privatized, many of these people lost a number of perks and a substantial amount of power. Perhaps they wish that Air Canada would still hold a flight for a late-arriving cabinet minister, as it did in the days before privatization. Imagine three hundred or so passengers and $100 million worth of aircraft waiting at the departure gate for a politician. I'm told that's how Air Canada was run twenty years ago, and some wish the company had maintained this policy as a sort of corporate legacy.

Despite this aggravating backdrop, we continued our efforts to improve relations with Ottawa, and I scheduled meetings with several cabinet ministers. Some of the people were terrific, and what you saw was what you got—as with John Manley, Allan Rock, Clifford Lincoln, Sheila Copps, and Senator Lise Bacon, five extremely logical and fair-minded politicians. With others, the meeting was pleasant and then you learned they were completely two-faced—as with Brian Tobin and David Collenette. I met Tobin for lunch soon after he became minister of industry, and he seemed genuinely interested in Air Canada and what we were up against. Afterwards he suggested to business leaders at various breakfasts and lunches that it was over for us and that we should file for CCAA. With yet others, you just walked away shaking your head. One such case was Herb Dhaliwal.

I had asked for a meeting with Dhaliwal to explain certain steps we were taking to improve our post-integration operations. Dhaliwal, I had been told, talked about being both an entrepreneur and a businessman with experience in the transportation industry, which I'm sure he is. Here, I believed, was someone who could understand the challenges Air Canada faced and the means we were using to overcome them.

At our meeting, I presented a detailed review of our situation, dissected the problems we faced, weighed the alternatives, and proposed some solutions that both Air Canada and the federal government could implement to benefit Canadian air travellers. Through it all, Dhaliwal provided little response. When I finished, he shook his head and said, "The problem with Air Canada is that you guys just don't take advantage of an opportunity when it's presented to you."

I asked what he meant by that.

"I remember," he replied, "coming back once from Bombay via London with two other MPs. When we got to Heathrow, we were very tired and facing a long flight home. The three of us asked for an upgrade so we could get some rest, and you guys refused. I mean, how could you miss an opportunity like that to put yourself in our good graces? It's beyond me how you could miss that chance!"

I was stunned. I had just completed a comprehensive review of our company and the manner in which our proposals either meshed or conflicted with positions taken by the federal government, and all Dhaliwal could do was complain that we hadn't upgraded him and two of his colleagues. What if there had been no seats available? Would he have proposed bumping three customers back to economy class just to make room for him and his colleagues? Perhaps he would. Perhaps he did. He certainly suggested that making such a gesture would have earned a more favourable response to our position. Is this the way he believes policy decisions should be made?

I asked when this "insult" to Dhaliwal occurred. He shrugged and replied, "Oh, about five years ago."

So there it was. The Honourable Herb Dhaliwal, federal cabinet minister and reputed confidant of the prime minister, had been stewing over an imagined slight for five years. This gives you a flavour of the kinds of things we encountered on some of our treks to Ottawa and, I hope, explains why I have tried to avoid the Chrétien crowd entirely. My hopes—and I can only hope—for Paul Martin's team are high, although he has gotten off to a rough start, principally, I feel, because of the legacy of the Chrétien years.

At times it seemed as though statements issued from the transport ministry were being drafted by comedy writers for the *Royal Canadian Air Farce*. At one stage in a meeting David Collenette wanted our chairman, Jack Fraser, to attend so that he could yell at us about our market share being too high after Canada 3000's failure, he actually suggested in all seriousness that Air Canada be limited to flying into just one city in each province. He was speaking to us in an elevated and agitated tone, but I couldn't help myself and burst into laughter. "That is the stupidest idea I have ever heard in my life," I said. "I guess we won't be able to fly to Ottawa then!" I could see that he hadn't thought of that.

9

HARD BARGAINING

THE ONEX takeover episode and its long and complex reverbera-
tions had diverted attention from completing the purchase of new
narrow-bodied aircraft that had been in the works. From a capital cost
standpoint, nothing is more critical than buying the right planes and
putting them on the right routes. Airlines burn cash if the aircraft are
too large, stifle demand if they are too small, and lose customers if
competing airlines offer more comfortable equipment. The capital and
operating costs are so immense that even minuscule advantages in cost
can generate big bottom line benefits.

The decision we needed to make in early 2000 was different from
the one Hollis Harris faced in 1995, when our last major aircraft purchase had been made. That was before the Canada–U.S. Open Skies
Agreement, signed later that year, which led to unfettered flights
between any U.S. and Canadian cities. Under the previous agreement,
a rigid set of rules dictated the routes that could be flown, or in certain

cases the size of aircraft that could be flown in the transborder market. Beyond the bilaterally agreed upon markets, there were some provisions whereby small markets could be served, but at the time, the only aircraft that could sensibly operate in these markets were turboprops. The introduction of the Bombardier Regional Jet (CRJ), a fifty-passenger jet, would turn the agreement and our industry on their heads, permitting jet speed to compete with slower turboprops. Hollis and I were excited about the jet, and he assigned me to identify routes where it would be most suitable and to conduct an evaluation to buy these airplanes—something I knew he would do even before we started the work.

Mike Hewitt, our director of schedule planning and design, joined me in working up a proposal. Mike is a true Air Canada gem, one of many senior people at Air Canada I have come across with a degree in mathematics, and a guy with so much talent and enthusiasm that I always had to hold him back when I assigned him a project. He generally worked on longer-term fleet development. I remember the first time I asked Mike to look at some future fleet planning, which is generally dealt with on a high-level basis. Unbeknownst to me, Mike worked about twenty-four hours straight to deliver a brick of paper that not only addressed my request but provided schedules for our entire aircraft fleet by day of the week for the next five years. A funny man, he is undoubtedly a genius in his own right as well as an example of the kind of talent and dedication we have at all levels of the company.

The plan Mike and I submitted proposed an initial fleet of fifteen CRJs to service high-potential routes. The new fleet represented a great opportunity for us, but at that stage we didn't have open skies, so there was clearly a large risk in acquiring these planes if the U.S. market didn't open up. Surprise—Hollis believed so deeply in the potential for this aircraft that he increased the order to twenty-four anyway. Mike couldn't believe it. He had entered Hollis's office expecting him to reject or scale back his plan, as all previous CEOs had always done. "In all my years with Air Canada," Mike said beaming, "I have never seen an aircraft order approved without endless debate. Not only did Hollis make a decision on the spot, he *increased* the order!"

I was more pleased than I could say, because I knew we had the strategy and the strategic weapons—the CRJs—to take on U.S. carriers in the transborder battleground and win.

We were among the first airlines in the world to buy the regional jet, so it took a substantial amount of courage for Hollis to make the decision. It worked perfectly. When the Open Skies Agreement took effect, many people expected us to be annihilated by American, Delta, United, US Airways, Continental, and the other airlines that expanded their presence in the Canadian market. Thanks to the efficiency of the CRJ and good network planning into and behind U.S. hubs, we captured two thirds of the cross-border traffic between Canada and the United States in no time at all. The Canada–U.S. market is the largest single international air travel market in the world, so the prize was enormous.

Although I admired Hollis's wisdom and courage in purchasing the CRJs, I had not agreed with his decision to add the Airbus A-340-300 to our fleet. The A-340 is essentially a four-engine version of the twin-engine A-330, which has the same fuselage, tail assembly, landing gear, flight deck, and wing geometry. The A-340 boasts a longer range than the A-330, but the A-340 is underpowered. Among other issues, this means that its engines are run at higher-than-ideal temperatures, making them prone to maintenance problems.

Looking back, Hollis's decision on the A-340 really resulted from his aggravation with Boeing. When he first arrived at Air Canada, Hollis tried to defer all expenditures, including delaying the purchase of six Boeing 767-300s the company had on order. Hollis felt that he had been a good friend and supporter of the folks at Boeing over the years and was furious when their then president, Ron Woodward, refused to cut Hollis, or Air Canada, any slack. Although I later convinced Hollis to take the 767s to enable us to grow internationally, the damage was done. The Airbus folks were gracious and were now selling terrific products, including the A-320, which Air Canada loved and first introduced first into the North American skies.

When Lamar became CEO our wide-body fleet, especially our 747 classics (100s and 200s), was in need of upgrading, and the choice was between two exceptional aircraft: the A-330-300 and one of my favourites, the Boeing 777. We were making the decision in a buyer's market, a perfect environment for me to lead my first aircraft order competition. The 777 was Boeing's first new product in years, designed to fit neatly between the 767 and 747 models, and the company wanted to score a major victory with us. At the same time, Airbus risked being squeezed out of North America entirely, after Delta, American, and Continental agreed to exclusive twenty-year deals with Boeing. (These deals were cancelled later on orders from the U.S. Justice Department when Boeing merged with McDonnell Douglas.) If we chose the 777, the impact on Airbus would be devastating economically, as well as morale-crushing, because Air Canada was still its key North American customer and at the time we were the only North American airline flying Airbus wide-bodies.

It was a classic no-holds-barred competition. Although both models have twin engines, the 777 is larger and heavier and will comfortably seat around 325 passengers; the A-330 seats around 280. Although the A-330 has a shorter range than the 777, it met most of our long-distance route requirements. If we needed more range, however, we could select the virtually identical (except for the engines) A-340, which was already part of the fleet. Throughout the negotiations, I expressed my admiration for the 777 every chance I got, putting pressure on the Airbus people to shave their prices even more. They truly believed I wanted the 777, and they were right. I pointed out how flexible the plane was for both relatively short-haul and long-haul routes, depending on the configuration, and admired its vastly superior range and exceptional comfort. What's more, a future stretched version of the 777 would effectively replace the aging 747, another element in its favour. I like an aircraft with maximum versatility, and few could beat the 777 on that measure.

As we moved towards the decision, the high stakes for both manufacturers were evident in the aggressiveness of their deals. We were cognizant of the risks to both, but Airbus and its team were listening to every single aspect of our requirement and Boeing wasn't.

In one sense, this competition and the way both companies were handling it highlighted the divergent paths they were on. Boeing had for years been developing derivatives of their original models, the classic being the 737, which moved first from the 100s and 200s to the 300/400/500 era and now the "next generation" of 600/700/800/900s. Clearly it is cheaper to upgrade old airplanes, but when the competition comes out with an altogether new aircraft, as Airbus did with the 320 family, you can be left in the dust. Increasingly, Boeing was eating dust, and this was most evident in Airbus's innovative and brilliant (albeit obvious) move to standardize their new aircraft cockpits in an approach called CCQ (common cockpit qualifications). This approach meant pilots could be simultaneously checked out, or "current," on aircraft as radically different in size and performance as the narrow-body A-320 and the wide-body A-330. The resulting cost reductions in training were enormous.

Finally, there was the matter of future commitments. I felt that beyond the battle between the wide-body 330 and the 777, I could go after Airbus on narrow-body pricing. I wanted committed, new, reduced pricing on all Airbus narrow-body models for ten years. As replacements for our aging DC-9s, Hollis had ordered thirty-five A-319s. We were still awaiting the delivery of the final ten units. In the heat of the aggressive pricing battle between Boeing and Airbus to seal a deal with us, we managed to obtain new pricing from Airbus for all future Airbus narrow-bodies, including the A-319. As it turned out, the new price was considerably lower than the original pricing on the first thirty-five, and during negotiations with the Airbus people for the wide-body order I leveraged them into applying their new pricing to the balance of our order for A-319s. Reducing the price of the remaining ten aircraft on the original order meant that we received one and a half of these new aircraft free, compared with the original order price. We also manoeuvred our way to lower prices on future A-340-300s by about 20 per cent from the original order.

When the final proposals were submitted, the net present value between the Boeing 777 order and the A-330s was over $300 million, in favour of Airbus.

On the day we were to announce our decision, the Airbus team members waited nervously in a seventh-floor room at our headquarters, pacing the floor. They were sure we would choose the 777. I walked in with a sombre face, as if I were going to deliver some bad news, and said: "Guys, I think the 777 really sucks—congratulations!" Everyone laughed, and I'm sure they felt relieved. Later I put a call in to Hollis and told him I had cleaned up the mess he had made when he paid too much for the A-340s and A-319s. He gave me a good ol' Hollis laugh. His pride was evident.

The lesson is that you play by the rules, but you play as hard as you possibly can, using every tool available to you. We had Boeing's aggressiveness and great product and Airbus's anxiousness, as well as undelivered A-319s, in our corner. We used these facts like a club to save hundreds of millions of dollars for the company. It's the only way to play the game, and it was fun.

Managing capital and operating expenses for an airline such as Air Canada is like riding a pendulum that swings constantly between spending top money for new aircraft and responding to new salary demands. I admire the people who fly and maintain aircraft as much as I love the planes themselves. Airline pilots tend to be genuinely nice people, more intent (as you might expect) on serious concerns—like guiding a 360-tonne (800,000-pound) aircraft carrying hundreds of people thousands of kilometres in comfort and safety—than on trivial day-to-day matters.

The senior-most captains also tend to have very attractive work schedules. A senior captain on one of our A-340s told me that he constantly took the Toronto-to-Tokyo non-stop flight because, with three round trips a month, he could fly enough hours to fulfill his monthly commitment. He could leave on a Monday at 1 PM, get to Tokyo around 3 PM on Tuesday, spend the night in an airport hotel, leave Tokyo Wednesday at 7 PM, and be back in Toronto Wednesday at 6:30 PM. Three trips totaling fifty-four hours, and the month's work was done. His approximate pay: $250,000 a year.

Do I fault the captain? Absolutely not. In fact, good for him. If I could spend three weeks at home every month, plus vacation, I would do so in a second. This situation, however, highlights the vulnerability of companies like Air Canada to what will come one day: international low-cost carriers conducting long-haul operations. But we are not there yet, and we will have to see how the legacy carriers adapt when it happens.

Only an extremely small percentage of Canada's pilots are hired and trained to become Air Canada pilots. Most will never fly big jets at all, and many good, capable people will bounce from one flying job to another, going from one failed airline to another.

But even for those fortunate enough to be hired at Air Canada, the road is far from easy. First you have to be selected from the cream of the crop. Then you have to pass our initial training. After that, you start out as a new first officer. With low seniority, you get the "leftover" flying, generally meaning overnight flights, layovers in lousy cities, and a brutal schedule away from home and family. Christmas, New Year's, or your children's birthdays at home you can almost certainly forget about. I can't imagine anything worse.

The journey to senior captain is a tough one. Along the way you've got check rides every six months to ensure your continuing competency and medicals every year. If your health goes, so does your career.

The company/management/pilot/union relationships are fascinating ones, in which disagreements between management and pilots tend to be based on the pursuit of goals designed to benefit the unions and their leaders more than individual pilots. The most counterproductive case is something called augmentation, the insistence on having extra pilots aboard certain flights. I steadfastly support it on flights of a certain duration. But pilot unions around the world have tried to take it one step too far by ignoring economics and achieving nothing more than creating jobs, opening the window for lower-cost, non-union operators to drive a truck through.

Pilots should rotate their duties on long flights, but augmentation with one extra pilot should be enough unless the flight takes longer than, say, fourteen hours through the middle of the night, or perhaps sixteen hours in daylight, in which case two extra pilots for a total of four makes sense.

Pilot unions, however, are pushing for augmentation on routes as short as eight hours and on aircraft that don't even have provisions for pilots to rest, like bunk beds. This is one of the areas where the hardline unionists underestimate the damage they do to pilot careers by undermining the airline's profitability. Their logic says that more pilots mean more pay for more pilots, driving them up the seniority/pay ladder. My logic says that having more pilots than are needed on an aircraft to ensure safe operation means that fewer routes are viable, fewer airplanes are needed, and so fewer pilots are employed and those employed are paid less.

The flying public may think the more pilots the better, but there is no correlation once certain limitations are exceeded. Most pilots I know would rather work on the flight deck than try to force themselves to sleep in the middle of a journey. Augmentation is all too often not about safety at all; it's about union featherbedding.

Augmentation isn't the only area where divergent logic applies. It also applies to pilot training and scheduling. Because seniority determines how much pilots are paid, they naturally want to fly bigger and bigger aircraft, which pay more, as their careers progress. In my view, this is also counterintuitive. It means pilots spend more time than they or the company would like training on different aircraft types (I have yet to meet a pilot who would prefer to be training instead of flying). It also means that they fly longer missions and are away from home for longer and longer periods, battling time changes as they get older. I'm a believer in seniority-based pay systems, where pay is based on how long an employee has been with the company. If you want to fly short-haul, small airplanes for your entire career, your pay isn't affected, as it is based on your years of service, not the size of your aircraft. Many pilots I have spoken to over the years would love to see some type of seniority-based system implemented—even if it was only, say, that they get paid the same rate for flying all wide-bodies—as you find at carriers like KLM and Lufthansa.

Unfortunately, this is not a place our union or most pilot unions want to go. Happily, ALPA, the union that represents the pilots at Jazz, our regional subsidiary, has chosen seniority-based pay, and I think it is a genuine win-win situation. Unions are all too often managed by some people whose prime motive is not to fly aircraft but to squeeze the "best" deal possible for their members. I understand and respect that motive. If I play hardball with suppliers like Boeing and Airbus, I expect our unions to play hardball too. I just don't understand it when some of them let logic get in the way of a beneficial outcome for their members.

10

MULTIPLYING BRANDS

IN THE interim between scoring our victory over the Onex-led takeover and the horror of September 11, we began implementing changes in Air Canada's pricing and flight structures that we had been considering for some time. The process has proven, in many ways, to be among the most controversial steps we have taken at the airline.

My years at Air Canada convinced me that the airline could—and should—become Canada's one-stop shop for aviation. Whatever air service Canadians need, we should be able to provide it at a competitive price and with better quality. If you need air cargo, corporate jet charters, no-frills bargain fares, or first-class comfort going anywhere in the world, or any other service associated with flying, the first name you think of should be Air Canada. This is not a naked effort to become a true monopoly but an ambition to earn and deserve the support of customers in the same manner that, say, Lufthansa and Singapore Airlines have in their home markets.

Few people in the aviation industry were getting the message about the low-cost carriers that were following the Southwest Airlines strategy. During the Onex battle in 1999, I first expressed my desire to get into the low-cost carrier game by starting an airline that would be based out of Hamilton and would serve the country. Everyone howled simultaneously—the politicians, the Competition Bureau, and our unions. Ottawa claimed I wanted Air Canada to dominate the industry. Not so. I wanted Air Canada to be the obvious choice in any segment of the business, and I could see that if we didn't protect our underside by offering legitimately low-fare service—which could only be sustainably done if our costs were low—the end was near.

David Collenette told us we should stick to full service. I shook my head in disbelief. In essence he was saying, "Who cares if you, the CEO of Air Canada, believe you've got to be competitive in the low-fare game? Government knows best!" It would be analogous to telling Petro-Canada that they couldn't sell self-service gas, or the Royal Bank that they couldn't offer ATMs.

Meanwhile, on another front, the unions were screaming that we were simply trying to undermine them and hurt our employees. I look back on this period satisfied in the knowledge that we tried to convince them to adapt and to protect the livelihood of our employees. But they looked the other way.

By 2000, the effect of the low-cost carriers had been apparent to me for years, yet as recently as 2003 Don Carty, then CEO of American Airlines, was still claiming that the legacy airlines—airlines with extensive seniority among their employees and substantial pension obligations as a result—could maintain a 30 per cent yield premium over the low-cost airlines, an impossible feat. Thanks to business class and international service, we may be able to sustain a 10 per cent premium, but that's about the limit. No matter what carriers like Air Canada and American Airlines do to reduce costs, they keep encountering that brick wall of employee seniority, unproductive work rules, pensions, and operating complexity.

We gain a lot from employee experience, especially in the case of pilots and mechanics. But in the seniority-driven airline world, the benefits of experience do not balance the cost disadvantage equation relative to low-cost carriers in the eyes of the consumer. Essentially, the travelling public says, if the government lets them fly, they must be safe (even though this may not be so) and I will choose them if they are cheaper. John and Jane Q. Traveller couldn't care less about seniority if it will save them $20. That's fine. But if the cost of every aspect of operations, from equipment leases and maintenance to operations and marketing, were identical at WestJet and Air Canada, it would still cost us over $1 billion per year more to run Air Canada as a result of workforce seniority alone. Air Canada has sixty-five years' experience; WestJet has eight. WestJet has been growing rapidly off a small base for years; we have grown as one of the world's largest carriers, but it has not been a continuous upward trajectory. WestJet keeps averaging down its workforce seniority with every aircraft it brings in, but we can't.

When I began making these points to employees, explaining that we needed to reduce costs and compete with the low-cost carriers, union leaders accused us of trying to squeeze the unions and their members for the sake of fatter corporate profits, even though I supposed they knew we were right. Unfortunately, their battles to retain the status quo in defiance of reality over all those years made the necessary cutbacks of 2003 more painful for their members than they should have been and left us in a weaker competitive position than was necessary. This was one of those times and issues, though, where the notion of "leading the horse to water" comes to mind. We told our employees and their union leadership of the looming threat of low-cost carriers in employee letters, public speeches, and any other form we could. We did it years before our peers, but few wanted to listen; and so we resigned ourselves to dealing with the consequences as best we could once the impact began to be felt.

AS WE MOVED into the late 1990s, customers were rapidly driving change in our business, as they were in other businesses. The growth of generic grocery products was a good example of customer-driven change, as many consumers rejected the elaborate packaging and persuasive imagery of national brands in favour of simple packaging, good quality, and low prices. More closely linked to the airline business has been the strategy of companies such as Marriott, the hotel–motel chain. For many years, Marriott operated as a middle-of-the-road brand, offering accommodation for "average" travellers, going head-to-head with Holiday Inn and several other chains. As upscale customers bypassed Marriott for the prestige and the amenities of Hilton, Westin, and Four Seasons, and as bargain hunters flocked to no-frills accommodation like Motel 6, Marriott management came up with a multi-brand approach to expand their market. Today, high-end travellers book a room at a Ritz-Carlton or a J.W. Marriott resort; those looking for an upscale but more reasonably priced experience find it at a Renaissance; business travellers on a budget gravitate to a Courtyard by Marriott; people wanting extended-time accommodation find it at Residence Inn; families are attracted to Fairfield Inns, and so on. At last count, Marriott was operating seventeen brands of hotels, inns, and resorts designed and managed to suit different categories of customers, but they were all linked to one centralized booking and management facility. Many Marriott customers undoubtedly don't realize that all these chains are controlled by one parent. More important, Marriott was making money at it. In spite of a severe drop-off in travel during early and mid-2003 due to the Iraq war, SARS, and a weakened economy, the company continued to earn profits for its shareholders.

Although the air travel market changed during the 1990s, and continues to change today, the traditional mainline sector remains important to the bottom line. At the same time, we could no longer afford to ignore the rapidly growing low-fare segment, because doing so would leave our core business exposed and vulnerable to attack. Our challenge, therefore, was how to appeal to both without taking away from either. Unless you dramatically lower your costs, you simply can't. With our obviously higher costs and legacy structures and without union co-operation to change that, our best bet was to develop different brands employing cost savings in all areas with the exception of labour—which is exactly what we did.

We began by forming a team to create the new venture under the code name Project JetRed. I had been closely studying the creation and evolution of JetBlue in the United States and decided that it was a model we could emulate. Starting with JetBlue and Southwest, we adapted the best practices of the low-cost carriers designed to cut costs and reduce passenger fares. They included 100 per cent Internet-based ticket sales and distribution, one-class service, food and beverages available only for sale, and maximum in-flight crew efficiency by using 159 seats on our A-320s, meaning four flight attendants could cover the aircraft under government regulations requiring one flight attendant for every forty passengers.

The success of charter operations like Air Transat and no-frills services like WestJet was evidence that customers would put up with more crowding and fewer amenities in return for substantial savings. Why not respond to that market while offering extra benefits like the same industry-leading seat pitch—the distance between each airline seat and the one in front of it (just as JetBlue did)—as regular Air Canada flights, plus Aeroplan miles, advance seat assignment, and more reliability?

As much as possible, we wanted to make the brands distinctive from the mainline operation not only to protect the Air Canada brand but also to distinguish the new product as a true low-fare, no-frill proposition. This led to the concept of a no-frills airline brand within a larger airline structure—not a new idea. Many legacy airlines in the United States had attempted similar airline-within-an-airline or brand-within-an-airline moves but abandoned the idea after racking up substantial losses. What made us think Air Canada could succeed where Delta, United, US Airways, Continental, and others had failed? Several things.

First, the structure of those previous efforts had been flawed. Their low-cost ventures permitted expensive interline connections not only on their own full-fare carrier but on other non-affiliated airlines. On the United Shuttle, for example, Japan Air Lines passengers could check in both themselves and their luggage at Tokyo and fly first-class to Las Vegas, changing to a United Shuttle flight in Los Angeles. United was offering two-class service, providing interline connection for luggage, using paper tickets, and paying commissions to travel agents. For thirty years, Southwest had been demonstrating that you can't do these things and still make a profit as a low-cost airline. Our brand would be true to the Southwest model in all these respects.

Next was the awkward and confusing execution by the early low-cost carrier offshoots, such as Continental's launch of Continental Lite in the mid-1990s. The company offered discount fares but failed to adequately separate its Lite brand from Continental itself, and passengers paying full fare had no idea whether they were on a full-service flight or a no-frills Lite flight until takeoff. The result was enormous resentment from full-fare customers, and Continental wasted a fortune before abandoning the idea.

Finally, things had changed. The low-cost carriers were eating the lunch of the legacy carriers in ways no one would have predicted ten years earlier. September 11 greatly accelerated the evolution, and technology was revolutionizing the way customers booked reservations and paid for tickets, thanks to Internet distribution and electronic ticketing, which sharply reduced two of the most expensive pre-flight functions. The time had come to revive the concept and make it work.

We remained tied in to union wages and work rules, meaning the labour floor to our cost structure was too high for us to compete with non-union companies. We had to reduce all of the non-union labour costs that we could, and I knew that we could achieve much of the savings using such advantages as the economies of scale that come with our large fleet. It would also help that our flight crews and maintenance workers were highly experienced and customers would know that. And clearly, we would have to create a new low-fare brand that offered the lowest possible fares and was distinctive from others under our corporate umbrella.

Into the mix came a guy named Noel O'Dea, from Target Marketing, in St. John's, Newfoundland. O'Dea had impressed me earlier with his work on the brand for our new regional carrier, Jazz, which was the result of an amalgamation of the various regional carriers Air Canada had formed over the years (Air BC, Air Ontario, Air Alliance, and Air Nova) and our acquisition, through Canadian Airlines, of Canadian Regional. At first, I wasn't overly encouraged when I discovered that O'Dea had never worked on an airline logo or branding project before. As sometimes happens, though, this last factor may have been an advantage, and his creativity on Jazz blew me away.

I was so impressed with O'Dea's efforts that I asked him to work on the low-cost brand we could use until such time as the unions came on side with new contract conditions permitting us to launch a separate low-fare carrier. With the changes taking place in the industry and Air Canada's continued inability to respond, we could no longer afford to wait for the unions to come on side. In addition to a unique and effective name, I was looking for a colour scheme that was fun but basic enough that we could change the aircraft logos literally overnight. I wanted this whole exercise to be low risk and to cost next to nothing.

O'Dea proposed three names: Bravo, Orange, and Tango. Bravo reminded me too much of the television channel. I loved Orange, but I was concerned (as were our lawyers) that we could be in conflict with the European telecom group of the same name, ironically owned at the time by Li Ka-shing (Victor Li's father). Tango was ideal, even though it shared its name with a British soft drink, especially with the great purple design submitted by O'Dea.

The strategy for Tango was to position it as a low-fare alternative, yet with attractions that the low-cost competition did not offer. This meant separating it dramatically from the mainline Air Canada brand and creating a brand within an airline, complete with distinctive aircraft, a different look and feel, and a different personality. This would allow Air Canada to establish credibility in the marketplace so that consumers could accept that we, too, or at least an operation affiliated with us, could offer low fares. Once that acceptance was established, we could always dissolve the separation between it and Air Canada so that Tango became strictly a fare class. One of the main challenges faced by legacy airlines in competing with low-cost carriers is the perception consumers have that airlines like Air Canada couldn't possibly offer truly low fares—even though our fares were as low as the competition's. That was one key advantage low-fare carriers have always had. Consumers seeking low fares simply ignored mainline offerings and went straight to the Southwests and WestJets of the world the same way deal-seeking consumers went straight to Wal-Mart, completely bypassing Eatons. We needed a vehicle to get deal-seeking consumers to give us a serious look and that vehicle became Tango.

To run Tango, I tapped a young fellow airline junkie named Ben Smith. Ben is one of the most dynamic entrepreneurs I have ever met. He started his career running his own travel agency in Ottawa and when I met him, I was instantly impressed by his knowledge of aircraft, schedules, and the industry as a whole. Ben spent several years looking at airline start-ups both inside and outside Canada, and he took to the new venture with relish. Within weeks, Ben (who himself brought on a human dynamo in the person of Zeina Gedeon—a fellow former travel agent who never took no for an answer) and his team had established the schedule, personality, and website for Tango—all at minimal cost and investment. Tango had truly become a separate brand within the Air Canada fold—with its own aircraft, signage, website, and call centre (in reality, a subsection of our call centre in Saint John, New Brunswick)—overnight.

The success of any new brand depends on quickly cementing it in the consciousness of consumers, because the sooner they understand what it represents, the sooner the thing can start paying for our market share, prices, and perceived service deficiencies. Almost overnight, people became aware that we had a low-cost service that could compete with others, such as Canada 3000, on price and still deliver more comfort, advanced seat selection, Aeroplan miles, and other perks. Tango was a winner, and the proof was in the number of travellers choosing the new brand.

Tango taught us a lot, not the least of which is that the halo that sits upon the heads of low-cost carriers is largely the result of lowered expectations. Even when Air Canada offered dollar-for-dollar price-competitive seats versus the no-frills carriers, perceptions remained high: I'm flying Air Canada; I want food, Aeroplan points, Maple Leaf lounge access, and all the accoutrements of a full-service carrier. In the more than two years we operated Tango, the same employees who flew mainline aircraft, whether they were pilots or flight attendants, and the same ground staff transported over three million people, and I never received a single complaint on my desk. Same people, same planes, but with a different name, different paint job, and low prices, and you could do no wrong. But everyone involved with Tango—customers and employees alike—felt a difference. Not just because of the purple aircraft but because the fares, service, and expectations were all aligned. The low-cost carrier game isn't complicated, and lowered expectations are part of their success.

Tango was launched in the fall of 2001. Around the same time, Sport Hawk International, a sports charter company, went bust as a result of its inability to withstand the shocks created by the events of September 11. This provided us with another opportunity to enter a new market niche using aircraft rendered surplus by those same September 11 aftershocks.

The Canadian Airlines fleet we had acquired included long-range Boeing 737-200s, which had two pilots and two engines and thus were more economical than the older 727s used by Sport Hawk, which had three of each. The 200s were reconfigured from 120 seats to 48 executive-class seats. In addition, Air Canada had immediate access to ready-made expertise in premium customer service with flight attendants already familiar with the rigours of our award-winning Executive First service and concierges trained to take care of our most frequent fliers. Armed with a solid plan and a reputation for reliability and world-class service, we made a pitch to the Toronto Maple Leafs and Edmonton Oilers NHL clubs and to the Toronto Raptors NBA club, winning contracts from all three. Air Canada Jetz was born—a name previously intended for our low-cost carrier.

Jetz has proven a money maker from day one, carrying sports teams to games and superstars like Bruce Springsteen to concerts. These are demanding passengers, yet without exception I have received nothing but rave reviews for the performance of the flight crews serving them. The crew members on Jetz were drawn from our normal roster of employees, and they and their managers have proven the tremendous wealth of talent we truly have. All they needed was the latitude to manage their own business and make things happen, and they did.

I foresee a possible future demand for an upscale service, perhaps an all-business-class brand, depending on the recovery of the airline

133

industry over the next few years, as well as a low-cost international product bringing holiday-seeking customers to the sun in the winter or Europe or South America in the summer. If and when this happens, we'll be ready.

We took flak for the multi-branding approach. Some people claimed that it was merely an attempt to force competitors like WestJet out of business. Others suggested that we risked cannibalizing our main brand with these moves. I would prefer any day to cannibalize myself on a controlled basis rather than have a competitor do it to me on their terms. Examples of companies that have profited from cannibalizing themselves abound and include Procter and Gamble, with its competing detergents, and Starbucks, which has stores every block or even across the street from each other in big cities. Our new brands were both defending and expanding our customer base by offering attractive alternatives to passengers. The fact is, we had little choice, and at least we were experimenting. One of the most fascinating aspects of all the noise we heard from our detractors was that none of them were offering any alternative ideas.

Either we compete with WestJet or we vacate the domestic business—our strategy comes down to that. Well, we're here to stay and we will compete, although our top emphasis for growth lies elsewhere, in the transborder and international markets.

The conflict between legacy airlines and stripped-to-the-bone low-fare operations is not a purely Canadian phenomenon; it's a global one, and Air Canada is leading in its response to that issue. Proof of this pours into my office every week, as other airlines around the world grow aware of our strategy and begin to emulate it. The CEO of Air France made a point of telling me how much he loved the names Jazz, Tango, and Zip and the graphic design executions of each, and before Delta copied our Tango concept with its Song, SAS with Snowflake, United with Ted, and British Midland with BMI Baby, all four airlines visited us to learn how to set up and market a low-cost operation. Our innovation has been compelling, and representatives from some of the world's leading airlines are visiting Canada to discover where the future of aviation is leading. Not all of these efforts will succeed, I suspect, for a variety of reasons. The aircraft assigned to Song, for example, are too large, in my opinion. But this doesn't alter the fact that Air Canada has helped redefine the structure for legacy carriers around the globe.

No better illustration of this fact exists than the changes taking place at Qantas, one of the world's most respected airlines. Qantas essentially mirrored our strategy in late 2003, when it rearranged the parent company into ten divisions. There are four flying businesses: Qantas Airlines (main international and domestic operations), Qantaslink (regional airline operations), Australian Airlines (international leisure carrier), and Jetstar, a domestic low-cost carrier. Sound familiar? There are also two flying services businesses: Engineering Technical Operations and Maintenance Services, and Airports and Catering, as well as four associated businesses: Qantas Freight, Qantas Holidays, Qantas Defence Services, and Qantas Consulting.

Besides the obvious replication of the strategy that Air Canada introduced three years earlier, the Qantas move is especially interesting because, like Air Canada, Qantas was privatized from a government-owned operation in the early 1990s. The difference is that when the Australian government said privatized, it meant privatized, and Qantas has never been saddled with obligations its competitors do not share. It intends to operate each business as an individual profit centre supported by a corporate umbrella providing staffing, computer, and financial services. Incidentally, Qantas has publicly declared that it will not permit its share of the domestic Australian market to drop below 65 per cent and will take whatever pricing and servicing steps it deems necessary to prevent that loss of business. To my knowledge, this statement has not generated cries of "Unfair!" or "Monopoly!" in Australia. I chuckle at the outcry that would ring out if I were to say the same thing in Canada.

If it needs to be said, I'll say it here: Air Canada is pro-competition. We welcome it not just from a philosophical standpoint but from a practical one: competition makes you better. It also makes you tougher, and this toughness is reflected in the way that we, or any other successful corporation, carry on business. The legal strategies of a company seeking to expand or defend its markets should not be misinterpreted or unfairly hung with terms such as "predatory."

The failure of Greyhound Airlines in 1997 was blamed on Air Canada's "predatory" efforts, which is totally untrue. Greyhound's problems were rooted in its use of old, inefficient Boeing 727-200 aircraft and its insistence on cross-connecting flights through Winnipeg. Objections raised against Greyhound's launch from a regulatory point of view originated with Canadian Airlines and WestJet, but not Air Canada. In fact, while Greyhound was waiting for approval to operate, everyone contacting its call centre heard: "Air Canada is the only domestic airline not objecting to our start-up, and we suggest you call their reservation number," an unlikely response from a company that considered us predatory.

No critic of Air Canada these days is more strident than Clive Beddoe of WestJet. I congratulate WestJet and its employees for trying to duplicate Herb Kelleher's Southwest model, but Beddoe's constant quibbling about Air Canada has grown wearisome. It would also be helpful if Beddoe presented his views with more honesty. For example, Beddoe has stated that Air Canada was privatized with billions of dollars in taxpayers' money and a clean balance sheet, which is total nonsense. In fact, we received less than $250 million as capital from share sales, while the federal government pocketed almost $500 million. Statements such as the one made by Beddoe, totally at odds with the facts and rarely challenged by media observers, are outrageous.

Clive Beddoe has stated that our hub system creates airport crowding and inefficiencies, leading to extra expense passed on to customers. He is correct to a degree: hub operations demand careful management and scheduling to avoid congestion and to control costs, but these can be achieved, as virtually every international airline in the world knows. It is amusing to watch WestJet increase its hubbing activity, especially at Pearson International in Toronto. How is it handling the "extra expense"?

WestJet also claims that Air Canada is seeking to dominate the domestic air travel market and eliminate competitors, an allegation that pricks up ears across the country. WestJet fails to mention that only Air Canada has actually *reduced* its domestic capacity across the board each year since 1999, while WestJet, Jetsgo, and CanJet are rapidly increasing their own. The fact is, WestJet is actively trying to put

Jetsgo and other low-cost carriers out of business, believing that this is its exclusive domain. I admit to becoming agitated when so-called industry experts declare, "Air Canada must reduce its capacity," leaving other airlines free to expand their own capacity without apparent restriction. If we cannot get our costs in line and compete, we will be gone—a basic rule of the marketplace that I accept. But to charge that Air Canada should not be permitted to seek growth in existing or new markets solely on the basis of our size and capacity is absurd. Let's remember that we are not attacking the markets of WestJet and other carriers—they are attacking *ours*. Do we have a right to protect those markets? If Canada wants to continue claiming that it is a free-enterprise economy, then we indeed have that right.

Clive Beddoe says he favours competition, but his actions do not support that idea. When we reacted to one of David Collenette's demands for greater competition in the domestic air travel market with our Open Skies Plus proposal, WestJet vetoed the idea before it got off the ground because it does not want U.S. competition to affect it.

Beddoe often complains about how we have tried to put him out of business. It's too bad the folks at WestJet do not recall the time in September 1996 when Transport Canada was about to shut WestJet down for irregularities in maintenance record-keeping procedures and the airline temporarily suspended operations. WestJet asked Canadian Airlines to assist it in carrying stranded passengers back to their original point of embarkation, but the people at Canadian rejected the idea. When West-Jet turned to us, we agreed to look after any stranded passengers, covering our expenses by drawing from a credit provided by WestJet and returning excess funds to them once the crisis had passed. Without our assistance, several thousand WestJet passengers might have found themselves with tickets but no flights to board, and there would be fewer WestJet fans around today. Clive Beddoe never mentions this arrangement. Some memories, it seems, are both short and selective.

THE RISE of discount airlines was one factor contributing to the sea change in the North American airline industry; another was the United Airlines pilots' contract negotiations fiasco in 2000. No airline can afford a prolonged pilots' strike, and through the 1990s companies paid whatever the union negotiators demanded. The cost, of course, was passed on to the passenger, leading to the rise of discount airlines and the United Airlines experience.

In early 2000, United's pilots, who owned a good chunk of the airline, signed the most expensive contract renewal in the history of the industry, providing an immediate pay raise of 22 to 28 per cent for every United Airlines pilot, plus an additional pay raise of 4.5 per cent each year through 2004. These were outrageous increases to employees who were already well paid, and they bore no relation to prevailing marketplace conditions. The mood of the period was captured perfectly by United pilots' union president Rick Dubinsky when he said, "We don't want to kill the golden goose [United]. We just want to choke it by the neck until it gives us every last egg."

When pay increases failed to arrive quickly enough to suit the union, it instructed pilots by stealth to "work to rule," which resulted in cancelled or delayed flights and major upheavals in the airline's flight schedules, followed by a rapid decline in passenger loads. Under work-to-rule, pilots would delay takeoffs, choose less direct routes, and generally raise costs (and passengers' ire). United became perhaps the most disliked airline in North America; yet other pilot unions, ignoring reality in pursuit of their own nest of golden eggs, began demanding similar contracts. It was like watching a line of corporate dominoes falling: when Delta pilots received raises of 24 to 39 per cent over five years, US Airways had to match this under a parity clause in its contract.

During this period when the pilots of United so severely damaged their own company, the most remarkable story I heard (perhaps it's even true) was about two captains getting into a loud argument at San Francisco. They had operated Chicago to San Francisco flights one hour apart, but by the time they arrived in San Francisco they were neck and neck. They were furious with each other and debated who had done the greater damage to the airline, as if this would somehow help their company, customers, or themselves. One captain said something along the lines of: "What were you doing? I flew as slowly as I could to increase the crew's pay [the longer the flight, the greater the pay], and by getting here so late, we've busted all sorts of passenger connections, which will cost us a fortune." The other captain replied that he had done more damage by flying faster, burning more fuel, and causing more wear and tear on the engines.

Pilots are a professional group and generally understand business well. Their unions know how far they can push things. After the appalling events of September 11, reality began to set in among union leaders, and salary cuts became suddenly acceptable to save jobs. "Now," one industry analyst commented, "those United pilots are furiously trying to shove the eggs back up into the bird."

With the collapse in air traffic after September 11 and the rise of air fares, driven in part by elevated labour costs among the unionized airlines, passengers were being asked to pay more than the market dictated was fair and necessary, creating a disconnect between passenger expectations and economic realities. Markets abhor this type of dislocation every bit as much as nature does, and rushing in to fill the empty space, as the high-cost legacy carriers pulled a whopping 20 per cent of their capacity from the marketplace, came entrepreneurs like David Neeleman at JetBlue, all imitating to one degree or another the model set by Southwest Airlines: cut operating expenses to the bone, keep debt off the books, avoid unions (although Southwest is heavily unionized), pay significantly lower wages (as much as 50 per cent lower) to employees, don't provide pension benefits, and offset the lower employee income by offering attractive stock options.

Nothing distinguishes large legacy airlines such as Air Canada from newer operations like WestJet and Southwest more clearly than employee costs. The difference is not simply a matter of one side being more or less generous than the other; it is the result of unions seeking better deals for members and the effect of their efforts compounding over decades. WestJet has been in operation since 1996, and the years since then mark not only the limit of seniority but also the years over which no pension obligations have accumulated. At Air Canada, we have employees with more than forty years of service. Their seniority entitles them to top wages, and their looming retirement age demands that the company come through on its obligations to them. I am not claiming that this situation is unfair or that it cannot be managed. My

139

point is that it is far more complex for a company like Air Canada to emulate the success of WestJet than our critics claim.

Gerard Arpey, a good guy and the new CEO of American Airlines, told me he was recently on a panel with Joe Leonard, the CEO of the profitable low-cost carrier AirTran. Apparently, Joe was bragging about how successful they were and would continue to be and about how the legacy carriers just couldn't get it together. Gerard responded by saying that he could be a genius too if he had the seniority levels and pay scales of AirTran and didn't provide pension benefits for employees. The difference between the success of low-cost carriers and the woes of the legacy carriers isn't rocket science; it can be distilled down to this one key facet of our respective circumstances.

David Neeleman of JetBlue, who has become a good friend, reminds me all the time: "Hey, it's easy to run a profitable airline, Robert. All you need is new planes, new employees, and no debt." And he's right. My challenge is to turn a great legacy carrier, Air Canada, into a sustainably profitable company in a totally different operating environment.

Airlines tend to focus on technology, which risks underestimating the importance of people. In the early nineties I sensed that many of our senior in-flight staff needed to recharge their batteries so that they might return to work fuelled with enthusiasm. The company had never offered leaves of absence to this group, and when I introduced the idea hundreds took advantage of it over the summer months. We won at both ends with this idea—younger people earning lower wages filling in for them gained confidence and experience, and senior people returned feeling better about themselves, their jobs, and the company.

I'm a firm believer in the dynamics of market forces, whether in determining the price of corn or in adjusting employee salaries to reflect similar workloads, and I expect these forces to make themselves felt soon. Companies such as AirTran and WestJet may be paying their people half as much to work twice as hard as employees with the legacy airlines, but this imbalance cannot continue forever. The economic chasm between the small newer airlines—the ones that won't fly to airports with bad weather or high service fees—and the larger airlines that can carry you around the world is immense. It costs companies such as United and American about 11 cents (US) to carry each passenger 1 mile; Southwest can do the same thing for less than 7.5 cents.

Dislocations such as this one will not remain static, and the gap is beginning to close. Large international airlines are finding ways to reduce costs in dozens of areas, from charging for meals on shorter flights to rolling back wages and salaries at all levels. None of this can be achieved without pain and frustration, because no one enjoys being told he or she has to work harder for less money. In my experience, employees understand and accept realities if the facts are presented in language with a B.S. quotient of zero, if the sacrifices are fair and equitable across the company, and if there is the promise of an upside in the future. In our case, the upside consists of an improved potential for long-term job security, and we have always tried to explain this to Air Canada employees when looking for ways of reducing our costs.

11

SEPTEMBER 11

AND ITS

REPERCUSSIONS

WHENEVER I travel to London on business, my hotel of choice is not in Mayfair or Knightsbridge, and it's not the Savoy, the Dorchester, or even the Hilton. It's the Renaissance at Heathrow airport, an undistinguished place except for one thing: it is the best hotel in the world for watching aircraft take off and land. When I was a kid living in London, it was called the Heathrow Penta. I used to dream of one day being able to afford the £20 a night to stay there instead of loitering around the cold, wet terraces of Heathrow's Queen's building or the parking lots to watch the airplanes.

At the Renaissance, I always request room 3208, overlooking runway 27R. If my family is travelling with me, they insist that we stay in London with normal people, "normal" meaning anyone who won't sit for hours staring out at airplanes. When I travel alone, I prefer the Heathrow Renaissance.

My trips to London have generally been routine, with one notable exception. On this trip, I had planned to meet up with Rob Peterson, our CFO, and talk with the Royal Bank of Scotland to arrange financing for some Airbus A-321 aircraft we had ordered. Most complex problems from the merger with Canadian Airlines were behind us. Things were looking positive again—traffic and profits were improving, and the routes to Asia and South America that we had coveted so much were in place and performing nicely.

I left for London on flight 864 out of Montreal. It was a fine flight, smooth and uneventful, as most transatlantic flights are.

At Heathrow I checked into the Renaissance, kicked off my shoes, ate some breakfast, and watched aircraft coming and going for an hour or so before curling up to catch a nap before my meeting. It was September 11, 2001.

The telephone call that awakened me about four hours later was from my secretary, Pauline Boisvert, informing me that an aircraft had just crashed into New York City's World Trade Center. I assumed the incident involved a private plane, probably a Cessna or some other small craft. I knew the Empire State Building had been struck by a military plane in thick fog in the 1940s, and I expected this would be just another weather-related accident. Unfortunate and tragic, of course, but an accident. Rolling over, I reached for the remote control and switched on the television. The screen flickered to life at the same instant the second jet struck the south tower of the World Trade Center.

I leaped off the bed, phoned Pauline, and asked her to put me through to Rob Giguere, at the time our executive vice-president of operations in Montreal. Rob confirmed that he had already sent an order to Air Canada pilots instructing them to lock their cockpit doors. Rob had spoken to United Airlines Flight Operations, and they were having trouble finding all their aircraft. We both agreed to dispatch messages via our Datalink system to all aircraft on North American routes, instructing them to land immediately. Shortly thereafter, as we know, all aircraft were ordered to land. Then I sat and watched and listened, as the rest of the dreadful day unfolded, including the crashes at the Pentagon and in a Pennsylvania field, while staying in touch with Air Canada headquarters in Montreal. Taking in the appalling terror of those images, I tried to fathom the impact on the future of the airline industry generally and on Air Canada in particular. What would happen now? What could we do for our passengers and our employees? How would we handle whatever was to come next?

The events of that day could not have been anticipated, yet in a small way they were not entirely surprising. For years, many had feared that the airline system was vulnerable to any group of fanatics with the determination to carry out such an insane scheme. Until September 11, you could drive a tank onto almost any airfield in North America without being challenged. Having grown up overseas and having heard bombs go off in London, I always worried that the United States, which is so insular and naïve about the ways of the world and the world's views of the country, would some day be shocked. But never in my wildest dreams did I, or any other decent person, ever conjure up the horrors of September 11.

I spent the rest of that terrible day speaking to my family, to Rob Giguere, to Duncan Dee, at the time my executive assistant, and to the rest of the team, confirming that every Air Canada passenger and crew member was safe. As CEO, I was ultimately responsible for overseeing the safe return of Air Canada passengers, aircraft, and crew from locations all over the globe, a duty I could effectively perform only from Montreal, so it was important that I return to Montreal as quickly as possible. Rob (since retired) and the entire Air Canada operations group were tremendously experienced, and I wasn't worried that they couldn't handle the situation. Air Canada's people are often at their best not when things are routine but when the chips are down, as they were then. Nevertheless, it was important that I find a way back as quickly as possible.

It would be difficult for me to get back to Montreal, however. Not only was Heathrow crammed with unscheduled aircraft and stranded passengers, but all transatlantic air traffic had been grounded until further notice.

I called Bob Brown, then president of Bombardier and more recently chairman of the board at Air Canada.

"Bob," I said, "is there any way you can get me back to Montreal from here?" Neither of us knew how long the commercial transatlantic service would be grounded—likely several days, perhaps a week or more. Bombardier happened to have a Challenger in Germany. If flight clearance could be obtained, he would make it available for me to travel back to Montreal. I passed this information on to Duncan Dee, who contacted the Ministry of Transport in Ottawa, where David Collenette kindly helped us obtain clearance from the armed forces in the United Kingdom, the United States, and Canada to fly out of Luton airport, about 80 kilometres (50 miles) north of London, direct to Montreal, the following day.

The next morning, I met the Challenger in Luton and introduced myself to its Bombardier crew, who were as pleased as I was to be heading home. Commercial aircraft had been grounded throughout Europe and North America, and military aircraft were being scrambled at the first hint of any unauthorized movement. I was comfortable, but Lizanne was not. When I told her of the plan, she had visions of a nervous F-18 pilot who had failed to get the message dropping out of the sky and locking missiles onto his target, which would be us.

I asked the pilot if he felt comfortable about the flight, and he shrugged and said, "I've got a fax that says it's okay." He showed me a letter-sized sheet of paper authorizing the flight. "If a fighter shows up off our wingtip, I guess I'll just hold it up to the window and let him read it."

The flight was uneventful but unsettling. During the dozens of times I had crossed the Atlantic seated in the flight deck, the air waves had been alive with routine radio transmissions and chatter between pilots or between pilots and air traffic controllers. On this flight, until we entered North American air space we heard only total silence, perhaps the first time this had occurred on a transatlantic flight since Charles Lindbergh's day. I think it's safe to assume we were the first civilians to cross the Atlantic after the attacks and probably for a couple more days as well.

We landed at Dorval airport without incident, although we surprised the small coterie of Canada Customs inspectors on duty there. "How the hell did you guys get here?" they asked when they boarded the aircraft.

The next few days were a whirlwind as we dealt not only with our own aircraft and passengers, grounded around the world, but with those of other airlines whose planes had set down in locations from Gander to Whitehorse and who were depending on Air Canada to get them back into the air. For all intents and purposes, we were the only operators of big aircraft at most of those airports. I also had to field requests from hundreds of people who knew me, or claimed to know me, asking if I could pull strings and help return their family, friends, and employees from wherever they happened to be stuck.

It took almost four days for things to settle down before normal commercial air flights could resume in North America. Although many people assumed that the industry remained in a state of suspended animation through that period, this was not true. Like others, we were managing the needs of our own operations and caring for the various demands of our competitors. I happen to believe, however, that Air Canada faced a unique combination of challenges and that we succeeded at least as well as everybody else and better than most.

First, our own situation: 16 of our aircraft, along with 110 crew and 2200 passengers, were stranded outside Canada. We knew where they were, and we had been assured that everyone was safe. Other than request that local consulates and any of our personnel stationed in the area address the needs of our passengers, we could only monitor the situation and trust that the passengers were receiving adequate care under the circumstances and that our aircraft would be serviced properly for the return journey.

Here in Canada, we were dealing with 220 foreign aircraft that had been ordered to set down in 16 Canadian airports, including 42 aircraft at Halifax, 40 at Gander, 38 at Vancouver, and 27 at St. John's. In many of these airports, Air Canada was the only operator capable of offloading aircraft, processing stranded passengers, and providing necessary line maintenance work on the diverted planes. Once again, Air Canada's people rose to the occasion. Arriving with these planes were 44,000 passengers and crew members, and to my knowledge all of them had nothing but praise for the manner in which they were treated during their unscheduled stay.

Although those numbers are impressive, they fail to convey all the complexities of the situation, because those 220 foreign aircraft were in place alongside hundreds of Air Canada aircraft and their passengers and crew as well. The aircraft required service and maintenance, and the baggage needed handling both off and back on the planes. To complicate things further, many of the aircraft were parked at locations at the airport not designated or equipped for the required service and maintenance.

The efforts of Air Canada employees everywhere in the organization were exemplary. Employees cancelled their vacation plans to pitch in, some of them working twenty-four-hour days until things returned to normal. Many of them opened their own homes to stranded passengers. In Halifax, the entire Air Canada team assumed responsibility for over eight thousand passengers on the flights diverted there, ensuring that everyone had comfortable lodging and care throughout their ordeal.

The company's performance, and the contribution made by Air Canada employees, earned recognition and appreciation from airlines the world over, although I suspect that our achievement came as no surprise to them: Air Canada has always been more highly regarded beyond Canada's borders than within them. Following is a letter that came to us from the Air Transport Association of America and the CEOs of several U.S. airlines:

Dear Minister Collenette:

Along with the Chief Executives of several of the largest U.S. carriers, I am writing to thank the Government, people and airlines of Canada for the tremendous assistance and courtesies provided during this particularly difficult period. We would especially like to underscore the unbelievable level of assistance our carriers have received from our friends at Air Canada.

The events of September 11th have had a profound and lasting impact on all Americans and, in particular, the U.S. airline industry. As our flights were diverted to Canadian airports, we were heartened by the welcome and support we received from the Canadian people and Air Canada. Air Canada's support in servicing our customers, assisting with logistics, and servicing our aircraft was critical during a time of great stress and strain. The stories we have heard from crews and customers of the kindness they saw while in Canada will remain with us all.

147

Then, a classic incident occurred. Amid the letters of thanks and appreciation to me from airline executives and passengers came an official notice from ACPA announcing that it was filing a grievance against Air Canada. Its complaint: I had been a passenger on a flight not commanded by an Air Canada pilot—the one arranged for me by Bombardier—contrary to the union agreement.

The entire world, and our industry in particular, had changed forever, as all the commentators kept telling us. As well as witnessing the appalling loss of thousands of innocent lives, September 11, 2001, marked the biggest single-day crisis in the airline industry—in fact the entire global travel industry. None of this appeared important to the union executive.

I doubt that the rank-and-file members of ACPA were aware of the grievance being filed, and I suspect that they would have disagreed with it. Our pilots are good people, and they are professionals. I'm sure they would have supported my efforts to get back to Montreal as quickly as possible, if not for me to be with Air Canada, at least for me to be with my family.

Meanwhile, anyone could see that we were in danger not only of losing individual airlines but of seeing an entire industry collapse. Nor would this be a relatively short-term tremor; its implications would extend for years, driving customers away from international travel generally and air travel specifically.

Through the balance of September 2001, I watched the contrasting attitudes of Canada and the United States towards the airline industry in each country. The United States is considered a bastion of free enterprise, and it is slow to provide taxpayer money to support private industry, but among the changes that resulted from September 11 was a new opinion of that country's airlines. On September 10, 2001, most U.S. airlines were despised for their deteriorating service and constant financial woes. On September 12, 2001, the same airline industry was the object of compassion and support, and when airline executives marched almost arm-in-arm to Congress later that month, they received a sympathetic hearing. Within days, they were promised $5 billion in cash and $10 billion in loan guarantees. An additional

$3 billion in cash would come later, along with significant tax relief, and a total of almost $30 billion in support was pledged. This was more than a matter of propping up a devastated critical part of the U.S. economy; it was a concerted effort to restore public confidence in all the airlines and to ensure that commercial aviation continued to provide necessary lubrication to the country's economy.

The International Air Transport Association (IATA) estimated that the week following September 11 cost the world's airlines about $10 billion in lost revenues and extra costs. Midway Airlines, already operating under Chapter 11 bankruptcy proceedings in the United States, gave up all hope on September 12, saying the terrorist attacks had eliminated any chance of recovery. Swissair grounded its fleet, Ansett of Australia failed, the New Zealand government invested heavily in that country's airline to prevent its collapse, and an estimated 100,000 airline employees in the United States had lost their jobs by September 25. When Air Canada finally resumed flying on something resembling normal schedules, our passenger load was down by 60 per cent and we had lost $100 million in four days as a direct result of September 11.

Meanwhile, no one at Transport Canada seemed to be aware of just how much damage had occurred and was continuing to occur within our industry. Transport Canada kept operating with the same apparent philosophy that it always has, crisis or no crisis. This approach is best described as *Do nothing until it is too late to do anything at all.* We had to do something. On September 26, we took action to save the airline by grounding eighty-four aircraft, reducing our capacity by 20 per cent, and reluctantly laying off five thousand employees.

I went to Ottawa and began making a case for financial support proportional to that being provided to the U.S. airlines. The events of September 11, I pointed out, were a stake through the heart of the airline industry all across the world, but especially in North America. I was not pleading exclusively for Air Canada, although we stood to lose more than anyone else. I was seeking support for the Canadian airline industry in the same degree that Washington was backing the U.S. lines, because the impact in this country was comparable to that in the

149

United States. I told David Collenette, "You need to stabilize the entire industry or we will start losing airlines."

I had to try to engage Collenette again when the U.S. announced that it was putting air marshals on all flights. Upon hearing the news, I contacted the minister and told him we would require air marshals on our transborder flights at least. His response was to state that there would be no air marshals on board any Canadian commercial flights.

"Look," I countered, "the consumer has a choice to fly with an airline that has a security officer on board or one that does not. Which one do you think the consumer will choose on the basis of safety? We need air marshals because our competition will have them."

Collenette's reply was, "No way."

Of course, when Air Canada was permitted to fly into Washington's Reagan National airport and the U.S. insisted that air marshals must be on board every flight, Collenette relented.

I took a lot of flak for speaking out, especially about the need for financial guarantees. WestJet, which at the time still flew only domestically in western Canada and faced no U.S. competition, sneered that we were asking the Canadian taxpayer to solve problems that began long before September 11. Almost no one seemed to realize that we were operating more than six hundred flights between Canada and the United States every day of the year, probably more flights to American destinations than by all other foreign airlines put together. As a result, U.S. airlines were our primary competition, not only on routes from the United States to Canada but also on those from Canada to the rest of the world via U.S. hubs. In fact, almost two thirds, or over $6 billion, of our revenues were generated against the U.S. industry, now highly subsidized, not just on transborder traffic but around the world. They had just received billions in cash and guarantees to get back up and running while we had received nothing.

Our passengers were disappearing as fast as those south of the border, and we were operating (supposedly) in a free-trade environment under NAFTA. On that basis, I argued that Ottawa should provide proportional financial support for the Canadian industry, representing a market a tenth the size of the U.S. market. Behind the scenes, Angus

Kinnear, CEO of Canada 3000, and Jean-Marc Eustache of Air Transat kept urging me on, convinced that they would receive a proportional share of whatever we got. As much as they wanted money, they wanted to save themselves from the media scrutiny. Meanwhile, I got my head beaten in. Who could blame them for hiding?

Through it all, only one individual from the federal government ever asked me about our status and whether we needed any assistance to ensure the airline's survival. To the surprise of many people, I suspect, it was Gilles Duceppe.

Collenette, as usual, made his presence felt but not in a manner that could be construed as helpful. With traffic and revenues vanishing, and our U.S. competition enjoying access to billions of dollars in government backup, we had little choice but to announce layoffs, something I deeply regretted but could not avoid.

Before making our announcement, we notified Ottawa, and Collenette was on the telephone to me in no time at all. In fact, he called me at home. He was livid. "If you lay off any employees," he screamed at me through the receiver, "you will be breaking the law of Canada and you will personally pay the consequences!" He was referring to the commitment we had made when acquiring Canadian Airlines not to lay off anyone. Post–September 11, given everything going on, this was indicative of the help we got from the minister of transport. We immediately appealed to the solicitor general for a ruling, according to the extreme circumstances of September 11 and its consequences, and received an exemption with little difficulty. Collenette had achieved nothing beyond making a good deal of noise.

Once again, I am not in favour of government handouts to private enterprise. If I stated this on one hand and asked for government support under normal conditions on the other hand, I would rightly be accused of the same kind of hypocrisy that I find so irritating in certain quarters. The aftermath of September 11 generated anything *but* normal conditions. We were faced with two unprecedented situations: a cataclysmic event and massive financial support to major competition.

We presented Ottawa with our case for support, based on three factors: a crippling drop-off of passenger bookings right across the industry, major financial support being offered to our U.S. competition, and substantial fees and taxes that were already restricting our operations.

In response, the Canadian airline industry was offered $160 million in emergency aid, with $100 million earmarked for Air Canada. In addition, Ottawa agreed to follow the lead of every other nation in the world by promising to cover increases in insurance premiums. No reduction in taxes or fees was offered, so the federal government continued to suck cash from the industry after Sepember 11 as it had before.

No, that's not quite true. Ottawa began collecting *more* per passenger when it slapped a supplementary tax of $24 on every airline ticket sold, generating nearly half a billion dollars in federal revenue, earned on the backs of airline employees and shareholders. What did passengers and the airline industry receive for their money? Employees of the Canadian Air Transport Security Authority (CATSA), basically the same people who had been doing airport security in the past, dressed up in new uniforms. It was all classic Collenette.

People assume that the arrival of CATSA meant that airlines were relieved of the expense of security measures, but this is not so. Among other steps, Air Canada was directed to collect data from every customer who boards a flight to or from Canada, including name, gender, passport number, date of birth, and nationality, and to forward this information to the federal government. We now require more agents to process international customers than we did in the past. Added to other directed measures, this procedure has more than doubled our security costs. Meanwhile, Ottawa collects a fee to perform a service that we and other airlines used to do in the past for a fraction of the cost, absorbing the cost in the price of the ticket. It is truly bizarre when you consider that government is generally viewed as responsible for public security and provides it without surcharge everywhere, except in the airline business.

We estimate that Ottawa now nets hundreds of millions of dollars more each year from air travel than it did before September 11, 2001, calculated after deducting government assistance to cover higher insurance premiums and loan guarantees. I wish I could say that Air Canada and other airlines benefit from this largesse, but we do not.

The government's inaction was at least partially responsible for the almost overnight disappearance of Canada 3000. The airline had been in serious trouble for some time, and it can be argued that the events of September 11 simply hastened the inevitable. But its demise under the circumstances demonstrated not only the dangers facing the airline industry but the attitude of the then minister of transport towards the situation.

Since the integration of Canadian Airlines and Air Canada, numerous voices in Ottawa had been grumbling about our "dominant" share of the market and the dangers it posed to the country. Making this kind of complaint enabled the government to portray itself as a consumer watchdog, even though that "dominance" was illusory.

By late 2001, after September 11 and the introduction of Tango and its low fares, complaints about our market share had faded away as our competitors expanded. Canada 3000 had swallowed Royal Airlines and CanJet, expanding its schedules and market share accordingly. Meanwhile, WestJet maintained its growth, and the U.S. airlines continued to represent strong cross-border competition and our market share became less of an issue. This was the same levelling effect of market forces that we claimed would happen back when we were being roasted in Ottawa and by the media for supposedly acting like a monopoly.

The market expansion was no proof that all of the players were financially healthy. We continued to struggle with our legacy carrier costs and balance sheet structure, but we were more financially sound than Canada 3000, in spite of claims by some so-called experts at Transport Canada that the airline was a roaring success.

Canada 3000 had begun life as a charter carrier and did a reasonably good job at it. Unfortunately, management decided that the company could be just as successful as a scheduled airline serving first domestic and later international destinations, yet still operate efficiently as a chartered vacation carrier. These three types of services demand three very different business and operating strategies, as well as the skills and experience to go along with them. Canada 3000 tried to implement all three simultaneously on a learn-as-we-go basis and struggled from the beginning.

Flying vacation charters is a relatively low-risk operation. Tour operators commit months in advance to fill the aircraft seats, the service is generally one-class, and the airline can really crank up utilization of the aircraft, flying at all hours of the day or night. Passengers paying full fare on scheduled airlines would never put up with these inconveniences, but they accept it on a charter flight. Had Canada 3000 remained a charter operation, I suspect it would still be flying today.

An all-charter airline is not a glamorous business, and growth is limited. Like charter operations the world over inevitably seem to, Canada 3000 tried to transform itself into a scheduled carrier, flying head-to-head with us and, on international flights, against airlines like British Airways, Air France, and the U.S. lines. As a result, its risk levels shot through the roof, and when it added India to its schedule, Canada 3000 seriously overextended itself. On top of this, the absorption of Royal Airlines and CanJet diverted management's attention from the complexities of converting Canada 3000 to a scheduled airline, stretching the company's human and financial resources.

By September 2001, Canada 3000 was a house of cards ready to fold with the first strong wind. That's not just my opinion. Top executives of the airline knew long before September 11 that they would be broke by the end of the year—an opinion confirmed by an internal letter from its late chairman, John Lecky, to his board, sent in the summer of 2001. The letter questioned the strategic direction of then CEO Angus Kinnear, and acknowledged that the company would be out of cash by the end of the year. This letter was later published in the *National Post*.

When the shaky foundations began to collapse in the weeks following September 11, Canada 3000 management approached Transport Canada with a business plan stating that it would face massive layoffs and pay cuts of 20 per cent unless it received assistance. On October 25, 2001, David Collenette came through, announcing loan guarantees of $75 million to help Canada 3000 through a "short-term cash crunch" resulting from the decline in air travel following September 11. In announcing the guarantee, Collenette borrowed a few key words from the presentation I had made just a few weeks earlier while pleading for financial support in line with that awarded U.S. airlines. The key word I had been repeating was "stabilize," and so Collenette stated: "This is all part of the plan to stabilize the industry. [Canada 3000] is a well-run company that, through no fault of its own, has gotten to this particular stage." In obvious gratitude, Canada 3000 released a statement acknowledging the government's support, noting: "Canada 3000 will repay any amounts loaned against the guarantee."

Fat chance. Within hours Canada 3000 sought protection under the Companies' Creditors Arrangement Act (CCAA), which in this case was like raising an umbrella to ward off an avalanche. Just twelve hours after its CCAA filing, the "well-run company" that Collenette had chosen to support was out of business for good. Those internal memos predicting the airline's demise by year-end were proven correct, and thousands of Canadians all over the world found themselves stranded.

I was outraged. If Canada 3000 was eligible for $75 million in loan guarantees, we should have qualified for $750 million on a proportional basis, yet all we received was a brush-off and a bill for higher government fees and charges. In addition, $750 million would have been approximately proportional to the relief we would have received from Ottawa if it had treated us like the U.S. government treated U.S. carriers. Clearly, this was evidence that Collenette wouldn't help us, but he gave Canada 3000 exactly what we were asking for. On top of that, Collenette's office noted with shock and surprise that former Canada 3000 passengers were now flying Air Canada, among other airlines, and raising our share of market. Had the failure of Canada 3000 been the result of some Air Canada conspiracy to knock off competition? You might think so, on the basis of statements, some attributed to Collenette himself, that emerged from Transport Canada. Our introduction of Tango, the rumours said, had been a strategic move aimed at driving Canada 3000 out of the market, and the Competition Bureau claimed that if Canada 3000 had not gone out of business, the government would have shut down Tango. No one seemed to care that Canada 3000's problems had been home-grown, the result of expanding too far and too fast and then, like most of us, being clobbered by September 11 and not being able to withstand the blow.

Separately, I felt that Ottawa's move to throw cash at Canada 3000 as a result of its blind obsession to maintain competition for Air Canada highlighted the probability that if we had walked away from buying Canadian two years earlier, the government would have infused capital to keep it going.

In December 2001, I attended a reception at the U.S. ambassador's home in Ottawa. It was to introduce Canadian business and government leaders to Tom Ridge, Secretary of Homeland Security, and was one of those generally pleasant occasions when we all try to put our differences behind us in the spirit of Christmas and enjoy some degree of camaraderie for a few days.

David Collenette walked across the room to chat with me. Outside of committee rooms our conversations were always polite, and he wished me the best of the season. Then he leaned closer to say in a low voice, "Did you see that article in the *National Post* today about Canada 3000's debts?" He was referring to a story revealing that, for some time before going under, the company had been in more serious financial straits than had been publicly revealed.

"The one about them owing $145 million?" I said. "Yes, I saw it."

"Boy," he said, "can you imagine how fast they would have gone through that $75 million if we'd given it to them?"

I suppose I could have reminded him that he had praised Canada 3000 as a well-run company with only "a short-term cash crunch" before Parliament and the country just days before it threw in the towel Instead, I just nodded. It was Christmas, after all.

Collenette wasn't finished. "Oh, by the way," he said, smiling, "I realize that Tango didn't put Canada 3000 out of business." Then he put his hand on my arm, leaned even closer, and added: "Of course, I would never say that publicly."

12

POLISHING

OUR PUBLIC IMAGE

I WAS AS horrified as anyone in April 2002 upon learning that four Canadian Forces personnel from the Princess Patricia's Canadian Light Infantry had been killed in Afghanistan when a U.S. aircraft dropped a laser-guided bomb on them during night exercises. The entire country shared the sorrow of that event and the grief that the victims' families were suffering.

I called my then executive assistant, Duncan Dee, at home on a Saturday asking him to contact the Department of National Defence and offer whatever assistance would be helpful, especially for the families. Duncan called the office of the chief of defence staff and the Canadian Forces Base in Edmonton, where the Princess Pats were stationed. He was put through to a captain who happened to be married to an Air Canada flight attendant. The captain commented that the Department of National Defence had not planned to transport members of the soldiers' own regiment to serve as honour guards at the victims' funerals across the country. Pallbearers and honour guards would be drawn from whatever local Canadian Forces Base was nearest to the burial site. This meant that honour guards for the two Nova Scotia infantry victims would not be drawn from the same regiment as those who died but more likely from naval personnel stationed in Halifax.

We asked the captain if members of the Princess Pats would like to act as the honour guards for their fallen comrades, and he replied that they would very much appreciate being able to do so. So we offered to fly them wherever directed, free of charge, along with any other military personnel who wished to travel to the funeral. The only stipulation was that the soldiers wear their uniform on the aircraft, making it easy to confirm they were entitled to the flight. We also thought that the soldiers' presence would be good for everyone's morale and that many Canadians would want to express their feelings to the soldiers during their journey.

The regiment made arrangements at their end and the four victims received the observance they deserved, with members of their own regiment honouring the men and mourning their loss. We could have made a big deal about the arrangement, but we chose not to. This was not a public relations gesture but a corporate expression of the same sorrow that the rest of the country was feeling.

Unbelievably, this gesture almost backfired. On one of the flights from Edmonton, a passenger noticed the soldiers in their uniforms and discovered the purpose of their journey. She assumed that we had charged full-fare tickets to the Canadian Forces. Without making any inquiries, she sent e-mails to practically every media outlet across Canada to complain that Air Canada was gouging our soldiers at a time of national need. How dare we try to make a profit from such a national tragedy!

The fallout was immediate. Switchboards at the Canadian Forces and Air Canada offices began lighting up like Christmas trees thanks to calls from people across the country prepared to believe the worst about Air Canada. We asked the Canadian Forces communications people to respond on our behalf, and they did a great job of setting everyone straight. The media, however, did a less-than-effective job of explaining things. No media outlet in Canada ever ran the truth—that we had provided free return transportation for regiment members to mourn the loss of their comrades.

"I cannot believe what you people put up with," the Canadian Forces communications officer from Edmonton commented to someone in Air Canada media relations. I considered inviting her to spend a day or two here so that she could see for herself, but I decided against it.

This was admittedly a unique type of criticism directed at Air Canada, but it did not entirely surprise me. It was just another area of complaint, and dealing with complaints is a major part of every airline's operation.

Most complaints tend to be about relatively small problems presented as major concerns, such as not receiving the seat that was requested or an interruption of refreshment service due to turbulence. Any failure to satisfy a customer is regrettable, but some people exaggerate a situation in the hope of earning compensation beyond the scope of their problem. We do not live in a perfect world, which makes it difficult to run a perfect airline. If we are the source of major problems in providing service, the passenger deserves an appropriate and timely response. Minor errors, especially in situations that are beyond our control, deserve a sincere "We're sorry," and I insist that we express such an apology wherever appropriate.

I sometimes find myself protecting airline employees from unfair and outrageous demands and treatment. I recall being seated on a flight out of Toronto when a customer boarded and began acting as though he were the only passenger on the aircraft, making demands on the flight attendant and complaining loudly when they weren't met to his satisfaction. He wanted special service and he wanted it *now!* I watched this individual make himself as unpleasant as possible for several minutes. Then I stood up, identified myself, suggested he cease being difficult, and asked him to disembark for a chat.

This shocked him. He had tried bullying tactics, perhaps thinking other passengers would support him, but this plan had backfired.

When we got onto the jetway (the bridge connecting the airplane to the terminal), I told him I appreciated the fact that he had purchased a ticket on the airline but I would not accept anyone abusing our employees, just as I would not put up with Air Canada staff abusing customers. "The customer is not always right," I said. "Sometimes employees can be right as well. What's really bothering you?"

"Your employees don't smile enough," he replied. "Nobody smiled at check-in."

I suspect he didn't deserve a smile. Then I pointed out that Toronto had been struck with a number of storms that day, playing havoc with our schedule. Passengers were demanding information about rescheduled departure times, and our staff was being pushed to the limit. "These people are under a lot of stress right now, and if they can't smile at you as nicely as you want them to, be reasonable." I asked what else was bothering him, noting that he was holding a business class boarding pass.

"They took too long to give me my upgrade," he said.

"If that's your biggest issue," I said, "I suggest we get back on the plane and not hold everyone up. Give me your number, and I'll phone you tomorrow and deal with whatever is really bothering you."

He gave me his card and we reboarded the plane, flying to Montreal without further incident. I personally phoned him the following day, which shocked him again. This time he was calm, and he admitted rather sheepishly that he had overreacted the previous day.

Nothing pleases me more than to read letters complimenting us on our service or expressing appreciation for exceptional performance from our employees. It may be surprising to some, but we receive thousands of these letters during the year. If the customer mentions a specific crew or individual, I forward it to the appropriate Air Canada employees, letting them know that their efforts were appreciated by both the customer and me.

We have many letters on file from passengers praising Air Canada employees for going beyond the passengers' expectations, and each letter helps balance the negative reports that appear so often in the media. The letters relate some amazing tales of Air Canada personnel performing like heroes and treating the experience as part of their job, from helping to deliver babies in flight and taking young children home when a parent or guardian forgets to show up at the airport to working three days without a break when situations such as September 11 demanded it.

Throughout my tenure I have tried to be proactive in response to legitimate customer complaints and have encouraged Air Canada staff to be the same. As COO, I chaired a weekly operations review, and during one of those sessions I became very upset upon hearing that a boy had been struck on the head by a box falling out of an overhead bin. When I asked what we had done in response, the vice-president responsible for in-flight services, an otherwise nice man, shrugged and said we had given the boy's parents some release forms from our claims department to sign.

"That's it?" I asked. "That's all we did?" I launched into a speech I have repeated many times over the years, reminding everybody that we have to treat our customers exactly the way we would want to be treated ourselves—handing parents some release forms to cover our legal obligations was not good enough, and it never would be. I asked for assurances that the boy was all right. When I learned he was, I had a large Air Canada model plane sent to him with our apologies for the accident.

A horrific incident occurred some time later, when one of our airstair vehicles failed as a young boy was disembarking at St. John's, Newfoundland. He fell directly onto the concrete and suffered a severe injury to his arm. Given the height from which he had tumbled, the injury could have been worse, but I was mortified that such an accident could happen at all and immediately dispatched a vice-president to the Newfoundland hospital where the boy had been admitted. "I want you with the family, next to the boy's bed," I said. "Provide whatever the family needs, because that kind of thing is not what this company is about." Ultimately, we enabled this boy to travel, at our expense, to Toronto to receive the best possible medical care, and we kept an eye on him as he recuperated.

Negative letters concern me, positive ones reassure me, and sometimes letters arrive that simply confound or amuse me, like one from a loyal Air Canada passenger who flew regularly with a companion listed as John Stradivarius. Both were enrolled in our Aeroplan program and had built up a fair number of points in their travel. When the first passenger attempted to claim his companion's Aeroplan points, however, we realized that "John Stradivarius" was not a human being, but a cello. The human passenger valued his instrument so much that he purchased a separate ticket for it on each flight, strapping the cello into the seat next to him. All very well and good, but we had to explain to him that qualifying passengers have to be people.

The last word on airline complaints was made at an IATA board dinner meeting in Madrid a few years ago. We get a lot of business done at these sessions, and in between we have time to trade stories about our industry. At this dinner I was seated with Jürgen Weber, who was then CEO of Lufthansa; C.K. Chong, then CEO of Singapore Airlines; and Carly Fiorina, CEO of Hewlett-Packard, who was making a pitch to IATA on behalf of HP computers.

Put a few airline executives together and they soon start trading tales of customer problems and complaints and how they were handled. Jürgen and I tossed a couple of stories back and forth between us, and Carly mentioned that HP received its share of customer complaints as well. "Fortunately," she said, "I have a wonderful person heading up a customer service group reporting directly to me. She never loses her cool and knows exactly how to handle customers who have totally lost it."

In one instance, Carly told us, an outraged HP customer was making totally unacceptable demands to compensate for a problem he had encountered with his HP product. Nothing that the HP customer service person offered satisfied the customer, who screamed through the telephone: "Listen, if you don't fix this thing to my satisfaction, I'm going to come down to your office with this warranty, roll it up, and shove it up your ass!"

Without losing her cool, the HP complaints manager replied: "Sir, if you do that, it will be voided."

We all had a good laugh over the story, but C.K. Chong remained bent over the table, holding his head in his hands. "I am so tired," he said, "of going to cocktail parties, receptions, meetings, anywhere at all, and having people approach me to complain about their last flight on Singapore Airlines. They'll tell me how upset they were because the flight was late, or that we misplaced their luggage, or they weren't happy with their meal. They find all kinds of things to complain about, and it never stops—all I hear are customer complaints!"

To put this in its proper context: Singapore Airlines is generally rated ahead of every other airline in the world for customer service. Nobody does in-flight service as well as that airline, and it has won every possible award in virtually every year it has been operating.

At C.K.'s words I clasped my hands together and bowed to him. "On behalf of every airline executive in the room," I said, "I thank you for letting us know that even the CEO of Singapore Airlines puts up with the same stuff as the rest of us."

IN ADDITION to dealing with customer complaints, I try to help with problems in other areas. My home computer has access to the same detailed operations data posted on the terminal in my office at Dorval, which is the same as the information available to our folks at Systems Operations Control in Toronto, who monitor our worldwide operations. At home, I'll often slip into my den to check departures, arrivals, and passenger loads of Air Canada flights around the world. If I spot a problem, I will take steps to fix it. The people in operations know I do this, and instead of being concerned that the boss is looking over their shoulder, I think they appreciate the fact that I take an interest in their work and have an understanding of the challenges they face.

Some time ago, I remember hearing that we had severely overbooked a flight from Montreal to Haiti that day. Overbooking is standard practice in the airline industry, and the degree varies according to the destination, among other parameters. On specific flights and destinations, the number of no-shows can be predicted with relative accuracy, and the goal of overbooking is to operate each flight with the maximum possible passenger load without leaving anyone behind. The trick is to estimate, with reasonable accuracy, the number of passengers who will not arrive for the flight.

Flights to and from Haiti are notoriously difficult for airlines to manage. It is a country faced with endless challenges at every level, and several international airlines have simply given up on the destination.

Montreal has a large community of Haitians who wish to travel back to their country and bring relatives to Canada for a visit, so we maintain the service in response to strong demand from this community and in spite of a high no-show rate. When I joined Air Canada in 1992, we were providing weekly 747 service from Montreal to Port-au-Prince, booking as many as 750 passengers on a 482-seat aircraft because we could easily expect 300 no-shows on every flight.

On this particular day, the no-show rate was uncharacteristically low, resulting in a full aircraft and dozens of disappointed people standing around Dorval when it took off. This is not a reasonable way of treating people, and I instructed our airport manager to provide a refund to everyone who had been bumped from the flight and offer to fly them to Haiti at our expense aboard a special flight for them.

There comes a time when you have to balance the human aspect of business against the need to minimize expenses. Not only is showing this kind of respect for your customers civilized, it is also good business practice. Keeping current customers is easier than attracting new ones. When business decisions are based on that awareness, it becomes logical to accept short-term pain for long-term gain.

13

SARS AND
FILING FOR CCAA

IN 2002 we expanded Tango service to smaller markets like Thunder Bay, London, and Windsor in Ontario, Charlottetown in Prince Edward Island, Deer Lake and Gander in Newfoundland, and Kelowna and Abbotsford in British Columbia, making Tango a truly national service in response to strong customer demand.

May brought more awards to the airline: the readers of the *Official Airline Guide* (OAG), a group that represents the most frequent flyers in the world, named us the best airline in North America and Aeroplan the best frequent flyer program. "Best Airline" was gratifying, since North America is the most fiercely competitive airline market in the world. The Aeroplan award meant that we beat out every other program for member benefits, ease of use, and other factors, despite nonstop criticism in the national media about the service offered.

As a reflection of the prestige and significance of the OAG awards, they were announced at a glittering ceremony in London, England, presided over by HRH The Duke of York. The OAG had prepared a press release for worldwide distribution, and our media relations department added to it, with announcements sent to every daily newspaper and news organization in the country. It was news to be shared with pride. Or so I thought.

The next day I scanned the newspapers and checked the TV newscasts in vain. There was nothing. An international jury composed of thousands of people, all readers of the magazine who were frequent flyers, had praised Air Canada, and determined us to be best, but no one in the Canadian media cared to listen.

I was upset at the snub, and as sick as it made me to pay the newspapers anything, I instructed that a full-page advertisement should appear in newspapers across Canada the following day. The ad's headline, in large white letters on a red background, read:

SOME GOOD NEWS
DOESN'T MAKE THE NEWS

The rest of the ad talked about the awards and what they meant to us as an airline and to our customers as Canadians. We shouldn't have had to spend the money on a story with such substantial news value, given the endless criticism the media heaped on us, but we did. Because no one else wanted to talk about it.

WE MANAGED to survive the ravages of September 11 in spite of Ottawa's refusal to match the funding received by our U.S.-based competitors, and in 2002 we restored the airline to profitability over two quarters—an accomplishment unmatched by any of our North American peers, even with their considerable subsidies.

The financial progress we made in 2002 earned me a second consecutive Aviation Laureate award from *Aviation Week & Space Technology*, the leading industry periodical. The publication issues awards in various categories every year, and I had received one in 2001 for advocating modified sixth freedom rights, an attempt to liberalize the marketplace and open it to more competition. This time the award was for repositioning Air Canada through our branding approach and for restoring the company to profitability.

By the spring of 2003, however, with the threat of the Iraq war looming on the horizon, the company began to bleed again. Events unconnected to us both at home and abroad were undercutting the progress we had been making. Nobody said running an airline like Air Canada would be easy, but nobody expected one crisis after another to come at us either.

Our first goal was to slow the losses we were suffering and to maintain adequate cash balances. We began with textbook solutions, including selling equipment we owned and leasing it back to raise cash. We negotiated a deal on this basis with GE capital, which would have generated $600 million to carry us through to the profitable summer months. These kinds of steps were stopgap measures to get us over the hump. To ensure success over the longer term, though, we needed to set performance benchmarks, especially in the area of costs, and work towards them to ensure financial stability.

We found one by determining how much money we would save each year if our pay scales and work rules approximated those of West-Jet. The answer was $1.3 billion. Slashing employee salaries to those of WestJet was out of the question, however, because WestJet's pay levels were much too far beneath our own. I proposed aiming to save half that figure, or $650 million, which translated into salary cuts (or increased productivity), right across the board, of 22 per cent.

That is a major hit to ask of anyone. Many of our employees had families to support and debts to pay, and a reduction of that much in their incomes would not easily be absorbed. Yet the company could not continue as it had without running onto the rocks somewhere down the road, which would have a far greater effect on everyone. If we could re-store financial balance by slashing costs—including, among other things, salaries at every level—we could keep running things under the new order of a post–September 11 world featuring the constant threat of terrorism and low-cost carriers. We had precedents in the industry. United and US Airways had reached agreements with their unions and creditors while in Chapter 11, avoiding substantial involvement by the courts, and American did it without filing. Their experience could serve as both a model and a justification for the steps I felt we had to take.

We needed labour on our side for practical and moral reasons. The practical reason was obvious: to persuade union members that it was necessary for everyone to bite the bullet and accept lower incomes in exchange for greater job security and the hope of restoring at least a portion of that lost income in the future. The moral reason was connected to our need to renegotiate aircraft leases and supplier contracts. Many of our equipment leases had been signed years earlier, when interest rates were substantially higher; we wanted to renegotiate them to reflect the current low rates, a move that would save us millions. There was no incentive on the part of lessors to accommodate us, but if we went to them showing that labour was making major concessions to restructure our costs, we would be armed with moral pressure.

When we began our discussions with the unions in early 2003, we encountered predictable arguments against the idea. I wasn't surprised; no union wants to ask for sacrifices from employees. Union leaders are elected to get more for employees, not less. As time passed, however, we had a sense that the unions understood our case. I expected some give-and-take once serious talks began, especially when it became clear that we were not crying wolf but were serious about the drastic steps needed to save the company. Then, in early March, something happened that essentially gutted the best chance we had for a serious dialogue with the unions. The source was the office of transport minister David Collenette.

Asked by a reporter about the company's struggles, Collenette shrugged them off and said, in effect, that Ottawa would never permit Air Canada to fail. This contradicted all the indications given to me by him and others at Transport Canada. More critically, it undercut our negotiations with the unions, from whom I had been asking concessions. Now Collenette was telling the unions and their members, in effect, "There is nothing to worry about—don't give Milton an inch!" Yet his office had been giving us every indication that we were a private enterprise with no claim to government support.

I was in Singapore for Spring Break of 2003 when the war in Iraq began and when severe acute respiratory syndrome (SARS) first appeared. This was a one–two punch that I knew would devastate international air travel. Passenger air traffic through Hong Kong and Singapore dropped right through the floor after SARS and its devastating effects appeared in those cities, and when SARS hit Toronto, no one had to draw me a picture of the impending disaster. I cut my trip short and immediately returned to Montreal.

Most provincial and municipal politicians I spoke to understood the risk that SARS would pose to the travel and tourism business in Canada. Billions of dollars would be lost if people around the world chose not to travel to or within Canada because they feared contracting this potentially fatal disease. All of us were dismayed by the slow action from the federal government.

SARS levelled a direct blow against Canada's best-known attributes. Next to the scenic attractions the country offers, Canada brings visitors from abroad as a result of three qualities above all others: safety, open spaces, and cleanliness. These are the country's primary assets, and without them the Canadian travel and tourism industry could not survive in the face of increased competition and decreased demand. When an event damages an entire industry's primary assets, management had better respond quickly and effectively or just close up shop. Everyone in business knows this.

The impact of SARS on travel had little to do with reality and everything to do with perception. On a micro scale, SARS was a tragedy to every one of the victims who succumbed to it, and to their families. On a macro level, in Canada it was restricted to a relatively small area of a single city, affecting a few hundred people in a municipal population of five million, yet every corner of the country suffered. Visitors were at no more risk to their health in downtown Toronto than they were in Amsterdam or Anaheim. It didn't matter. If potential travellers to Canada believed that Canada was no longer a safe place to visit, they would cancel their journey.

Coincidentally, when I left Singapore for Canada I was travelling between the two locations in the world outside China whose populations were hit most severely by SARS, and through the first few weeks of the crisis I watched fascinated and alarmed at the striking contrasts between the response of each government. To put it bluntly, Singapore made decisions and Ottawa dithered. Within a day or two, Singapore had installed thermal scanning machines at airports to examine arrivals, and the whereabouts of visitors were tracked while they were in the country. All possible SARS cases were quarantined in their homes, where webcams were installed. Health officials had the right to telephone each individual at random and order him or her to appear in front of the webcam to be identified. Anyone breaking quarantine was considered to be endangering the health of others and could be heavily fined or put in jail.

Was this heavy-handed? It depends on your point of view. If you believe, as I do, that the measures saved lives and helped maintain Singapore's image as a safe, well-run nation, it was not heavy-handed at all. Those observing Singapore's response became convinced that its government was taking the situation seriously. The government was decisive in its actions, and visitors had relatively little to be concerned about.

After covering Singapore's decisive handling of the crisis, CNN would switch to its correspondent in Toronto and show Ontario government officials and hard-working health professionals, all with the classic deer-in-the-headlights expression, announce that yet another person had died of SARS and that a dozen or so more were suspected to have the illness. With every appearance of these scenes, I could almost hear our reservations computers tally up another thousand or so passenger cancellations.

When the traffic and revenue figures came in, they were even worse than I had feared. The combination of concern about a war in Iraq and the impact of SARS in Canada produced a revenue loss to us of over $400 million in the first quarter of 2003. Travellers whose destination was somewhere else in Canada cancelled their trip even if it didn't involve Toronto, and thousands of Canadians who had planned to visit other countries on business or to visit family and friends were persuaded to change their plans, in case they carried SARS with them. It was all irrational, of course, but that's what happens when perception overrides reality.

I suspected, and figures compiled later in the year confirmed, that Air Canada, along with Singapore Airlines and Cathay Pacific, would suffer more reservations losses as a result of SARS than other airlines in the world. Through late 2003, traffic on our Asian routes, accounting for over $1 billion in annual revenue, plunged 60 per cent and the number of people boarding or deplaning at Toronto was down 25 per cent.

It was clear at the outset that even if Canada should be declared SARS-free the next day, the effects of the outbreak would linger for months because of the timing. March and April are the months that most people begin planning their summer vacations, and few people outside Canada were feeling comfortable about touring Quebec or the Rockies or anywhere in between while those frightening images of masked SARS workers were being broadcast. They began looking at other destinations, and having changed their plans once, they were unlikely to change them again. Everyone in the Canadian tourism industry would suffer losses through the entire year, and Air Canada's own figures revealed a drop of 19 per cent in revenue for the third quarter of 2003 compared with the previous year—a decrease of $517 million. From couples operating bed-and-breakfasts to international-tour operators, everyone recognized this danger, and we all waited for Ottawa to do something. All we got were platitudes and confusion.

Things really went downhill when Health Canada challenged the World Health Organization (WHO) on whether or not Toronto should be on WHO's restricted travel list. While the debate raged on, its only achievement was to elevate the story to the top of the list at the BBC, CNN, and other news organizations around the world. When WHO refused to back down, the country received more bad ink and our bookings plunged even further.

My efforts generated nothing beyond a little head nodding and some mumbled words of agreement. The simple fact was that nobody wanted to do anything. I have seen individual Canadians react to help neighbours in trouble or express their support, as 100,000 did on Parliament Hill a few days after the September 11 attacks. I know it is in the Canadian psyche to do something when the need is obvious. It just didn't seem to be the policy of some in the Chrétien government to act in the same way. Too often the attitude appeared to be, "If we talk about it long enough and do as little as possible, it will eventually go away."

SARS WASN'T the only crisis I faced in March 2003. That month, a letter from the Office of the Superintendent of Financial Institutions (OSFI) appeared on my desk informing me that, based on its current estimates, Air Canada had to make funding payments of hundreds of millions of dollars to its employee pension plans. The value of most companies' pension plans had dropped dramatically because of the bear market in stocks, which dated back to mid-2000, and low interest rates. OSFI informed us that we had a shortfall to make up as a result, based on the valuation of the plan's assets as of March 2003, and that we should act on it right away. We countered that we were fully compliant in having performed all the valuation tests and having met all the funding measures required under current pension legislation. OFSI, perhaps prompted by all the negative coverage provided by the media, insisted that we conduct some fund valuations that were not otherwise necessary.

The OSFI challenge was a problem to be dealt with, but it was not the dramatic crisis that some members of the business press claimed, and we had continued to meet all our obligations. Nothing was amiss. Air Canada and its employees were feeling the impact of depressed stock prices and interest rates that every other corporate pension plan in Canada was feeling and, indeed, that every Canadian with an RRSP was experiencing. Diverting funds to the plan on the scale that OSFI requested was out of the question. We had just completed arrangements for an additional $600 million in cash to carry us through the summer, anticipating that international travel would continue its recovery. We could not fund our summer operations and meet the OSFI directives out of the same pot of money.

We eventually started an acceptable dialogue with OSFI, pointing out that if Air Canada ceased operations our pension funds would indeed be in deficit in excess of $1.5 billion, but as a going concern we were underfunded by just $250 million. SARS, however, proved one complication too many. The bottom continued falling out of our revenue base at an uncontrollable rate, and I realized I could not accept in good faith the $600 million being made available to us by GE Capital. We still had over $3 billion in unencumbered assets with which we could raise cash, but

SARS was making things too ugly too quickly. With no end to the bleeding in sight, CCAA protection was becoming the obvious choice.

Filing under CCAA is equivalent to Chapter 11 filing for corporations in the United States. Like Chapter 11, it enables corporations to keep operating while they restructure, free from creditor pressures and the need to satisfy creditors' demands immediately. Under CCAA protection, a company may increase the amount ultimately paid to creditors and preserve employees' jobs. Applying CCAA represents neither surrender nor death, but I desperately wanted to solve our financial problems without it.

The roots of the CCAA experience can be traced back to the events of September 11, 2001, and their impact on us and on the industry generally. Among the various responses to the crisis we considered was restructuring the company under CCAA. We rejected the idea at the time, believing we could manage our way through the difficult months ahead, perhaps with the same kind of federal assistance that the U.S. airlines received. Reviewing CCAA had been a simple precautionary move, one I hoped we would never have to take.

Although filing for CCAA is a discouraging procedure under any circumstances and is nothing that any CEO ever wants to do, it appeared to be our only option in light of the continuing drop in revenue due to SARS and tension about Iraq. We were unsure how far it would drop and how long it would take to turn around, and given our existing financial status we had to plan for the worst.

Right to the end, I did not want to file. It simply was not in my nature. The board of directors, however, was concerned about the risk of personal liability that each member (including me) would face if we encountered bankruptcy. The decision to seek protection under CCAA quickly evolved from an option to a necessity unless I could obtain an immediate 22 per cent reduction in labour costs from our unions.

Meanwhile, American Airlines was swinging back and forth between filing and not filing for Chapter 11 protection in the United States. When I talked with American's president, Don Carty, he indicated that the airline might be able to swing a deal with its unions to avoid Chapter 11, and later that very day they succeeded. American

Airlines convinced the unions that the best way to protect employee pensions was to accept salary and wage cuts deep enough to reduce American's costs to the point that American could avoid filing for protection, thanks to a critical difference between Chapter 11 and the CCAA rules. Under a Chapter 11 provision (1113), the corporation seeking protection can ask a judge to undo labour contracts, an option not available to Canadian companies under CCAA.

American's success, though achieved under different circumstances, motivated me to try the same thing, and I put the idea to the board. Returning to my earlier calculations, I explained that if we were to obtain the necessary cuts in union wages and salaries, or an equivalent increase in productivity, we would be in a position to ride things out. With that assurance, the board gave me another opportunity to talk with our unions. As soon as the stock market closed that day, March 31, I contacted every union leader and laid it out as clearly as I could: unless we could get 22 per cent pay cuts across the board, we would file for CCAA protection the following day. I reminded them that I had been talking about a 22 per cent improvement for months, and now it was down to the crunch. "This is the best way to protect employees' jobs," I said to each of the leaders, "and protect their pensions. We can convert the 22 per cent to productivity improvements later and nobody will have to take a cut in pay. Let's work it out. But right now I need that commitment from all of you because CCAA will not be good for any Air Canada employee."

I made my case as straightforwardly as I could, but I could not keep my emotions out of the discussions. If Air Canada were to be restructured and saved, if it were to emerge intact from this chain of catastrophes and challenges, I wanted to do it on terms that reflected the needs and interests of its employees and shareholders. I especially wanted to protect the pensions and standard of living for working Air Canada employees—and I told our union leaders that—because if we slipped into bankruptcy it would be a no-holds-barred situation when creditors swooped in to seize and carve up every last asset under our corporate roof. I was also dealing with a stacked deck unique in the industry: a SARS outbreak in the home hub of a weakened airline battling against

U.S. airlines enjoying billions in government support that we weren't getting. Singapore Airlines and Cathay Pacific might have been dealing with SARS as well, but financially they had always been built like Fort Knox. They were also operating in the Asian economic boom territory, 8,000 kilometres away from a U.S. market still staggering from the collapse of the tech market and the trauma of September 11.

That day I also called the prime minister. As CEO of the country's sole international airline and a key component of Canada's transportation system and economy, I believed that he would want to be aware that we faced filing under CCAA and would be interested in discussing the implications. He apparently did not—neither he nor anyone at his office returned my call.

I remained on the telephone with union leaders almost non-stop for twelve hours. The talks with the unions went on through the night and into the early hours of April 1. The International Association of Machinists and Aerospace Workers (IAM) was pragmatic and supportive from the beginning, as was the CAW, which represents our call centre and counter staff. Both unions assured me that if everyone else agreed to the same conditions, I could count on them. The pilots' union set a number of conditions; some could be accommodated and others were more difficult, but at least we had a bargaining position. Only the Canadian Union of Public Employees (CUPE), representing Air Canada flight attendants, was intransigent, saying no from the very beginning, and it never varied its response. All night long, I made the case to the CUPE representatives on the telephone. Time after time they agreed to get back to me, but when they did it was always to read aloud some emotionally charged polemic that concluded by repeating their original refusal. "I implore you," I recall saying at one point, "for the benefit of all the employees and their pensions, please take the 22 per cent and let's modify the payout into productivity." Their answer was to play back yet another speech that led to the same emphatic no.

No one mentioned it, but I suspect that every union, especially CUPE, was recalling David Collenette's remarks of a few weeks earlier that Air Canada would not be permitted to fail. Sometime after 4 AM, I realized that CUPE was not going to co-operate under any conditions,

175

and without CUPE on board, I could expect nothing from the others. Totally drained, I had no choice but to report to the board that we had failed to win over the unions.

The long evening had been emotionally exhausting. I felt I had run a marathon or two without travelling any distance. I didn't get any sleep that night, and as the sun began creeping over the horizon the following morning I broke the news first to the board and then to the rest of the world. At least I could take some satisfaction in having provided the unions with an opportunity to rise to the occasion. I was also pleased that we had not gone through a long-drawn-out "Will they file? Won't they file?" drama. We explored every avenue searching for an alternative solution, and when it was clear that none existed, we made a decision and filed. It caught a lot of people off guard, but what would have been the point of procrastinating?

Dawn also brought Montie Brewer, our executive vice-president, commercial, who arrived carrying a box of doughnuts and hot coffee. When I told him about having to file for CCAA, he was neither deflated nor surprised. Instead he shrugged and said, "This is going to be okay. It's the only place to go."

Montie is a true industry star, doing amazing things at Air Canada. He came to us from United primarily because he wanted to be part of an airline willing to change, and I know I'll never forget his words to me that morning. He had come to grips with a fact that I had yet to embrace: to be truly "fixed," North American legacy airlines need to go through a full-fledged restructuring process.

With Montie's words still echoing in my head, I began to admit that CCAA was not only unavoidable but essential. The morning we filed for bankruptcy protection may have been the most depressing in my entire career, but it soon became apparent that it was the most liberating thing that had ever happened to the company.

As it turns out, we filed for CCAA at what turned out to be perhaps the best time in the industry's history from the standpoint of restructuring aircraft leases. Over the preceding years, aircraft manufacturers and lessors had looked to the Asian market as their safety valve. Other than during the brief economic blip of the late 90s, Asia's airlines had been booming and had a seemingly insatiable appetite for new equipment. But now, in the midst of the SARS crisis, with no one knowing how long it would last, the Asian carriers were trying to cancel orders and return equipment.

It was the perfect time to negotiate new lease rates, and we did, at rates near the market's bottom. When I review with people familiar with the industry some of the rates we settled on with lessors, their eyes widen. On a pre-filing annual lease cost base of about $1.4 billion, we are set to emerge from CCAA at about $700 million per annum.

Through the restructuring, we were also able to reduce vendor contract costs ranging from IT services to pretzels by about $500 million per year.

On the labour front, our objective had been to reduce annual labour costs by $1.1 billion. In the end, this was done in two rounds. In the first, it was principally achieved through work rule changes that enhanced productivity. No longer would we have nineteen categories of mechanics, some of whom could cut sheet metal but not paint it. Now, if a mechanic is qualified to do the work, they are able to do so without having to pass it on to another person based on their classification. ACPA was the only group that sought to take their portion of the cost reduction target in the form of a pay cut. Thus, the pilots' pay was reduced by 15 per cent, but with the mutually agreed upon understanding that if they wished, the 15 per cent could be translated into productivity changes of equal value. In the second round of labour cost reduction negotiations, reductions came in the form of a combination of pay decreases and work rule changes. I reduced my pay by 15 per cent in round one and 5 per cent in round two.

All in all, these changes in our labour, vendor, and aircraft lease contracts produced an annualized cost reduction of an impressive $2.2 billion. At the same time, through this restructuring, our corporate debt was lowered from approximately $13 billion to $5 billion.

177

From today's vantage point, I recognize that the decision had been inevitable, just as restructuring will prove inevitable for the majority of airlines all over the world. The movement is already happening in the United States, Europe, South America, and Australia. The last market to feel its impact will be Asia, but it will happen there as well when the explosive growth of low-cost carriers gains momentum in that market.

"There's nothing like a good Chapter 11," a representative of a U.S. investment house once said to me. The statement reminded me of the words of Robert Duvall's character in *Apocalypse Now*—"I love the smell of napalm in the morning!" It made my stomach turn, but I knew what he meant.

Later that day, I called a few associates in the industry to deliver the news directly. One of these was Jürgen Weber of Lufthansa. When I told Jürgen the unions would not move, he replied, "Robert, everybody in this business is going to have to do what you did." Jürgen added some bitter words about unions generally, a comment that appeared out of character until I recalled the experience he had undergone recently.

No one in the business had a better reputation for dealing with employees than Jürgen Weber had for his treatment of Lufthansa people. He loved them and they had reason to love him for all he had done for them, but in the summer of 2002, Lufthansa pilots followed the dictums of their union leaders by striking, damaging the airline heavily. At the time, Jürgen later told me, they cut him off too, even jeering him at town hall meetings. Jürgen's experience highlighted the futility of garnering employee support at legacy carriers. In fact, sadly, there are no examples of great employee/management rapport at any legacy carrier.

Ironically, it is this evolution towards pilot scheduling like that illustrated in the three-times-a-month Toronto-to-Tokyo flying that gets companies like Air Canada into a more difficult situation in attempting to maintain good company/employee relationships.

Think about it: how many businesses can you think of where perhaps a third of the employees rarely, if ever, come onto the company's premises and are at work for just ten days a month? The connection for these employees is reporting in for duty, flying, and then resting. The crew can interact on their journey or at the hotel at the destination, but otherwise how can they connect with the company and learn about what's going on? Unfortunately, all too often, this is done solely via the newspaper! The company can spew out communications all day long; whether those communications are actually read is another issue.

This situation highlights one of the challenges of legacy carriers. The crews of short-haul low-cost carriers are generally closer to home and take off and land multiple times a day, generally resulting in more frequent interactions with other colleagues—and the company. I think the answer for legacy carriers will be the increased use of the Internet, or an intranet, as the case may be, and we're working hard to develop our capabilities in that regard. A site that provides current, topical information and that is interactive will enable employees to connect with each other and their company, in real time, for the first time, and I think this will be highly beneficial for legacy carriers like Air Canada and our relationship with our employees.

WHEN WE FILED FOR CCAA protection, we had spent only seventy-two hours setting up debtor in possession (DIP) financing. During the pre-filing period, which happened so quickly because of SARS, we managed to speak to a couple of large banks, but they failed to come through with an adequate offer. When I could see that the banks weren't going to deliver, I dispatched Calin Rovinescu and Rob Peterson to GE Capital, which literally overnight approved the $1.05 billion in financing we needed. GE is an amazing company with incredibly capable people. It is no fluke that it is as successful as it is.

We had maintained a dialogue with Ottawa, explaining that our problems were complicated by SARS, Iraq, and the lack of post–September 11 assistance. The people at Transport Canada seemed to have trouble getting their heads around the situation and finally came back with a plan offering us a $300 million loan guarantee over ninety days. This was nothing more than a useless Band-Aid. To qualify for it, we would have to agree not only to declare bankruptcy but to permit a government representative to sit on the board and oversee our every move, as well as give Ottawa the power to designate the chief restructuring officer.

The idea would have been disastrous for a multitude of reasons, none of which seemed to have concerned the folks at Transport Canada. If we announced that we had a backstop of $300 million for only ninety days, the news would have launched a feeding frenzy among everybody who claimed we owed them a buck. Creditors would have lined up at our front door anxious to seize every penny before the ninety days ran out. With government bureaucrats second-guessing our decisions and a restructuring more responsive to Ottawa's concerns than to our own, it was clear that accepting such a deal offered would be totally foolish, devastating both to the franchise and to our employees. We didn't want a government handout anyway. We wanted a 100 per cent private-sector solution, and we got one.

As usual, Louis Ranger, David Collenette's deputy minister, completely misread the situation. Once private-sector financing was in place and I explained the absurdity of the government's offer, he back-pedalled like crazy, saying, "Well, that's not the way we understood things."

During the throes of our restructuring under CCAA, I set a priority on our continued association with Star Alliance, insisting that we honour our financial commitment to Lufthansa and other alliance members. This meant leapfrogging other creditors, who understandably resented the decision. Ensuring that we continued to share not only the marketing benefits of the alliance membership but also the economic rewards in commissions and revenue was the correct thing to do.

Skeptics still point out that WestJet survived SARS without a crisis, so why couldn't Air Canada? That's like saying Vancouver wasn't affected by last week's blizzard, so why was Montreal? Toronto was both our primary entry point for international and transborder traffic and the focus of all the concern about SARS. We were the only airline feeding substantial volumes of passengers into Toronto, and suddenly the world didn't want to go there. Domestic travel felt barely a ripple, because Canadians knew what and where the real danger was, and they did not stop flying within their own country. As a result, WestJet lost virtually nothing from its passenger load while our load factors plummeted.

FILING FOR CCAA PROTECTION highlighted the fiscal imbalance between older legacy airlines and newer operations, but this is only half the challenge facing the industry. The other half concerns a sea change in travel that provides start-up airlines with advantages they would not have enjoyed a decade ago.

Airlines have been launched by entrepreneurs since commercial aviation became a reality in the 1920s. Fledgling operations, usually undercapitalized, struggled to fill a niche and lived hand to mouth until, if they were fortunate, they were absorbed by a larger competitor. If they were not so fortunate, one day they discovered that they were so weighed down by red ink that they could not take off. This had little or nothing to do with the quality of the service or the expertise of the management and a great deal to do with market clout and distribution.

Start-up airlines of twenty or thirty years ago failed to seriously threaten larger scheduled airlines because the middlemen in the industry—travel agents who represented the vital link between passengers and the means to carry them to their destination—resisted those airlines. They simply couldn't afford to upset the big airlines, which provided their bread and butter. When you called a travel agency in the 1960s, '70s, and '80s and asked it to book you on a flight to New York on Tuesday, returning on Thursday, the agency turned to an Air Canada or American Airlines timetable, depending on your needs, the agency's preference, and, from the early 1980s on, your frequent flyer membership. It certainly wouldn't book you on Acme Airways or some other start-up operation unless you asked it to. Today, that function has virtually disappeared. Passengers make their airline reservations via the Internet, where schedules and pricing are totally transparent.

Every airline executive in the world acknowledges this recent revolution and the way in which this seemingly small change in procedure has altered how new airlines grow and operate. Airlines no longer rely solely on travel agents, and start-up airlines no longer depend on establishing a presence in the marketplace beyond launching a website.

14

AN IMPRESSIVE
AIRPORT
OR A MONUMENT
TO EXCESS?

THE SUCCESSFUL operation of commercial airlines in Canada is subject to a number of factors the airlines cannot control, including the privatized and ungoverned air traffic control (ATC) system (Nav Canada) and airports. These are true, natural monopolies. There is no alternative to them, the government does not appropriately govern them, and they behave accordingly.

Toronto's Pearson International airport and its management have become something of a joke in the industry, thanks to the inefficiency of the airport's operations. One aspect of Pearson operations that has been extremely frustrating over the years is ATC. It's not the employees—they are as capable as those anywhere on the planet—from an operational standpoint, it's the systems and procedures they must use, and from a cost standpoint it's a lack of management fortitude.

There is an old joke about an American Airlines pilot who called Pearson ATC as he left the area: "Toronto Centre, this is American 250 leaving five for eight. Just wanted to say that you guys are without a doubt the second-best ATC operation in the world."

After a short pause, the Pearson ATC controller asked: "Who's number one?"

The American captain replied: "Everybody else."

There are other problems too. Canadians pay more government-mandated air travel fees than anyone else in the world. At times, the federal government's greed in reaping a windfall from airline passengers is almost breathtaking. The simplest, most effective step in helping to restore the airline industry in this country would be for the federal government to reduce, to a reasonable level, the fees it collects from paying passengers. This would help Air Canada, it would help our passengers, and it would help the entire travel industry, including every commercial airline, every tour operator, every hotel, every car rental branch, all the way down to retired couples operating B&Bs everywhere from Victoria to St. John's.

The ultimate statement on how ridiculous government-mandated taxes and "private" airports and air traffic control providers' fees have become was made clear during the early days of Tango when we did a $1 ticket promotion. This was clearly a price to generate publicity and drive eyeballs to Tango's website. Soon, however, it became clear that on a $1 ticket from Toronto to Vancouver, the all-in price was $98. A $1 ticket for $98! One dollar for Air Canada, ninety-seven more dollars out of the consumer's pocket into the government's, airports', and Nav Canada's coffers. The consumer is being let down by the government in a big way in this picture and this hurts the airlines as well.

I once discussed these charges with Alex Himelfarb, one of my favourite people in Ottawa, who is clerk of the Privy Council and secretary to the cabinet. Alex had lectured in sociology at the University of New Brunswick for several years before entering the federal government, and his résumé lists all the left-wing social activist positions that someone like me would look at with suspicion. You might expect Alex and me to lock horns whenever we meet, but we enjoy each other's company immensely. Alex is one of the smartest people I have met in government, and his commitment to serving the people is genuine.

In our conversation, I pointed out to Alex that many of our attempts to correct Air Canada's financial status seemed to trip over expenses that we were unable to control, including airport fees and ATC charges that are among the highest in the world.

Alex smiled with sympathy, and said, only half joking, "You have to understand, Robert, that if we as a government came out and changed the way fees are levied at airports or at NavCan or changed the way they are governed, it would mean that we did not privatize the airports correctly. Politically, we cannot say anything except that current Air Canada management screwed things up."

In late 2003, Doug Young, the former minister of transport who oversaw the privatization of the ATC system and the airports, admitted that these policies had been failures. He said he had been fooled by the big banks that led these privatizations and that he regretted that things had been handled the way they were. He cited the lack of governance and the airports' inability to control costs, show interest in their customers, or build only the infrastructure required as opposed to the opulent facilities that were appearing all over the country.

I was impressed. I felt this showed tremendous courage on his part, and I congratulated him for his words. He thanked me, and in our one-on-one conversation continued to attack these bodies and their management without mincing words.

Even the ATC charges, which are spiralling out of control, are dwarfed by the difficulties and expenses that we and other airlines face when dealing with Toronto's Pearson International airport. As one of our captains quipped to me one day, Pearson is a construction site that happens to have a few runways.

In September 2003, the Greater Toronto Airport Authority (GTAA) imposed yet another fee increase, exacerbating a feud that had been simmering between Air Canada and Pearson International for years. The problems go back a long way, but they really began to gain momentum in January 1999, when a snowstorm caught Pearson airport management flat-footed. Dozens of flights were cancelled as a result, and the people at Pearson claimed the chaos was caused by Air Canada. I was not aware that any earthbound corporation could influence the weather, but the GTAA tried to convince everyone that we can and did. The facts are that the GTAA had just changed contracts for snow-clearing at the airport, and a new, inexperienced crew was on the job that day. In addition, the airport authority had just assumed, on a for-profit basis, responsibility for de-icing aircraft, a task Air Canada had performed without major incident for years.

On the night of the storm, the contracted de-icing operation imploded. The overwhelmed contractor was unprepared for the crisis, and many of our aircraft pulled away from the gate with passengers and luggage on board, only to sit awaiting de-icing before returning to the gates six or eight hours later, layered with newly fallen snow and ice.

Meanwhile, jumbo jets of Cathay Pacific, Korean Air, and Lufthansa, all fully loaded with people returning from Christmas vacations, began returning to their gates, also at our primary terminal, Terminal 2. Now thousands of passengers were being disgorged into the terminal with nowhere to go—the roads were impassable and the hotels filled to capacity—and the GTAA kept proclaiming that the airport was open. This is an old trick of airport authorities. By keeping one runway open they claim the airport is "open," even if taxiways are impassable and you can't get to the runway!

Things grew worse. With our aircraft returning to the gates, arriving aircraft had nowhere to go. The new snow-removal contractor began clearing apron areas but, in doing so, piled the snow up around the gates so that aircraft at the gates couldn't move out. We had passengers, airplanes, and crew all isolated at the airport, and people at the GTAA kept saying, "Hey, we've got a runway open—we've done our job!" The worst part was that Terminal 3, a much newer facility being used by both Canadian Airlines and American Airlines, had been set up to permit de-icing at the gate, and so their flights, although delayed, were able to move. The implication was that Air Canada had messed up and that the GTAA people were on top of things.

Our biggest concern at the time was not flight delays, as costly and disruptive as they might have been to us and to our passengers. It was safety. We refuse to accept the risk of inadequate de-icing of our aircraft, and our flight crews were concerned about the ability of the contracted firm to carry out these duties correctly. We immediately expressed our concern to Transport Canada and the GTAA; clearly, the people responsible for the procedure were poorly trained, inexperienced, and unfamiliar with airport procedures under these weather conditions. Initially the GTAA wouldn't let our experienced people help oversee the process, but eventually we managed to make that happen. We also wrote to the GTAA, asking for assurances that things would be corrected before the next onslaught of winter.

Instead of acknowledging that safety was indeed an issue worth addressing and engaging in some kind of dialogue to avoid a repeat of that fiasco, Pearson's then CEO, Lou Turpen, denied that there had been any risk to the public at all. And he didn't stop there. In a letter sent to us and leaked to the press by the GTAA, Turpen claimed that we were the cause of the problem. "Air Canada's attempt to deflect criticism to other organizations for its failure to perform," Turpen charged, "and to hide behind the issue of safety, is totally inappropriate."

Any decisions that involve flying in severe weather are based on questions of safety, and Turpen's claim that the public's safety was never at risk was dead wrong. Airport operators are not responsible for assessing and ensuring passenger safety. That is the primary duty of the airline and its pilots, and Turpen's inference that he, not Air Canada and its pilots, was the final arbiter of safe conditions set the tone from that point forward.

An even more dramatic example of how badly Pearson is operated occurred in the spring of 2003, when Pearson International ran out of glycol, which is used for de-icing procedures. This situation did not occur when we handled our own de-icing, and the GTAA's incompetence in stockpiling sufficient glycol meant that dozens of our flights were delayed, resulting in enormous expense for us and inconvenience for our passengers.

186

Pearson under Turpen was simply a horribly run operation that treated its biggest customer, Air Canada, with contempt. He was able to do this only because there is no regulatory oversight (Transport Canada refuses to go near the airports now that they are "privatized"). I know many of the capable people who work for the GTAA—some of whom started their careers at Air Canada. As I write this book, the GTAA has announced the departure of Lou Turpen and his replacement by John Kaldeway. I have high hopes for Kaldeway and am convinced that with Turpen's departure, the experienced people of the GTAA will begin to freely express their views on how to improve the airport operation and the airport's relationship with the airlines.

When the GTAA unveiled its plans for the expansion of Pearson, Turpen and his team announced that the program would be one of the largest public works projects in Canadian history, boasting that the new terminal would cover 33 hectares (82 acres) of land, feature 15 kilometres (9 miles) of conveyor belts to handle 18,000 bags per hour, and contain enough concrete to build two CN Towers, plus enough steel to construct three and a half Eiffel Towers.

Dozens of other claims were made by the GTAA. Two claims it could not make were that the cost of the expansion represented fair value to the people who footed the bill and that the facility would address the needs of the airlines paying the rent.

I was appalled at the initial concept. Although I wanted to see an impressive facility at Pearson to benefit Toronto, the GTAA's design bordered on the grandiose and had been drafted with little attention to the individual needs of the airlines that Pearson would serve—especially the needs of Air Canada, which not only provides 70 per cent of the GTAA's revenue but also accounts for 70 per cent of the traffic flowing through the airport. If you operated a business—a corner store, a plumbing service, even a lemonade stand—and one of your customers represented seven out of every ten dollars you earned, wouldn't you pay attention to the needs of that customer? I had hoped that the GTAA would be at least curious about Air Canada's needs, especially when satisfying them would generate benefits for passengers and retail tenants at the facility. Instead, Lou Turpen was building a monument to his own ego at Pearson, and Canadians will pay for its excess ornamentation and poor design for decades.

Our first response, when we were provided with details of the Pearson expansion plan, was to consider an alternative that would be less extravagant and more practical for both the airlines and the passengers—and who counts more in an airport's success? We suggested a central processing area connected by underground links to separate infield terminals. Each terminal would serve an individual airline or multiple airlines that were grouped according to common elements. Arriving passengers would be ticketed and have their baggage checked at the central processing facility, pass through security, then ride in comfortable computer-programmed rail cars to the appropriate terminal. We estimated its cost to be around $1 billion, and it would have been finished years ago.

The best model for this concept is Atlanta's Hartsfield-Jackson airport. Handling 2,400 flights each day, Hartsfield-Jackson qualifies as the world's busiest airport facility, yet it operates at remarkably high levels of efficiency, passenger convenience, and comfort. Atlanta is a hub airport, and the distinction between hub and gateway airports is important to understand when evaluating Pearson.

Airports are designed according to two operating functions: gateways and hubs. Most airports are gateways, which serve as ultimate destination points for passengers and don't qualify as hubs, where one or sometimes two airlines have significant connecting complexes. In North America, such gateway airports include Los Angeles and Boston.

The largest and busiest airports generally operate as hubs for major airlines. For example, Atlanta is a hub for Delta and AirTran, Chicago's O'Hare for American and Delta, and Paris's Charles de Gaulle for Air France. Although some passengers disembark at hub airports—around 30 per cent of the passengers at an airport like Atlanta—many more simply pass through the hub, changing planes and continuing on to their destination. Hubs are vital to the operation of a large airline because they provide smooth transfer between flights to other cities. Hubs provide the most efficient distribution network that can be designed. Each city at the end of every "spoke" from that hub is one stop away from any other city in that network. As the entry point to Canada's largest city, Pearson International airport is a hub for Canada and for the country's only national airline. For a hub airport to operate successfully, however, it requires certain basic design elements, including the ability to smoothly transfer between incoming and outgoing flights.

Ideally, passengers should be able to change planes without having to retrieve baggage, change buildings, or take other time-consuming steps. That's the way hub airports work, and it's the way Pearson should have been designed and built, but it was not.

Almost nothing in the GTAA design addressed Pearson's role as a primary hub airport. In fact, Lou Turpen steadfastly refused to recognize Air Canada as a hub carrier at Toronto, much as he refused to accept United's status as a hub player at San Francisco. As he frequently said, if Air Canada goes out of business, someone else will come along. This may well be correct, but it's no way to run a business. But Turpen and other Canadian airport managers really aren't running a business, they're running natural monopolies. Where else can we go? Buttonville? I don't think so, and the lack of choice was confirmed by WestJet when it gave up developing Hamilton as an alternative and went to Pearson in the end.

Our suggestions that the airport design be scaled back to a lower, more practical cost than Turpen's nightmare were ignored. We were informed that even though seven of every ten passengers through the airport would be clutching an Air Canada boarding pass, our suggestions would receive no more attention than any from Aeroflot, which flies into Pearson a couple times a week.

The idea of an airline asking that its needs be accommodated in an airport design may be unusual in Canada, but it's practically de rigueur elsewhere in the world. Detroit built an entire hub facility for Northwest Airlines, according to that airline's specifications, and it's a beauty, a perfect connecting complex, and it cost only a billion dollars to build, unlike Turpen's $4.4 billion Taj Mahal, which opened late and has clearly overrun its construction and operating budgets. Singapore Airlines effectively designed its own airport, which always grows one step ahead of the carrier's needs.

189

Turpen arrived at Toronto as the genius behind the development of San Francisco International airport (SFO). But many people in the industry agree that SFO's operating efficiency is a disaster. Turpen hardly qualifies as a visionary based on his claim that "current San Francisco International's runway configurations will adequately handle projected airline operations well into the next century." He said this with great confidence in 1993. Three years later, San Francisco airport officials announced that they desperately needed more runways, and San Francisco International, Turpen's creation, is the only airport I know of that Southwest pulled out of because of its inability to operate there reliably.

At the annual meeting of the International Air Transport Association (IATA) in May 2004, I was amused to discover that the San Francisco airport won the Eagle Award, the prize given to the airport facility deemed most improved in cost reductions and general efficiency. Good for them—they had taken about ten years to clean up the mess left by Louis Turpen, but they had finally succeeded.

Pearson International, in many respects, is a direct extension of Turpen's ego. Once, when questioned about the need for certain luxury installments planned at Pearson—facilities that Air Canada and its customers would obviously pay for, one way or another—Turpen responded that he had enough authority to build a baseball stadium inside the airport and charge Air Canada for it, if he wanted to. Turpen also boasted to me once, "Remember, I've got the only business around where the revenue line is the plug figure." By "plug figure" he meant the amount of revenue could be anything he needed to cover his anticipated expenses and make his operating plan work. Don't you wish you could run your home or business that way? This was all possible due to the way the federal government, under the guidance of another Louis, Louis Ranger, now the deputy minister of transport, designed the airport authorities. Louis Turpen and Louis Ranger just don't seem to realize that it is the travelling public that ultimately pays the price for what is happening at the GTAA. For example, the GTAA has a private box at the Air Canada Centre in Toronto, which costs $350,000 a year. Each traveller passing through Pearson picks up his or her proportional share of a not-for-profit airport authority's ability to go to Leafs games as well as the proportional share of other unnecessary costs these incur and pass along.

Between September 1997 and September 2003, the GTAA raised the fees it charged landing aircraft an average of 45 per cent per year. When it announced yet another fee increase in September 2003, a number of people noted that this would be almost enough to push Pearson onto the list of the World's Ten Most Expensive Airports. Projections indicated that, by the end of 2004, Pearson would undergo yet another increase, one sufficient to make it the fifth most expensive airport in the entire world. Given how reasonable costs are in Canada, even in Toronto, it is shocking to think that the GTAA could have so badly mismanaged its costs.

The arrogance of Turpen and his crew in setting these outrageous rate increases generated criticism from several quarters. Our concerns were echoed by a statement from WestJet, which warned that it was considering cutting back on flights through Pearson, then conceded that it had little room to manoeuvre. Several international airlines joined us in expressing dismay at the enormous landing fee increases proposed by the GTAA. When the International Air Transport Association (IATA) commented that it found Pearson International's landing fees excessive, adding that it had suggested for some time that airports roll back fees in light of the challenges facing airlines everywhere in the world, the GTAA threw what can only be described as an organizational hissy fit. Instead of acknowledging that IATA's comment about Pearson's fees was part of a global concern or attempting to justify the steep increases in some manner, the GTAA launched a personal attack on me as the instigator of the criticism. "We believe Robert Milton is the architect of this attack," a GTAA spokesman announced. "We feel this [the IATA comment on Pearson's skyrocketing fees] is a clandestine action by Air Canada using IATA as a surrogate. It amounts to an attack on the national airports policy, the federal government, Pearson airport, and the city of Toronto."

I was amused and flattered that the GTAA believed I could orchestrate the entire world airline community to attack it. At the Board of IATA I have for several years been extremely vocal about the need for airlines to work in solidarity to attempt to stand up to these monopolists. We have not done an effective job of it, and until we do, they will maintain their "divide and conquer" approach. My amusement was tempered, however, by the realization that the annual user fees Air Canada was paying Pearson had risen by $100 million per year over the previous five years. Sometimes when people look back to the "good old days" of the industry and Air Canada they forget they are looking at a regulated past. Think about it: increases in cost of $100 million per year!

The GTAA's claim that I had somehow insulted the federal government proved as ridiculous as it sounded when, just a couple of days later, I received at least the echo of support from an unusual source: David Collenette. The then minister of transport suggested that it was perhaps time to review the rents Ottawa charged airports across the country. The clear implication was that lowered rents would produce reduced landing fees for the airlines. "I think we really should make some adjustments," Collenette was quoted as saying, "so whether it's capping or reductions of rents, you know, all of those issues, I think we have to examine [them]." Then he added that the current federal rents policy was "flawed." I quickly had Duncan Dee, by then our vice-president in charge of corporate affairs, get back to Transport Canada to ensure that if they lowered land rents the benefits would flow through to the airlines and not stop with the airport authorities—something that seemed obvious to me but that I was sure they hadn't considered.

I took moral support from Collenette's words but not much else. After all, by that date Ottawa had been reviewing its rent policy for over a year and a half and had yet to make a decision. Later in the same interview, Collenette carved himself an exit when he said that the airport rent issue was "really a Minister of Finance decision for a budget because there's $214 million paid this year and the question is, if you reduce or cap it, what does it do to your revenue flow?" In other words, don't hold your breath. Finally, there was a very practical issue here. In October 2003, Paul Martin was about to become prime minister, and gossip on Parliament Hill said that of all the ministers in Jean Chrétien's cabinet, few had less chance of holding on to their portfolios than David Collenette. The gossip proved to be correct. Whether or not Ottawa ever adjusted its airport rent policy, Collenette was not going to be around to implement it, so he could say whatever he wanted. Deep down, I believed that Collenette's departure from the transport ministry would do more for Air Canada than any reduction in aircraft tariffs would.

Today we have Minister Jean Lapierre, who I hope will make some of the required moves for the industry. But I was extremely impressed with Tony Valeri, who held the Transport portfolio for only a short time in between Collenette and Lapierre. He was quiet and thoughtful, understood business and the issues we faced, and was obviously intelligent. He was very helpful during his short tenure.

Everybody ignored Collenette's comments, and Turpen and his people at the GTAA kept shooting the messengers instead of attempting to deal with the problem. To penalize IATA for criticizing Pearson's fees in its role as the representative of most of the world's airlines, Turpen announced that IATA no longer had status at Pearson. IATA, on Turpen's command, was banned from participation in any GTAA meetings and other activities, including consultations on how to maximize the airport's efficiency for passengers and airlines. In his letter to IATA announcing the ban, Turpen claimed that IATA's comments had been "misleading, unhelpful and further evidence of [its] confrontational approach to the airline/airports relationship."

In response, Giovanni Bisignani, who has become a good friend and is the highly effective CEO of IATA, pointed out that Canadians already paid the highest security fees in the world and that their flagship airport was about to become one of the world's most expensive facilities. Bisignani noted that we were working our way out from under CCAA protection, "and now [Air Canada] faces higher landing charges so that the Toronto airport can avoid having to reduce its own costs and gain efficiency. It's like *Alice In Wonderland.*" Turpen's response was to tell Bisignani, in effect, to mind his own business and claim that IATA's public information campaign on the GTAA's pricing and attitude was illegal.

It is incomprehensible that any business enterprise would tell its customers that they have no right to comment on the prices being charged them, especially when the charges are being applied by an organization with a monopoly on the services. Remember that these were not insignificant increases, nor were they expected to taper off in future years. The GTAA has promised to increase landing fees 25 per cent in 2004 and has warned that they could be much higher than that.

15

POWER, IN
AND OUT OF
OTTAWA

THE SUMMER of 2003 was dominated by Murphy, whoever he was, and his law. From post–September 11 security standards to the aftermath of the CCAA filing on April 1, we watched as the impact of SARS cut deeply into our international and transborder passenger volume.

A few commentators in the media claimed that Air Canada was using SARS as an excuse for other ills, even though it was clear that the world had stopped visiting Toronto and, for that matter, Canada. Only when our May 2004 figures showed that traffic was up 25 per cent over the disastrous May 2003 figures did anyone, including the "experts," realize how severely SARS had affected our company. By then, we had endured more than a year of grief. In any case, those who are genuinely interested in the truth will acknowledge that no other airlines in the world were struck as gravely by the SARS outbreak as we were, along with Chinese airlines, and Singapore Airlines and Cathay Pacific, both of which have hubs in what were SARS hotbeds.

In August 2003, during our restructuring, we introduced a shift change we had negotiated as part of our post-CCAA new labour agreements, which the CAW did not like and which it had not believed we would implement. When the union members realized that we intended to make the change, they grudgingly agreed to it. The shift change was unpopular with some of the membership, and the CAW turned to negotiating via the press. This led to a number of stories in the Toronto *Star*. One Toronto *Star* reporter showed up at a session where employees gathered to discuss the new rules with managers. These meetings are always a cathartic process, in which a good deal of anger and frustration is expressed before everyone gets down to the business of making the new schedule work. I understand and respect the need for this kind of venting. I consider it human, healthy, and necessary, and I support unions and managers conducting these sessions when new rules are proposed.

For two days the *Star* ran pot-stirring articles about customer service problems brewing at Pearson airport, and the next day, a Sunday, our check-in counters at Pearson International airport were crawling with reporters and television cameras capturing scenes of line-ups. Every story filed the next day claimed that our flights were being delayed because the company was demanding too much from overworked check-in personnel. Not one story, to my knowledge, noted that our service *and the service of every other airline at the airport* had been halted five times that Sunday, when the media were crowding the airport, by lightning storms passing through the Toronto area. Both air traffic control and the good sense of our employees determined that aircraft would not take off until the storm passed, but everything was blamed on the shift change.

Did hitches develop from the new shift arrangement? Without a doubt, but they were not nearly as damaging to our schedule as the closing down of the airport five times due to thunderstorms. Ironically, as a result of the shift change, we actually had more staff on hand during peak hours than before, thanks to the new union agreement that enabled us to reduce personnel when traffic was light and to bring part-timers in when loads became heavier.

Our counter staff did a phenomenal job working on the backlog, and by the following day things were almost back to normal. Nobody covered that. By Wednesday we were functioning at total efficiency, but by then the press had turned to other matters. We almost began to relax.

The next day was Thursday, August 14. That afternoon, Ontario and much of the U.S. northeast suffered the biggest electric power blackout in history.

Alerted to the situation, I tuned the TV set in my office to CNN and had this "here we go again" feeling. Meanwhile, our operations people began taking charge. Since the Toronto and Ottawa airports were closed, flights headed their way were rerouted to open airports elsewhere. Air Canada's systems operation control (SOC) in Toronto, located across the road from Pearson International airport, switched to standby power produced by an on-site generator that had been installed several years earlier to handle situations like this one. Systems operation control is the airline's nerve centre, keeping in contact with aircrew and ground personnel to coordinate virtually every activity. It began positioning aircraft throughout North America and, at my suggestion, even ferried a few empty aircraft over to Europe to be ready to move people once the power came back on and airports came back on line.

Our employees did everything they could under the circumstances, and most of the passengers were patient though understandably frustrated. No one was blaming Air Canada for the biggest power outage in North American history, although a few media outlets seemed intent on exploring that possibility. In Ottawa, TV crews captured images of long lines of passengers waiting for the airport to open, while a reporter marched up and down shouting, "Does anybody have any horror stories to tell us?"

The backup generator at systems operation control in Toronto was providing enough power to maintain essential functions, as it had been intended to; we had a long-term contract with a supposedly reputable maintenance company to keep the generator prepared for just such an occurrence. The next morning, in one of those great ironies of life that can persuade you that Somebody Up There doesn't like you, power was restored at Pearson airport, directly across the street from our operations centre, but not at SOC, leaving the centre itself to run exclusively on its own generating system, which abruptly shut down at the crack of dawn the next morning because of a failure in the fuel system. Less than a hundred metres away the lights were on, the air conditioning was humming, the restaurants were preparing food, and Pearson was quickly returning to normal, but our operations centre was entirely without power.

Now we were in total crisis mode. We were unable to dispatch an Air Canada aircraft anywhere in the world because we could not prepare flight plans, calculate aircraft weight and balance information, or monitor our flights enroute. (Both Jazz and Zip, using their own dispatch facility in Halifax to coordinate aircraft operations, were able to keep functioning.)

We desperately needed a way to get SOC up and running again, and Bob Brown, our chairman, wondered if the military could help. Canadian Forces had mobile generators that could be transported anywhere, Bob noted, as well as the cable needed to feed power throughout our operations facility. Could the military lend us one of their units? It sounded like a good idea, so I called Alex Himelfarb to see if he could help us. Alex promised to look into it and began speaking to his contacts in Ottawa.

Within minutes of talking to Alex I received a call from Louis Ranger, deputy minister of transport. "I understand you were looking for help," Ranger said.

"I contacted Alex Himelfarb," I explained, "to see if he could arrange some power generation from the military and get our operations centre up and running."

"Oh, that's all right then," Ranger replied. "The impression I had was that you wanted us to contact somebody in Toronto and help you leapfrog over other people to get power back at your operations centre, and we would not do that."

I could not believe it. The nation's largest air carrier, the country's only true national air service, was on its knees, and the deputy minister of transport was practically boasting that he would not raise a finger to help if it meant showing preference. Perhaps he took some pride in refusing to give even the hint of assisting Air Canada—and for all intents and purposes the nation's air transportation system—in a serious crisis. If so, I hope he was also proud that thousands of our passengers remained waiting in lounges for much longer than they should have, maybe even comforting themselves with the knowledge that the country's top transport bureaucrat was insisting that he not get involved.

After I talked to Toronto mayor Mel Lastman and the various power authority CEOS I could reach—all of whom tried to be genuinely help-ful—power was finally restored at the operations centre around one o'clock that afternoon, and we aimed to get flights in the air by four. Getting an airline up and running again after a full stop is an incredibly complex process, and I don't believe any airline of our size and network coverage had ever before gone from zero to 100 per cent of operations during the peak of the summer traffic load. You can push a button and turn on a baggage conveyor belt as soon as you have electricity, but starting an airline from a full stop requires methodical progress through a series of stages. While this was happening, our staff at Pear-son did an exceptional job of accommodating people under conditions that would make many employees throw up their hands and go home. Managers and vice-presidents were pitching in where they could help. I headed out to Dorval, walked through the terminal talking to cus-tomers and employees, handled bags from arriving flights for a few hours, and on the way home drove a mother and her child, who had been sleeping on top of a baggage cart, downtown in the early morning hours. Everyone was working hard to help our customers, and it was a great triumph over more adversity.

The incident created problems for everyone, not least those thou-sands of people who had been counting on us to carry them to their destination. Air Canada had nothing to do with the power outage, but that didn't matter. We had a contract to provide service, and even though those passengers had seen us working our hearts out, I knew they would remember the night spent in the Air Canada terminal at Pearson International airport for a very long time.

I SUSPECT others in Ottawa besides Ranger and Collenette wish Air Canada were still a Crown corporation. At a meeting with Collenette and our respective assistants to discuss Air Canada's market share after the collapse of Canada 3000, I explained that there were numerous ways to evaluate the question. I felt that many of our Ottawa critics were using the wrong way of assessing market share. The media was buying the criticism at face value, and the combination of political and media pressure was not helpful in our efforts to reposition the company. I explained that the 80 per cent market share attributed to us was based on available seat miles (ASMs) and that this measure was not the only way to assess true market share. An ASM is the measure of how many miles you move available seats through the air, or the number of seats on the aircraft multiplied by the number of miles flown. If in a day's utilization we flew one 747 with 425 seats return from Toronto to Vancouver, while WestJet (as an example) flew a 737 with 140 seats between Calgary and Vancouver over five return flights in the same time period, we would have dispatched 850 seats while WestJet flew 1,400 seats.

In this example, WestJet would have dispatched 62 per cent of the total 2,250 seats. Measured as ASMs, if Toronto to Vancouver is 2,085 miles and Calgary to Vancouver is 428 miles, then the Air Canada 747 would produce a total of 1,772,250 ASMs and the WestJet 737 would produce 599,200 ASMs. So, in this illustration, our round trip 747 to Vancouver would produce an ASM share of 74.7 per cent (the figure Collenette and the media loved to quote), but in that same time period the WestJet 737 would dispatch 60 per cent more seats, even though it would have produced only 25.3 per cent of the ASMs. What is more important in a competitive marketplace: Air Canada racking up big ASM counts flying big airplanes long distances, or putting more seats in the air?

I saw in Collenette's eyes that the penny had dropped, and I left the meeting convinced that at least one misunderstanding had been cleared up. At his press conference that afternoon, however, the transport minister ignored our discussion and continued blasting our share of the market. Nothing he had acknowledged was presented to the media. Collenette restricted his views to a general condemnation of Air Canada's market position and a glowing tribute to his own efforts to "tame" us.

It is no secret that former transport minister David Collenette and I had problems working together. Usually I shrugged them off, but sometimes the pettiness surprised and exasperated me. Here's a good example:

One of my favourite people in the Canadian airline business is Jean-Marc Eustache, president of Air Transat. I enjoy his company, and we meet from time to time. On one of these occasions in early 2003, Jean-Marc and I were discussing the board meetings of the Canadian Tourism Commission (CTC), a government agency that promotes the Canadian tourism industry by marketing the country's attractions and facilities both within and beyond the country. "Why aren't you at those board meetings?" Jean-Marc asked.

I explained that I wasn't at the meetings because I was not a board member.

"But I submitted your name to be invited to the board long ago," Jean-Marc said. "Didn't anybody contact you?"

I assured Jean-Marc that no one had invited me to join the CTC board of directors. It didn't matter to me whether I sat on the board or not. Although I support the CTC's efforts, and many in the organization no doubt are capable people, the CTC has so far failed to live up to its mandate of promoting Canada as a tourism destination while countries such as Australia have continued to excel. I knew that Air Canada would be able to make worthwhile contributions to the country's travel and tourism industry if we participated at the board level. So why hadn't I received the invitation? It seemed strange that the board of an organization dedicated to building Canada as a tourist destination did not include a high-level executive from the country's largest domestic and international airline, especially when a prominent member had submitted the executive's name for nomination.

Duncan Dee has terrific connections in Ottawa, and I asked him to find out if I had been proposed as a board member of the CTC. He is an amazing guy who, in addition to English, speaks French, Italian, Spanish, Russian, and the Hokkien dialect of Chinese.

My reliance on him to sort things out at every level was demonstrated once when my wife, Lizanne, was chatting with Mario Rosario's wife, Sabine, who is Swiss. Although she speaks English well, Sabine is not completely familiar with the nuances of the language. After hearing Lizanne often comment, "Duncan did this, Duncan did that, Duncan, Duncan, Duncan...," Sabine asked innocently, "What is a Duncan?" For the record, "a Duncan" is one of the brightest, hardest-working people I have encountered at Air Canada and undoubtedly in all of Canada, and he deserves recognition for all he has accomplished by the grand old age of thirty-three.

About Duncan's five languages, I feel compelled to tell a couple of stories. His Russian came in handy when we were in the midst of a battle about overflight rights with the Russians. They were naturally disarmed by this fellow from Air Canada conversing with them in their tongue. One of Duncan's areas of responsibility now is our international markets. Recently he visited South America, where he met with our big corporate accounts, travel agencies, and media. Our staff there could not contain their glee at having a Spanish-speaking vice-president. Just how linguistically gifted he is became even clearer, though, when I observed him conversing in Tagalog (the language of the Philippines, which he doesn't count as one of the five), but he seemed to make a mistake or two and didn't seem too pleased with himself.

"What's wrong?" I asked.

"I mixed in a few words of Albanian with the Tagalog, and I confused the other person," he said. He picked up the Albanian when he and Mary sponsored a refugee family from Kosovo who had settled in Canada. Who knows what else is in his head?

To get back to the story about the CTC, within a day or two, Duncan came back with the news. Yes, my name had been submitted, as Jean-Marc mentioned. An invitation had not been sent to me because the submission had been turned down by David Collenette's office.

Where benefits can be achieved for both sides, you ignore the differences and get down to work. I am sure that executive-level representation by Air Canada would have benefited the CTC in many ways. If Collenette had felt uncomfortable with me personally, he could have asked someone else from Air Canada to attend. Instead, Collenette or a member of his staff chose to blacklist representation from the biggest carrier of people into and throughout the country, a decision that did not help the CTC achieve its goals for Canada and most likely inhibited many of its efforts.

Over the years I have encountered many examples of negative attitudes at the transport ministry towards Air Canada and towards embracing change. One example is the Open Skies debate.

We have always supported an open-market situation with the United States, which does not permit foreign airlines to fly domestically from point A to point B. Regulators identify seven rights, or "freedoms," ranging from the privilege of flying across another country without landing—the first freedom—to taking on passengers and freight in one foreign country and carrying them directly to a third country—the seventh freedom. The sixth freedom means carrying passengers and freight from a foreign country and flying them to a third country via the country in which the airline is registered.

As Collenette droned on about our market share, I felt perhaps the only way to get large-scale, sustained competition (we had seen everyone except WestJet disappear from the domestic marketplace over the years) was to let the U.S. airlines into our market on a basis they would agree to. Thus was born our idea of "modified sixth freedom rights." Modified sixth freedoms would permit us to fly U.S. passengers from, say, New York to Los Angeles via Toronto. Naturally, we would offer reciprocal opportunities to U.S. airlines, meaning that American Airlines, for example, could carry passengers from Toronto to Vancouver, using Chicago's O'Hare airport as a transfer point; and Northwest could take someone from Montreal to Winnipeg with Minneapolis as a hub. We believed everyone could win with this arrangement and that we could simultaneously reduce our share of the Canadian market, which presumably would please Collenette and his department.

We began making inquiries among U.S. airlines and officials in Washington and with Paul Cellucci, the U.S. ambassador to Canada. "There is definitely interest in discussing this idea," Cellucci assured us. I received similar assurances from the CEOs of several U.S. carriers and the top levels of the U.S. Department of Transportation. When we approached Collenette with a request to begin negotiations, he claimed that the United States was *opposed* to extending the Open Skies concept in this manner. This was a fabrication. Collenette really believed that trying to maintain barriers between Canada and the United States was sustainable, and he treated Open Skies as a dead issue—or a non-issue— even though it would have been an effective step towards improving the financial health of Air Canada and towards reducing the domestic share of market we enjoyed—a share that disturbed him so much.

It appeared to me that David Collenette was not interested in building a relationship either with me or with the company and that he would bash Air Canada whenever he needed to in an attempt to elevate his own reputation. There is a certain maddening logic to this. In Parliament it is easy to attack somebody who is not there to defend himself or herself, in a setting where you are not subject to libel charges and where the most outrageous statements are certain to be aired on television later that day. It is more difficult, but far more productive, to sit down quietly, exchange views, consider the other side's position, and find a solution that benefits everyone. That's good management, but lousy drama, and people like Collenette opt for the drama.

One place in the world where substance overrules drama in the government-airline relationship is Australia. Throughout this book you'll notice I frequently mention Qantas. There is no airline I respect more, from both an operational and a financial performance standpoint. Pundits have a tendency to compare Air Canada and Qantas. It is entirely relevant from an operational standpoint, and I think Air Canada compares favourably. In the area of financial performance, however, the differences are significant and highlight the impact that decades of imprudent government oversight of Canada's airline industry has had on Air Canada and, perhaps, what could have been had things been done differently, as they were in Australia.

If one looks at a snapshot of Air Canada and Qantas today, in the post–Canadian Airlines and post-Ansett world, Qantas is one of the world's most profitable carriers and Air Canada is coming out of CCAA. Clearly, Qantas didn't have to deal with SARS or September 11 in the same way Air Canada did (September 11 was actually a windfall for them), but how we got to today is in remarkable contrast. We're both the national carriers of large-land-area, Commonwealth countries that are rich in natural resources and have small populations. But only one carrier's story, Air Canada's, involves constant governmental meddling. In contrast, Qantas has benefited from governmental support or, when appropriate, non-intervention.

For one thing, Qantas had Australia's entire international route portfolio for decades. Ansett made minor attempts to fly internationally to points in Asia in the 90s, but Qantas regained all international routes when Ansett collapsed after September 11. The bottom line was no "division of the world" nonsense. If Qantas wanted the route, it got it.

Other than in the United States, there have been no examples of countries successfully dividing international route rights, even among two carriers, on a sustainably profitable basis. Some tried, and the carriers underperformed, which generally resulted in the country's primary carrier taking over, as was the case with British Airways' acquisition of British Caledonian and Air France's acquisition of UTA. Essentially, though, the world over, it was one country, one airline.

As we moved into the 90s and air traffic worldwide continued to explode, especially in Asia, some countries allowed second carriers to develop international routes in competition with the incumbent national carrier. Often this led to a fair bit of instability (which I regarded as healthy, since it made for more competition!), as was the case with Asiana versus Korean Air in Korea and EVA Air versus China Airlines in Taiwan. But the key is that this was as recently as the 1990s and there are no other good examples—except in Canada—where two large incumbents had to duke it out decade after decade, wearing each other out, depleting funding, and underachieving as they fought for route rights and against each other in international markets.

It is no wonder that Air Canada and Canadian Airlines underperformed financially, and it is no wonder that foreign carriers expanded with ease on routes into Canada against the divided Canadian carriers. It is also no surprise that now that the lid of restriction has been lifted from Air Canada, it is successfully expanding internationally and has so much more opportunity to develop further. The opportunity to do this came late and, as history has shown, unfortunately occurred just before

September 11 and SARS, but the results on Air Canada's new routes to Bogotá, Caracas, San José (Costa Rica), Sydney (Australia), Buenos Aires, Santiago (Chile), Shanghai, and so on illustrate the past underachievement, as none of these cities was being served when Air Canada and Canadian came together in 2000.

Another facet of Australian government support was that it simply let a wobbly Ansett collapse after September 11. Even though this move gave Qantas overwhelming control of the domestic market, the government had the sense to recognize that with time the market would selfcorrect and competition would return, as it has a habit of doing. This didn't add financial burden to the country's key carrier, Qantas, and in fact let Qantas selectively pick up the pieces it wanted: which it turned out wasn't many.

There were no special Parliamentary hearings, no cumbersome conditions or undertakings, no new bureaucratic powers to "increase" competition, no government policy aimed at lowering Qantas's now overwhelming domestic market share. No, in Australia, the free market was allowed to decide.

In fact, right after September 11 and Ansett's collapse, I realized Qantas was going to be tremendously short of capacity as it tried to accommodate Ansett's traffic. We were terribly long on aircraft and employees at that point, as our North American markets reeled, and so I had Jon Turner, our talented, young, head of Aircraft Programs, quickly contact Qantas to see if they wanted to lease some aircraft. They immediately signed us up to fly four 767-300s on trans-Tasman routes and their Sydney to Honolulu run. This helped us to save hundreds of Air Canada jobs post–September 11 and was also very profitable flying for us at the end of 2001. Amusingly, we later heard that British Airways, which owned about 18 per cent of Qantas, and American Airlines, their OneWorld partner, who was also awash in 767s after September 11, were miffed that we had gotten the work. We just anticipated Qantas's need, perhaps because of what we ourselves had been through, and moved faster.

An additional way that the government of Australia helped is that when it sold off its interest in Qantas, it did so with a plan, not just with hope for it to succeed and with a view to raising funds for the government's coffers. And finally, governmental fees for ATC, security, and so on are considerably lower in Australia than in Canada.

Qantas also benefits from not operating right next to the biggest, most competitive air market in the world, the United States, as Air Canada does. In fact, they couldn't be further from it. The market they are closest to happens to be the most exciting and fastest-growing in the world: Asia. Also, perhaps because of the distances involved in travelling to and from Australia, their markets tend to be much better yielding, with more people travelling business and first class than is the case for Canada.

Qantas also benefits from being in the Southern Hemisphere, so that traffic is strong for both the northern and the southern summers. I learned long ago you can't give away seats to travel to some parts of Canada from November to February.

Finally, in 1989 Prime Minister Bob Hawke faced the actions of the federation representing the pilots at Australian Airlines (since absorbed by Qantas) and Ansett, the two key domestic players. Hawke acted much as Ronald Reagan had in the 1980s when PATCO, the union representing U.S. air traffic controllers, struck. Reagan replaced those workers first with management and military controllers and then with new permanent employees. When the pilots struck, Hawke permitted the two carriers to temporarily contract in foreign carriers to provide alternative capacity, and at the same time he used the Australian Air Force to provide additional airlift. Next, so that Australia's carriers could re-build, the two airlines were allowed to rapidly import foreign, particularly U.S., pilots to replace the striking pilots—who ultimately had to find jobs offshore to resume their careers.

Clearly this action was draconian, but as might be expected it resulted in far more realistic labour expectations going forward, and it also influenced subsequent behaviour. And it helped buttress Qantas and its competitiveness among the world's airlines.

So, despite being each country's respective national carrier and a lot of similarities in our operational standards and Commonwealth heritages, the two airlines arrived where they are in remarkably different ways. They make good case studies on how to do things and how not.

THE REAL STORY
OF TRINITY
AND CERBERUS

Aᴹ ɪ ᴅ the crises we juggled through the summer of 2003, from sᴀʀs and the war in Iraq to the teeth-grinding ironies of the August 14 power outage, we continued to work to find an equity plan sponsor to provide the funding we needed to recapitalize the company and successfully complete our ccᴀᴀ restructuring. By mid-July, a dozen would-be sources had expressed interest in bidding for the role. Among them was my old friend Gerry Schwartz and his Onex group.

I had grown to admire Gerry and his top people at Onex, specifically Nigel Wright and Tony Melman, since our encounter in 1999. In fact, Gerry and I have gotten along fine over the years. During negotiations to purchase a substantial share of Aeroplan, Gerry proved to me again that he is one of the shrewdest businesspeople in Canada. Anyone who questions Gerry's eagerness to invest in Aeroplan is clearly unfamiliar with the airline industry and the various benefits of frequent flyer programs.

If you examine all the components of a large, international airline— the ᴍ ʀ ᴏ (maintenance, repair, and overhaul of aircraft), regional carriers, cargo, frequent flyer programs, and others—you find that the sum of the parts is much greater than the whole. Making all of these components fly, as it were, instead of being dragged down by the weight of the operation of large aircraft, is vital to an airline's success. The idea is to maximize and release value from the operations, which I believe we can do as well as anybody in the business. Nothing illustrates this better than Aeroplan.

Back in 1992, when I joined Air Canada, Aeroplan consisted of not much more than a few people sitting in cubicles on the fifth floor of an office block in the marketing department, plus some third-party communications support. We reorganized it into a more independent operation, and over the years it grew. Early in the new millennium, Calin Rovinescu led the charge to break out key units into profit-focused businesses in their own right. To lead the charge, we named one of our brightest people, Rupert Duchesne, president of Aeroplan. Rupert changed the structure of Aeroplan by building a strong support team and dramatically raising revenues. He set the mould we wanted to adopt by running it as an independent profit centre under the Air Canada umbrella, a model we continued to apply among various divisions of the company. By 2002, Aeroplan's enterprise value was $1 billion—not bad for a division assessed at zero book value just a few years earlier.

The secret of Aeroplan's success was to offer the widest range of benefits plus tie-ins with strategic partners who would use the Aeroplan points program as a powerful promotional tool. Like other frequent flyer programs, Aeroplan's success is strongly aided by a factor known as "point breakage," which describes the tendency of participants to accumulate points but neglect redeeming them for awards. Our retail partners—banks, car rental agencies, hotels, and others—pay Air Canada for every Aeroplan mile awarded. They value the miles as a marketing tool whose cost returns good value in promotional and loyalty benefits. We receive payment for these Aeroplan miles immediately, but they may not be redeemed for years, if at all. Many members have accumulated more than a million Aeroplan miles without redeeming any, and that's their choice—a choice I love them to make.

As a result, our frequent flyer program has proven to be by far the most profitable operation within Air Canada. Gerry wanted a part of it, and in January 2003 we agreed to sell Onex 35 per cent of the operation for $245 million. Beyond the raw economics of the business, Aeroplan unquestionably possesses the richest database of high-spending, high-travelling Canadians. In fact, about 6 million people, or 20 per cent of Canada's population, are members.

In mid-2003, when we invited equity plan sponsor candidates to meet our investment parameters as part of our plan to emerge from CCAA, we helped Onex partner with the Texas Pacific Group (TPG), expecting them to achieve at least part of the goal that had eluded Gerry almost four years earlier. He could boast both Canadian citizenship and Ottawa connections if he needed them, and I suspect he was confident (as was I) that his Onex–TPG partnership would succeed. But he never saw Victor Li coming. For that matter, we didn't know either whether Victor's bid would materialize.

Victor's entry into the mix went back many years and came down many tracks. One of the tracks went back to Singapore, when my father was senior vice-president of PICA, the Private Investment Company of Asia. PICA was owned by a number of foreign corporations, banks, and investment firms and had seconded a young Holger Kluge from CIBC. After doing good work for PICA, Holger left to head up the CIBC operation in Hong Kong. There he began doing deals with Li Ka-shing, who was so impressed with CIBC that he bought a significant stake in the bank. Li Ka-shing's holding company, Cheung Kong Group, ranks among the top one hundred corporations in the world, with businesses in almost forty countries and over 165,000 employees. Among them is his son Victor. Many people expected Holger to become the next CEO of CIBC. When John Hunkin was selected instead, Holger left. John is a fine guy and a skilled banker, and he has worked with us supportively through these many years of adversity. But I understand that Li Ka-shing was so upset at Holger's departure that he significantly reduced his CIBC holdings.

Having known Holger since I was a teen was one track that linked me to Victor Li. More recently, there was Eva Kwok, a lovely lady who joined the Air Canada board in the late 1990s. Through her I was directly introduced to Victor Li sometime in mid-2001, when we lunched together in Hong Kong. At the time, Victor was not interested in buying or investing in an airline and we were in fairly good shape financially, so the idea that he or any of his companies might make an investment in the airline was not relevant. Nevertheless, the relationship was established.

Around the same time, Frank Sixt was appointed CFO of Hutchison Whampao, one of Li Ka-shing's holding companies. Frank had been a college roommate of Calin Rovinescu's and had been a tax lawyer with Stikeman Elliott. Meanwhile, Marvin Yontef, who was acting as counsel to Air Canada, knew Frank well also and had represented the Li group on many deals in the past. As we worked through this period and I got to know Frank, he, too, quickly qualified for inclusion on my shortlist of truly smart, fast, and tough businesspeople I have dealt with—and he is funny and nice as well.

All these relationships fell into place relatively independently. When it came time to look for equity investors under CCAA, I recalled meeting Victor and began inquiring if the Li family might be interested in submitting a proposal. Eva naturally abstained from involvement for obvious governance reasons, but Calin and Marvin approached Frank to see if he was interested. Many things seemed to fit, including the fact that a substantial portion of the Li family's portfolio consisted of businesses purchased or partnered when companies were in distress, and the fact that Victor held Canadian citizenship, a definite advantage in dealing with foreign-ownership restrictions under Canadian law.

When Calin and Marvin had an opportunity to meet with Frank Sixt in Hong Kong in May 2003, they went off to explore the idea with him. I remained behind in Montreal; these guys had all known each other for years, and I wanted their conversation to be as open and relaxed as possible. Calin and Marvin returned to say that Frank's reaction had been positive, and I arranged to meet Frank a few weeks later in London. In the meantime, Frank had gotten a thumbs-up from Victor to explore the idea and had done his homework. As a result, he asked me a lot of tough questions. Fortunately, he was satisfied with my answers, and the project began spooling upwards.

Back home, the process to choose an equity plan sponsor was gaining momentum. At the beginning of the CCAA process, we had retained the Seabury Group, a boutique investment banking–financial advisory operation that came highly recommended by a contact at TPG (Texas Pacific Group), arguably the most savvy airline investors around. Ernst & Young functioned as monitor for the court, sitting in on meetings involving all participants and reporting back to the court on progress. A deadline of September 16 was set for interested parties to submit their letters of intent, with a shortlist to be announced by the Air Canada board on September 26. The finalists would be invited to submit and negotiate their binding investment agreements starting the next day, and the chosen investor group would be named on November 7. On the basis of presentations made to the restructuring committee, the original twelve candidates were narrowed to two finalists: Li's Trinity Time Investments, represented by Frank Sixt; and Cerberus Capital Management, a New York–based asset management firm. Onex and TPG definitely had the inside track, but their valuations were hundreds of millions of dollars below the other two. They also insisted that we would have to reduce labour costs by hundreds of millions of dollars beyond the $1.1 billion we were aiming for.

Cerberus managed about US$14 billion of unleveraged capital scattered among more than forty companies in North America, Europe, and Asia. In Canada, Cerberus held a controlling interest in Teleglobe Canada, and the money it was prepared to invest in Air Canada would be made directly from Cerberus assets and would not be subject to financing conditions. One of the key advisers to Cerberus was Brian Mulroney, and there was speculation that he would become our chairman.

Mulroney was no stranger to either Air Canada or me. It was his government, after all, that had taken the initiative to privatize Air Canada. Over the years after I assumed the CEO position, he made a point of phoning from time to time with words of encouragement. He first contacted me after September 11, 2001, when I was asking for government

211

support comparable to the level our major U.S. competitors were receiving from their government and was being pilloried for it.

I had never met or even spoken to the man before, so when my secretary, Pauline, told me that Brian Mulroney was on the line and wanted to speak to me, I figured it was a friend calling me as a prank.

It was with some surprise, then, that I picked up the phone to hear Brian's deep, distinctive voice: "I just wanted to tell you, Robert, that I think you are doing the right things against impossible odds, with no support from your government. Hang tough and stay focused, and you'll come out the other side. I'm telling you this from experience. People will knock anyone who takes new and different positions, but at the end of it you will know and they will know that you were right— even if they never admit it." It was good to hear that from someone who understood first-hand what I was going through. Brian Mulroney is a gracious, considerate man. Calling me out of the blue like that, someone he didn't even know, speaks volumes about him. I would have had no trouble working with him. In fact, I would have looked forward to it.

Aside from differences in their pitches, Cerberus and Trinity were a study in contrast when it came to attitudes and personality. The Trinity people were silky smooth—gracious and unhurried, soft-spoken and correct. Their offices, with a swimming pool and rock garden on the seventieth floor of a Hong Kong skyscraper, included the finest of furnishings and works of art, with spectacular views of the Peak and the Hong Kong harbour through massive picture windows.

Cerberus was at the other end of the spectrum. As many have pointed out, its name is that of the mythical three-headed dog that guarded the gate of Hades, and its corporate personality reflected at least some of its namesake's attitude. These were aggressive guys, driven by the need to Get the Deal Done and make money, and I suspect they considered the sort of nuances practised by Trinity as time-wasting distractions.

As dissimilar as they were, I liked and admired both groups in different ways. My experience in Asia and my capitalist–competitive nature gave me respect for Trinity's approach, while my appreciation for trench warfare drew me towards the Cerberus attitude. At one point, one of the Cerberus guys said to me, "Hey, we might not be the smartest guys in this round, you know," which struck me as amusing, since they were smart with a capital s. In the field of international high finance, they were prepared to apply whatever was needed to get the deal and get it done. Once they hit their target, their success at making money was phenomenal. You had to admire their brashness, and I did.

Brett Ingersoll, who led the Cerberus bid, had read a lot of the Canadian business press coverage of me and of Air Canada's situation, and he was worried that I might be as dreadful as I was painted. If I were as good at my job as others claimed, why was I putting up with all the criticism? "With so much vitriol in the Canadian media about you," Brett asked me at one point, "why do you want to stay on with this company? Why not chuck it and go on to something else, make some real money, and have some fun?"

"Because," I said, "what you read in the business press here in Canada is not always what's happening in the real world. The vast majority of our employees and Canadians generally want this company to succeed, and knowing that persuades me to stay on and battle away."

We broke for lunch soon after this, and I suggested heading for a little bistro I like on Green Avenue in Westmount. As we walked in, the first guy I saw was Dan O'Neill, CEO of Molson's, who waved and smiled and called a friendly greeting to me. Brett and I had a good lunch, and just as we emerged from the bistro a black convertible with the top down screeched to a stop in front of us. The driver, some fellow I had never met before, with an attractive blonde in the passenger seat, stood up in his car and waved before giving me the "thumbs up" sign and shouting, "Keep going, Robert, we're all behind you! It's gonna be okay!" Then he roared away. When we were settled in my car, a guy in a black Volkswagen pulled up alongside us and called over, "Hey, Robert, how're you doing?" That driver was Gordon Young, who now heads our reservations department. I waved, said, "Good to see you!" and drove away.

Brett, sitting in the seat beside me, seemed amazed. After being pilloried in the press, I was now treated like some good old home-town boy whom everybody roots for. The only thing missing was black-and-white photography and Jimmy Stewart. "Wow," Brett said. "People seem to like you!"

As we worked through the equity solicitation process, no aspect generated more interest than the potential for management participation. Clearly, for all these highly sophisticated potential investors, that was done to ensure that Air Canada's top management team was deeply aligned with their interests. Each investor group had examined the company's performance over recent years, had reviewed our management strategy, had discussed our capabilities with others in the industry, and had liked what it saw and heard. All the proposals included some degree of ownership for management, and more specifically Calin and me.

Both the Li and Cerberus proposals required Calin and me to stay on and run the company and to realize the goals set for it. They also included 1 per cent stakes for each of us, and this information ultimately made almost daily headlines. When GE Capital provided debtor-in-possession financing for Air Canada in April 2003, the contract also stipulated that Calin and I would remain on board for the same reasons that Cerberus and Trinity had cited. The arrangement was definitely not a reward for brokering the deal. It was a form of insurance that Calin and I would continue to manage the company in a manner that would prove beneficial for everyone involved.

Some Air Canada employees were upset by the potential gain that I stood to earn from this deal. I agree that would have represented big money if it had happened, although it's small-time compared with the CEO remuneration paid by other airlines the size of Air Canada. Some members of the business press reacted with indignation (or perhaps jealousy) at the news, but they got the story from me and no one else. I did not conceal or avoid revealing details of the arrangement. I refused to join the crowd of CEOs who make headlines for not disclosing the amount of money they make or stand to make. I said immediately, "Here is the deal, and here is what Calin and I stand to gain from both finalists, if we do our job well enough." I will never hide anything about my dealings with Air Canada. In the end we are all paid precisely what the marketplace says we are worth, and our worth is determined by the individual or the organization who buys our services. That's how the system works, and the day I am not worth the amount I am being paid is the day I am out of a job.

No single event during my years at Air Canada generated the media coverage of this proposed arrangement, representing a potential $20 million incentive for Calin and me to remain at Air Canada. Some commentators called it a "finder's fee," a bonus, or even a severance package, none of which was anywhere close to the truth. I'll defend their right to express an opinion, but I became annoyed when their comments to me were dramatically different from the ones expressed to the public.

Eric Reguly, a high-profile pundit in the *Globe and Mail Report On Business*, called soon after the retention offer was announced, congratulating me and looking for some background to an article he was preparing. During our discussion I explained that I would not hide any aspect of the deal, including the potential to receive a substantial reward like this one. "I'll take the hits all day long," I said, "because I refuse to be one of those CEOs whom guys like you rip apart when they don't disclose things."

Reguly thanked me for the interview and then, just before hanging up, said: "By the way, if I were you I wouldn't give up the twenty million."

In his column the next day Reguly blasted me, saying: "Robert, do the right thing—give back the twenty million dollars."

I immediately called and asked how he could write such a thing after stating that he would have taken the money himself. His only response was to say that he should have called and told me about his criticism before it appeared. I did not receive the twenty million and I have not spoken to Reguly since. I suspect the chance of either occurring in the future is about equal.

Unfortunately, far too many members of the media in Canada do this country a great disservice. For them, there is a seemingly never-ending desire to challenge winners, revel in defeat, and generally overhype the negative side of almost anything, regardless of relevance. Canadians deserve better. Ever since I've been in Canada, I've noticed that some journalists often cover business stories in a tabloid-like fashion. One day they're going after Bob Brown at Bombardier; what is anyone supposed to do if the aerospace industry collapses as a result of September 11? The next day, they go after Jean Monty for convergence. Hey, he was trying something different... anyone remember him cashing out of Nortel? Then they're on to Dan O'Neill for buying up a Brazilian beer company. Looks like a good market to me! The point is that these are world-class business leaders trying to honestly lead their company through conditions often well beyond their control. Yet they're pummelled. In the United States, the media generally pummel business leaders when they get their hands caught in the cookie jar, not whenever things get tough or they're trying something new and innovative.

For me, the ultimate illustration of some in the media going down this track of negativism came during the Salt Lake City Olympic Games, in 2002, when Team Canada lost the opening men's hockey game to Sweden. Wayne Gretzky, a great Canadian and indisputably the greatest hockey player who ever lived, chided the media. What did the media respond with? Headlines like "Wayne the Whiner." Wayne the Whiner? This guy was doing a great job of pumping his team up on their way to ultimately winning gold. When the team did win, did those writers apologize, or even make reference to their unfortunate comments? Of course not.

The media are seemingly above reproach. In the case of Air Canada, almost anything can make the news if it's negative. I could recite at length the unfair stories about our company, but one illustration of some journalists' lack of professionalism has been the selective use of "quotes" lifted directly from aviation chat sites on the Internet referred to as "industry sources." Over and over, several journalists cite these sources—although they don't have a clue who posted them, whether it was a 10-year-old in Regina, a former Air Canada employee fired for cause, or a WestJet executive. Such "reporting" is ridiculous and unprofessional.

Not everyone was negative about the deal with Cerebus and Trinity. After the details were announced, many businesspeople called to say, "Way to go!" and "You deserve it!" and "It's about time!" More than one told me that "not even $20 million made the crap you put up with worth it." I also received e-mails from numerous Air Canada employees who, far from being resentful about the agreement, expressed their approval because they wanted to see me continue in the CEO position and restore the company to strength. The irony about all the fuss was that I didn't even ask for the deal. The offers, including the management component, were the result of a competitive bidding process among astute investors.

As the battle came down to the wire, we agreed to visit the offices of Cerberus and Trinity and conduct final discussions, reporting on the meetings to the board before it made a final decision. In early November 2003, Calin and I caught a Friday morning flight to New York. As we stepped out of the limo from the airport, I glanced across Park Avenue at the U.S. headquarters of Deutsche Bank AG. Deutsche Bank had agreed to backstop a $450 million rights offering linked to the Li deal, so it was as familiar as anyone with our situation, and the bank's location sparked an idea.

We spent a few hours in the New York offices of Cerberus discussing various aspects of their offer. They made their pitch, which was a good one. They were so clearly genuinely interested in buying Air Canada. They viewed it as a true trophy and a business that was capable of growing internally through acquisition and of generating strong profitability. Here again, these were tough and fast personalities, and they intended to win. We shook hands and left to catch a cab for the airport and our flight home. But I made a stop first, and it was directly across the street at Deutsche Bank.

It had been over seven months since we sought CCAA protection, and I was totally focused on reviving the airline and fulfilling the goals we had set for it. We had two solid contenders for the financing needed to complete the restructuring process, but anything could still happen and I wanted a fallback plan. If, by some incredible quirk of fate, neither of our finalists chose to participate as planned—and after September 11, SARS, and the August 14 power outage I was growing accustomed to such quirks—what would be our alternative?

Now, as we left the Cerberus offices, one of the world's best investment banks was standing right in front of us. Why not strengthen our relationship, in case we needed it? We crossed the street, Calin located

Deutsche Bank's director of North American operations, we introduced ourselves to him, and we sat down to discuss alternatives.

The day after our meeting at Cerberus in New York, we hopped an overnight flight to Hong Kong, arriving Sunday morning. In Hong Kong I stayed in the Presidential Suite of the Lis' beautiful Harbour Plaza hotel. The suite was enormous and included a sauna, a grand piano, and an amazing view of Hong Kong and its harbour. Life would be good working with Li and his group.

Our session with Victor Li and Frank lasted the rest of the day, and on Monday morning we were on a plane back to Montreal. Thanks to the International Date Line, we arrived home Monday night. Things were moving that quickly.

The following day we reviewed the offers with the Board's restructuring committee. Both were strong, competitive offers. The Cerberus deal, however, suffered what the board considered a deficiency relative to the Li proposal, and it was one Cerberus could do nothing about. There was no easy solution to the legal restriction against people who were not Canadian citizens owning or controlling more than 25 per cent of the company's voting shares. Through its association with Brian Mulroney, Cerberus planned to comply with the rule one way or another. Its prospects for success regarding this issue were good, but it could not answer the foreign-ownership question with complete assurance, as Victor Li could. At this stage, even though these were clearly good, smart guys with an excellent offer, accepting their proposal would mean accepting some element of risk that things might fall through in Ottawa, and no one on the Air Canada side wanted to become engaged in an extended legal–political struggle, especially considering what a Ping-Pong ball Air Canada could become if it got immersed in political games in Ottawa.

The Trinity offer had no such barrier; Victor Li's Canadian citizenship simplified the arrangement immensely, reducing to zero the risk that Ottawa would step in with an objection that might derail the process. There were other aspects to consider as well. Trinity was tied into a network of holdings that included 30 per cent of the world's port capacity, substantial telecommunications assets, and extensive real estate. It also provided an unparalleled opportunity to open doors in

China, the world's fastest-growing marketplace for virtually everything, including air travel. The bottom line, though, was that it came down to two excellent offers. Since my compensation was inherent in the proposals, I told the board I would be happy to work with either party and then I abstained from the board vote. With the participation of our investment advisers, the board chose Trinity and announced its decision on November 8, 2003.

Creditors wanted to keep things moving, especially Japan's Mizuho bank, which was holding $100 million in unsecured debt. "In our view," Mizuho wrote in an e-mail to us, "the UCC [Unsecured Creditors Committee] should move quickly to endorse these [Trinity] transactions, removing unhelpful speculation, de-risking the restructuring, and locking in the value embedded in these proposals for unsecured creditors." A Mizuho representative attached a letter stating: "We [Mizuho] have reviewed the [Cerberus and Trinity] proposals and we completely support the Victor T.K. Li and Deutsche Bank AG transactions." The rest of his correspondence urged a quick wrap-up to what was considered a fait accompli.

I remained cautious, convinced that Cerberus was simply too hungry to roll over. "This is not over," I commented to our team and the board when both were finding it difficult to contain their euphoria. And it wasn't.

Trinity had built into the agreement the option to top its own offer if necessary, which became the infamous "Paragraph 9 Item 4" clause. The clause had not been inserted to give a losing bidder a chance to up the ante but was designed to protect Trinity against a latecomer, such as a bondholder or bank, demanding a revised deal. However, to its credit, Cerberus successfully argued before the Ontario Superior Court that clause 9.4 provided the opportunity to submit a revised offer, sweetening the pot for unsecured creditors. It was supported in its pitch by some creditors; among the most vocal was Mizuho, the same group that had urged swift implementation of the Trinity offer just weeks earlier. Cerberus, backed by Mizuho and others, demanded to argue the point with Justice J.M. Farley, who was overseeing our restructuring under CCAA. The three-headed dog was baring its teeth.

Justice Farley had assumed, as had others, that matters had been resolved and had left for his winter vacation in Florida. He was not pleased to be yanked north from the beaches and tennis courts to preside over something he believed had been settled almost a month earlier. Hearing the Cerberus arguments in his chambers on December 4, he dryly observed that Cerberus had a point and agreed that they could submit a new bid. As for the apparent change of heart by Mizuho and others, Justice Farley wrote:

> It appears that some stakeholders had their appetites whetted for what they perceived might turn out to be a "straight" (courthouse or otherwise) auction when word got out that Cerberus was interested in reopening the bidding. Given the understanding reached in Chambers on December 4, 2003 I do not see that it would be fruitful to get involved in any involved [sic] discussion of the whys and wherefors [sic] of possible Cerberus activity in this regard. Suffice it to say that Cerberus acknowledged today that it saw its way clear to exercise the opportunity contained in para. 9 of the Trinity agreement to solicit an Investment Proposal this week with a view to having that evaluated as a Superior Proposal by the independent Board of Air Canada.

After inserting Mizuho's written exhortation of November 12 to keep the process moving, Justice Farley added, "It would seem that Mizuho has done a complete and abrupt about face, apparently on the basis that it expects that the possible reopening of a bidding before the Trinity agreement was considered by the court would potentially achieve a betterment for the unsecured creditors…"

The rest of Justice Farley's comments expressed the hope that Cerberus would "put forward its absolute very best proposal before the end of this week," observed that "it is dangerous to have so many people attempting to grasp the steering wheel to drive the car," and concluded:

> As Mr. Griffin, attorney for the Monitor [i.e., Ernst & Young] observed, there is much merit in the adage of "a bird in the hand is worth two in the bush." Similarly, Aesop's dog had its mind clouded by its

perceiving that there was another bone (held by the dog in its mouth) that was up for grabs [recalling the fable of the greedy dog who dropped his bone in favour of the one in the reflection from the water, thus losing both]. No one here should have their vision so distorted.

When the Cerberus people made their "best and final" offer, which was in reality, very cleverly, three offers, they argued that Trinity could not raise *its* offer in response, saying that Cerberus had a right under clause 9.4 of Trinity's proposal and that Trinity had no similar right to top the Cerberus offer unless Cerberus retained the right to top *that* offer as well. What they wanted was an out-and-out bidding war, but we had already conducted a formal bidding process, and when news of this demand reached Justice Farley he laid down the law. The proposal selected by the board, he noted, would be the conclusion; there would be no more "final" bidding.

Trinity's subsequent offer sustained the $650 million for 31 per cent of the restructured airline but raised the potential amount that creditors could acquire from 56 per cent to 66 per cent. The board accepted this revised Trinity offer on December 22. Getting closure was just about the best Christmas gift I could hope for.

GOODBYE VICTOR,
HELLO BUZZ

THE YEAR 2004 seemed to hold so much promise for Air Canada
that I felt more energized than I had since becoming CEO. I still
regretted the need to restructure under the CCAA, but I accepted that
the process was necessary. Victor Li was offering not only the funding
needed to move us into the black but also the commitment to build Air
Canada into a successful global competitor. I looked forward to a new
Air Canada emerging from under the shadow of its Crown corporation
tradition. We would set new goals and achieve them. We would expand
our services and solidify our position. We would build expanded opportunities for our employees. We would prove the skeptics wrong. Air
Canada would again be cost competitive, and a legacy carrier could win
against the low-cost carriers.

Things began to unravel in February, though, with a directive from
Trinity to switch the Air Canada pension program from a defined-
benefit plan to a defined-contribution structure. Like most corporations whose roots extended back several decades, Air Canada offered a

defined-benefit pension program that provided employees with a retirement income based on a fixed formula. Defined-benefit plans are comforting to many employees because they are familiar and predictable. By applying a formula based on recent salary levels at retirement, years of employment, and age, employees can calculate the pension income due to them at retirement.

In the last few years, many defined-benefit programs have been replaced by defined-contribution plans, in which an employee and the employer place funds into a plan managed by the employee.

Defined-contribution plans provide advantages for both sides: the employer is relieved of long-term financial commitments that represent a potentially volatile future liability, and employees are assured of their retirement assets even if they are no longer working for the same corporation when they reach retirement age. The defined-contribution concept is a response to changes that have occurred in society over the years. In our parents' time, most people spent their working lives with one company exclusively and saw their pension income as a natural extension of the salary or wages earned over thirty or forty years. In recent years, employees have been more likely to change their jobs or careers. With a defined-benefit plan, they must give up their pension rights when they change employers. A defined-contribution plan enables them to retain these assets.

Not everyone is comfortable with a defined-contribution plan, especially those who are close to retirement and who have worked for many years at the same company. An agreement with Air Canada unions, as part of the comprehensive $1.1 billion in wage-cost reductions, in mid-2003 had stated that employee pension plans would not be altered. However, we now had an investor who we hadn't imagined being there a year earlier and who required a change to the pension plans as part of his long-term commitment to the company. To assuage Victor Li's concerns about future fiscal obligations, some changes would have to be made. The goal was to make the change with as little impact on the employees as possible.

Victor Li proposed a sixty-year formula: those employees whose age and years of service with Air Canada totalled sixty or more would retain the defined-benefit plan. As the heat mounted between Victor and the unions, and as I could see we were going nowhere and our $650 million investment by Trinity and $450 million from Deutsche Bank might be in the verge of evaporating, I tried to suggest the compromise of giving employees a choice between defined-benefit and defined-contribution plans. Trinity proposed paying a bonus of 10 per cent of their base to current employees who chose to switch from the defined-benefit to the defined-contribution plan. The bonus would be paid at the time of an initial public offering (IPO) of new Air Canada stock, provided the total amount did not exceed 10 per cent of the IPO.

I believed that this choice was fair to both sides. The unions were strongly opposed, but I knew many employees felt differently. We needed to find out precisely what they thought, so we set up a website where everyone at Air Canada could express their preferences before any changes were made. This single well-meaning gesture launched an avalanche of events that Calin Rovinescu correctly described as Kafkaesque.

The survey question was simple and specific: "Would you, as an Air Canada employee, like to have a choice between a defined-benefit pension fund and a defined-contribution fund?" The possible answers were yes, no, or a request for more information. Employees began responding immediately, with early responses in the thousands indicating that they overwhelmingly liked the idea of choosing the pension plan format for themselves or at a minimum wanted more information. The support was right across the board—pilots, flight attendants, machinists—everyone wanted a choice between the two types of plans.

But within a few days of launching the site, we were directed by the Canada Industrial Relations Board, at the insistence of the unions, to shut it down because it represented "an unfair labour practice." Not only that, but we were prevented from disclosing the results of the poll to anyone. Furthermore, unbelievably, the CIRB ordered us not to communicate directly with our employees on the subject of pensions. Thanks to the CIRB, we could not even ask our employees what they wanted! How was it unfair for an employer to ask its employees about their preference, as well as to reveal the findings to the same people who had been invited to express their opinions?

It was not unfair, of course. But it was contrary to the ideological stance of the unions, who were opposed in principle to anything other than defined-benefits plans. It became clear that any move that would set a precedent on pension plan structures risked opening the door to negotiations with other companies in other industries that had been trying to adopt a defined-contribution plan. It also seemed to me that many of our union leaders, who tend to be senior, wanted to retain defined-benefit plans, while defined-contribution plans, which are portable, tended to be attractive to younger employees.

The pension question was a legitimate deal breaker, and when it became obvious that the unions were digging in their heels on this matter, I asked Ontario Superior Court Justice Warren Winkler, who had helped us reach our new labour contracts designed to reduce labour costs by $1.1 billion in the second quarter of 2003, if he was prepared to help resolve the situation. I felt Farley and Winkler and most observers were mis-reading the gravity of the situation and that we might lose Trinity. But the idea that Trinity was just posturing prevailed. As helpful as Winkler had been, though, he did not want to get in the middle of the union-Trinity tussle.

Things went back and forth and around and around before Jean Jallet of the International Association of Machinists and Aerospace Workers (IAM) approached Kevin Howlett, our vice-president of labour relations. The IAM represents almost twelve thousand Air Canada employees in technical operations, airport ground service, and finances and clerical personnel. "If I can get an understanding from the company," Jean told Kevin, "that the full option would be provided to our people as Robert Milton suggested, I would be prepared to sign up on behalf of the IAM."

Jallet had confirmed his members' support for the idea of choosing between the two plans, and his actions were a bold move to demonstrate leadership. In his announcement of this acceptance, Jallet stated that there would be no losers in the deal. "The restructuring process has been difficult for our members," he noted, "but throughout the process I have been committed to empowering the membership to make their own decisions, and that is what this agreement is about."

I saluted Jean for his courage and insight in taking this position, noting that I could not imagine a better outcome for our employees than having the freedom to choose the pension program best suited to their personal needs. Jean Jallet became a hero in my books and among his own members, who cheered when his offer was announced. But back in Toronto, the IAM's international leadership declared that he had overstepped his authority. Within a day of making the announcement, Jean Jallet and "all general chairpersons" were yanked from positions of authority in their own union and replaced by representatives from the national office.

The IAM claimed the action was justified "to ensure that the interests of the members of District 140 are protected, following the disclosure of the unauthorized secret negotiations between the suspended directing general chairman of District Lodge 140 and Air Canada management." How could the union "protect" members who had already approved their leader's decision?

Jean Jallet said the union had torpedoed a democratic vote. "I listened to my members," he explained. "They're the people I represent and these are their wishes. I have done exactly what they've asked me to do, to give them the right to make their own decisions." Unfortunately, he was made to pay with his position for representing his members.

During the pension debate I received many thoughtful messages from employees and retirees sharing their views. Of these, one of the most poignant said: "Robert, I worked for Air Canada for thirty years. I love the company, I loved my job, and now I am happily retired. During those thirty years I knew a lot of wonderful and amazing people who had talents well beyond their job requirements at Air Canada. Because those talented people were married to the Air Canada pension plan they could never leave and pursue their life's dreams. Choice is the right way to go."

I was struck by this message, and this notion of enabling employees to chase their life's dreams was a key reason I felt offering a choice to everyone was the right way to go.

The unions did not accept the subtext of the pension option, which, had they acted rationally, would have benefited their members. Victor Li wanted to address the pension plan because he intended to be part of

Air Canada for an extended period. Pledging $650 million of his own money, he was acting as a committed long-term investor, which was precisely what the company needed to succeed, expand, and provide security for its employees. If he were planning to step out of the picture in a year or two, he would not have cared at all about the pension plan. His interest in addressing it proved his commitment. No one on the union side acknowledged this point.

Although I disagree with many union goals and tactics, I understand the unions' role as representatives of employee concerns. In the adversarial give-and-take of tough negotiations, emotions can, and often do, run high. Both sides accept this eventuality and, once the deal is done, put it behind them and get down to work. I cannot accept, however, some of the abuse directed towards Victor Li and his representatives during the long round of discussions about the pension question. It was nothing less than shameful, with racist undertones that no one should tolerate or excuse. At one point, a union representative suggested that a Trinity negotiator "tell Victor Li to take his money and get on the next boat back to China." This and similar comments made me embarrassed for the employees the union guy represented. The employees themselves were embarrassed—I know, because they sent me e-mails expressing their mortification.

Sadly, this stuff was buried beneath union cries about a foreign billionaire trying to seize the pensions of hard-working Canadians, a massive distortion of the facts. No one entitled to a defined-benefit pension stood to lose a penny, in spite of the unions' assertion that Victor Li was seeking to make himself wealthy at the expense of hard-working Air Canada employees. Yet those were the claims that dominated the media coverage.

In private, the situation was quite different. Union representatives felt that Victor Li was the best solution to our financial situation, and they told me so. They recognized the same qualities in Victor that I did: he was a long-term investor, he had the resources to make things work, and he had proven that he could help make companies successful. The unions' hardball tactics did not impress their own members and offended Victor Li.

Between the insults and the misrepresentations appearing in the press, Victor's enthusiasm for the plan waned. He was, after all, committing $650 million of his personal capital, money that would flow into the company not from some third-party source but directly out of Victor's own pocket. Would he have benefited from the company's success? Of course he would have, as would every Air Canada employee. Clearly, the more strident union leaders missed the point that Air Canada and their members needed Victor Li far more than he needed Air Canada.

No progress was being made on the pension issue, and as time passed it became clear that there was little hope of achieving any. On March 31 I attended a meeting in London with Victor and his team of advisers, which included personnel from the investment house Goldman Sachs. I was accompanied by Calin Rovinescu, Paul Brotto, Rob Peterson, and Montie Brewer. Victor was as relaxed as I had seen him, but he was clearly growing frustrated with the attitude of the unions. We reviewed our business plan and plotted the company's financial progress through the first quarter of 2004. Things looked good. Our revenue was on target and we had cut expenses through new leasing and debt arrangements, although we had yet to fully meet our labour cost targets.

Victor, who believes in motivating and rewarding individual employees for their efforts, made it clear that he was not prepared to deal forever with the inflexible unions, and given their intransigence, the outlook was not promising. Returning to Montreal, I reported my misgivings to the board, which, like the judge and his key advisers, did not totally believe that Victor Li would pull out, just as the unions did not believe it. But I was not surprised to receive a telephone call from Victor Li and Frank Sixt at my home the next evening.

Unless there was a major change in the unions' position, Victor and Frank informed me, Trinity would withdraw its proposal. It was not, on the surface, a complete walkaway from the deal—in legal language it released Trinity from its exclusivity covenant—but I knew it was over for Air Canada with Victor. Most clearly, it was no bluff, as some claimed. Victor Li had other investments to consider, and he wanted to pursue them rather than continue to deal with the insulting attitudes of some union leaders. I wish he had not acted in such an abrupt fashion, going "cold turkey" as it were, by completely withdrawing, because I knew he would lose the support of the Air Canada board and the judge and destabilize the entire situation. That is precisely what happened.

As soon as word of Trinity's pullout spread, I began receiving telephone calls from union leaders and their attorneys asking how we could re-engage Victor. Some offered to travel to Hong Kong and meet him personally. This strategy wouldn't have worked because the unions wanted negotiations with no preconditions, and Victor Li wanted no discussions unless the long-term pension obligations were settled first. Nothing would have been achieved.

Ironically, the day Victor Li announced his withdrawal from the picture marked the first anniversary of our decision to seek CCAA protection. We had accomplished a good deal of institutional change in that time, but after all the crises we had endured and the decisions we had reached over that period, we were almost back to square one in securing new long-term investors. The entire experience was like an extended carnival ride: merry-go-rounds that took us right back to where we had begun and roller-coasters that elevated our emotions only to plunge them back to earth without warning.

OVER THE YEARS since 1999, when I persuaded Calin Rovinescu to join Air Canada, we had created an exceptional working relationship; there are few people whose abilities and perception I admire more than Calin's. His insight into matters such as how to realize the value inherent in Aeroplan and Air Canada Technical Services helped change the structure of the company in one three-year period more than it had changed in the previous sixty years. His contribution in the last year alone had been enormous; he led the way in restructuring $4 billion in debt and renegotiating 350 aircraft leases, obtained necessary wage concessions, arranged the deal with GE Capital, developed the contacts at Deutsche Bank, and spearheaded the move to bring Victor Li into the picture as the potential primary investor.

Applying my father's three measures for a successful businessperson—smart, fast, and tough—Calin is all three. They may appear to be basic characteristics, but through my years in the business world I have been amazed by how few top people in both government and business bring all three to the table. In fact, not many can deliver two out of the three characteristics, which makes Calin even more impressive.

During some of the more acrimonious exchanges with the unions, I noticed Calin growing more and more uncomfortable. Like everyone else, he wanted to start building Air Canada into the successful enterprise we both knew it could become. In fact, several weeks before Victor Li's announcement that he would withdraw his financing offer, Calin informed me that, should our arrangement with Trinity fail, he would seek a new position outside the company. So it was no surprise to me when Calin entered my office in early April to announce that he would be leaving to pursue new opportunities—and he had several to choose from. Many people were saying we would have to trash everything we had achieved in the past twelve months and tackle the entire restructuring process from the beginning. This was too much for Calin. "Life is too short," he said, and he didn't have to say anything else. I was at that moment on my way into a board meeting, where I announced Calin's decision, which was accepted with regret by the board members. In his resignation letter, Calin described the process as akin to playing "full-contact multidimensional chess in a fishbowl," and he was exactly right.

He also pointed out that his departure could open the door for new attitudes and tactics in replacing Victor Li and Trinity as our primary investor. Calin had been closely associated with the Trinity bid. I agreed with him on that score; sometimes a fresh face can help both sides become more flexible. But his departure was still, in my opinion, an immeasurable price to pay.

I persuaded Calin to remain as an adviser to ensure an orderly transition—you don't fill the shoes of a Calin Rovinescu overnight—and he agreed. I assigned Paul Brotto responsibility for day-to-day restructuring, wished Calin well, and settled down to find a replacement for Trinity as the airline's funding source.

While many in the media were declaring the imminent death of Air Canada, we began negotiations with Deutsche Bank (DB). That premonition I had had months earlier that we might need DB in a new, bigger, or different way was coming true. We re-commenced our dialogue with

Julian Nichols, a capable young banker with DB in London. As an active participant in Victor Li's financing package, DB was familiar with our achievements and our goals; in fact, bank officials had expressed an appetite for a bigger deal than the $450 million portion they would have received through Trinity's plan. Using the same basic contractual language already in place, we were able to kick-start the entire negotiating process by eliminating the reference to Victor Li and Trinity, and we raised DB's commitment to $850 million.

The new DB rights offering deal was designed with a view that we would attempt to raise a further $250 million from a new equity participant. Doing so would return us to an equity raise of $1.1 billion, the largest one I'm aware of in the passenger airline industry's history, and $400 million more than we had set out to raise when we first started the equity-raising process.

It turns out this additional $250 million raise was readily achievable, and in the final analysis we had two interested parties. Once again Cerberus was there, and because of the superiority of its offer and commitment to keep us on track for a September 30 emergence from CCAA, it was selected. I cannot overstate my respect and admiration for the tenacity, focus, and dedication with which Brett Ingersoll and the Cerberus team pursued this investment.

Some have questioned why the pension situation, which had proved such a problem in the negotiations with Trinity, was not even on the table with DB. The reason is simple: although DB may retain some ownership of Air Canada, for them this is essentially a transaction for which they will make a considerable sum. They do not have the same long-term focus as Victor, who was concerned about pensions because he expected to be actively involved in the company ten or twenty years down the road. When your investment horizon is only a year or two, such concerns are irrelevant. And so with Trinity's departure and DB's increasing role, the pension problem went away—at least for the foreseeable future.

DB set a goal of realizing $200 million of the originally targeted (but not achieved) $1.1 billion in annual labour cost reductions before committing its support, and our negotiating teams were sent back to work with the unions to find these savings. DB suggested a deadline of midnight on Saturday, May 15, 2004. This time, the unions were more amenable to the process. The IAM proved to be methodical and rational about the negotiations, as did the pilots' union. CUPE, representing the flight attendants, managed to spin everyone's wheels until the last minute.

Even then, CUPE leaders attempted to re-jig the deal until they were dragged into Judge Farley's chambers, where they were reminded that they had signed an agreement and were expected to live up to it. This incident highlighted one of the more satisfying aspects of the CCAA process, the one that required the court to oversee negotiations with labour. Throughout the process the court demanded acceptable levels of behaviour, but those who witnessed the process for the first time— the court-appointed monitor, lawyers, and investor representatives— were shocked at the behaviour of the union leaders.

The leverage of airline unions is near-absolute, leading to one-sided agreements that are the basis for many of the crises facing the legacy airlines. In essence, airlines like Air Canada are operating with deregu-lated revenues and pre-deregulation labour relationships, a recipe for financial disaster unless they are by some means injected with a dose of reality.

The CAW, under Buzz Hargrove, stated quite simply that it would not participate, and Buzz instructed his team to pull out of the process, claiming he knew of various investors prepared to step in if we were unable to reach the $200 million cost savings target. This was excep-tional brinksmanship, even for Hargrove, who has made a career of talking tough in front of a microphone but showing a more reasonable face during private negotiations.

Hargrove was playing it close to the line. The original Saturday mid-night deadline had come and gone, and the other unions had agreed to concessions. If Hargrove single-handedly managed to drive the airline into liquidation and toss everyone out of work, he would not have many friends left in organized labour. Meanwhile, DB was becoming impatient, as was GE Capital, and warnings began to circulate that both might step out of the picture.

For several days in mid-May, Buzz lived up to his title of the Human Microphone, bestowed on him by the media, by making public declarations at every moment. He claimed, for example, that the company was asking $10,000 in wage cuts from employees who earned between $35,000 and $49,000 annually. This was nonsense and Hargrove knew it. We could achieve the savings target in many ways that avoided direct salary reductions of that magnitude from current employees. He also stated that DB and GE Capital were bluffing and that the federal government would never permit Air Canada to collapse. Both funding sources were serious about their impatience, as even Buzz must have known. In the background, Buzz was calling every contact he had in Ottawa in an attempt to get the government to open its chequebook. Any hope that Ottawa would bail out the company was futile. With a federal election weeks away and the Liberals being attacked for outrageous spending, a rescue by Ottawa would be a fatal mistake if Paul Martin was to have any hope of retaining his position as prime minister.

The stories grew even wilder when Hargrove began tossing out names of potential investors, including Gerald Greenwald, former chairman of United Airlines and now head of Greenbriar Investment Group; Gerry Schwartz and Onex; the Ontario Teachers' Federation Pension Board; and Texas Pacific Group. According to Hargrove, the last three would all be cobbled together in some sort of partnership that only he appeared to know about, since all three denied any interest in replacing DB. On Wednesday, May 16, I described all of Hargrove's claims about other saviours waiting in the wings as fantasies, and the talks broke off.

Ontario Superior Court Justice Warren Winkler, who was supervising the company's restructuring from a labour standpoint, instructed Buzz and me to meet with him at the Toronto Hilton in a last-ditch effort to resolve things (and setting off newspaper headlines announcing "Hargrove and Milton at the Hilton"). Paul Brotto and I flew down the next morning for our session with Buzz. It may have been high drama to some people, but Buzz and I already knew each other well. For all his bluster, Hargrove is a practical and serious guy who knows how to get things done.

As soon as I saw Buzz in the Toronto Hilton, I was more confident we would have a deal. During the previous two weeks, whenever Buzz appeared on TV, he had worn golf shirts and casual slacks. On this day, however, he sported a nice suit, tie, and starched shirt. I figured either he wanted to appear respectable in front of Justice Winkler or he wanted to look good for the TV cameras when the deal was done. I hoped for, and assumed, the latter.

My initial statement to Buzz, in the small conference room on the top floor of the hotel, was to stress the seriousness of our situation. I pointed out that he and I, in the presence of Justice Winkler, could agree on any number between zero and $45 million in annual cuts, the $45 million representing the CAW's share of the $200 million cost reduction demanded by DB. "But if we don't reach $45 million in credible savings," I said, "I'll lose the other unions and it's over." I questioned the other funding sources Buzz had been boasting about, all of whom had denied any serious interest in providing cash. Drawing on the old TV game show *Let's Make a Deal,* I said, "Buzz, we looked behind curtain number one and we insulted them," meaning Victor Li and Trinity. "Now we're dealing with the people behind curtain number two [DB]. I do not believe there is or will be a curtain number three to look behind."

"Let's be clear," Buzz said in reply. "I don't want to look for a curtain number three. I just want to get this deal done." The tone was set and the markers were down. We needed to get a deal, and it had to be $45 million. I thanked him, and we got down to work.

And so we began a long, productive session of exploring how we could cut $45 million from our agreement with the CAW, working with mutual respect for each other's interests. We even managed to inject a bit of levity from time to time. On returning to the room after a break, I brought in a box of Krispy Kreme doughnuts someone had picked up for us just as Justice Winkler said, "Man, is anybody going to serve us lunch?"

"Here I am," I said, and set the doughnuts in front of everybody. Then I turned to Buzz and said, "Whatever you do, Buzz, don't tell CUPE about this or they'll file a grievance against me for serving food!"

Buzz had a good laugh over that, and we resumed working our way through both the contracts and the doughnuts.

Things picked up as the day progressed. We both negotiated fairly, cutting to the chase when we saw an opportunity for an agreement with no posturing or mucking around. At the end of the day, we had it—a deal both of us could live with.

It was now time to meet the media. I suggested that Buzz be the first to go downstairs to the lobby level, announce that we had a deal, and explain the details to the media. I wanted to focus on describing where Air Canada was going now that everything was finally in place. Also, appearing in a joint press conference with Buzz would not, in my view, be fair to the other union leaders, who had managed to reach an agreement on schedule. Buzz agreed, we shook hands, and off he went in the direction of the elevators. His suit was buttoned, his tie was fastened, and his hair was as neat as when he arrived that morning.

When I caught him being interviewed on TV from the lobby barely ten minutes later, I almost fell down laughing. Now his tie was pulled askew, his collar was unbuttoned, and his hair was dishevelled; it looked as though he had been in a wrestling match with me all day. It was classic Buzz Hargrove, making it appear that he had survived the fight of his life instead of spending the day sipping coffee, munching doughnuts, and negotiating in a calm and forthright manner. Image is indeed everything, as much for labour negotiators as for corporations. During the interview Buzz said some complimentary things about me, actually praising me for my sensitivity and sincerity where the employees were concerned. The feeling was mutual.

Buzz always knows exactly what he is doing, and I respect him for that. Unlike other union leaders I have encountered, he knows what he wants for his members, knows how to negotiate towards that goal, and knows when to stop talking and start working to obtain a satisfactory result. More important, he knows how to conclude a deal.

Through those crisis days of mid-May 2004, the press was filled with speculation that Air Canada would receive a government bailout. We never raised the question or even hinted at it. My position was that Air Canada needed to fix itself. I believed it, the board of directors believed it, and my hat is off to Buzz Hargrove, who ultimately believed it as well. In all my years at Air Canada, the only time I ever formally asked for financial assistance from Ottawa was after September 11, 2001, which was purely an issue of establishing a level playing field between us and our U.S. competitors. Yet many commentators expressed outrage that Ottawa might feed us cash, even while we sought an exclusively private-sector solution to our problem. The entire subject was a straw man erected by some members of the media as a target they could knock down, probably with great delight. Its news value may have been measurable, but its authenticity was zero.

THE FUTURE,
BEFORE IT
WAS INTERRUPTED

A s I WRITE this, Air Canada is moving towards the close of the CCAA process. The air travel industry in this country continues to be harnessed by excessive fees and taxes payable to the federal government, but, on the plus side, we are beginning to repair the damage that resulted from having to reduce labour, aircraft leasing, and supplier costs. It was tough slogging for a while, but Air Canada now operates with the low-cost structure the unions agreed to at Zip and the low-fare structure of our Tango brand.

Over 60 per cent of our domestic sales are now made on the Internet, about three times the proportion of Internet sales of other legacy airlines. We are poised to achieve substantial international growth and are also preparing to take delivery of the first of our 105 new 70- to 100-seat regional jets. We have eliminated $8 billion of debt from our balance sheet, giving us the best balance sheet and making us the most financially stable of all the legacy airlines operating in North America.

No other airline of our size and capability is in the same enviable position. Other such airlines don't have that kind of Internet penetration, which generates real-time restriction-free sales. They don't have the opportunity for unfettered global expansion, including access to the United States, the world's largest passenger airline market. They don't have a fleet of up-to-date regional jets, which will lower our operating expenses dramatically. And they don't have our stature as a nation's airline.

We are also operating out of the new Pearson International terminal at Toronto. Expensive? Yes. But it's an improved entry and exit point for visitors and eventually it will be an attractive place to change planes.

Our strategy includes substantial growth on transborder and international routes, although such plans have a way of growing more complex and exasperating than they should, as our non-stop service to Delhi has shown.

We wanted to launch the Toronto/Delhi flights in late 2003, tracing a route over Russia. The Russians had been extorting exorbitant fees from international airlines crossing their territory for years, and many airlines took circuitous routes to avoid paying the fees. If you didn't have a grandfathered deal with Russia for overflights, the Russians demanded as much as they could get.

Knowing Russia's tough negotiating stance on such issues, we advised Ottawa of our intentions and asked the government to obtain an agreement from Russia that would be fair to both sides. Reciprocity should have been automatic, but by the fall of 2003 no deal had been signed.

We finally persuaded Ottawa to send Russia a letter saying that unless we negotiated reciprocal overflight arrangements within forty-eight hours, no Russian commercial aircraft would be permitted to overfly Canada on its way to U.S. destinations. But Ottawa wanted to wait to send the letter until after an upcoming meeting between both countries' leaders.

In October 2003, Jean Chrétien and Russian president Vladimir Putin met during talks in Thailand, and as promised Chrétien raised the matter. Putin knew nothing about the subject. It just wasn't an issue on his screen, and it became even less of an issue after Chrétien stated that there would be no retaliation from Canada and that he would appreciate it if Putin would look into the matter—hardly the way to apply pressure.

So all we had was an agreement to discuss the matter. I dispatched Yves Dufresne, our chief air negotiator, to Paris, where he was to meet with Aeroflot representatives. The Russians launched the discussion by announcing they wanted $9 million per flight in overflight fees from a flight that, on a good day, might generate $400,000 in revenue. They justified their position by claiming our Toronto/Delhi service would have a negative effect on their Moscow/Delhi routes. That's the way the Russians have worked since they've discovered capitalism: start with outrageous demands, come up with a rationale, and negotiate down from there.

Thanks to Alex Himelfarb and Rob Fonberg (at the time the deputy secretary to Cabinet Operations), the government finally sent a letter to the Russians demanding that either Aeroflot agree to reciprocal conditions with us or it would no longer be permitted to fly over Canadian air space. This time the Russians figured Canada meant business, but they still did nothing. As a result, Aeroflot's flights between Moscow and Seattle, San Francisco, Los Angeles, and New York were routed around Canada, causing delays and enormous increases in their fuel costs. The west coast flights were forced to fly north and up around Alaska. Eventually they agreed to lift all restrictions for thirty days while negotiating an agreement.

We were feeling pretty good about this concession and began a second round of negotiations with Aeroflot to get an accord in place. Soon we had a draft agreement permitting Aeroflot to fly over Canada without being charged fees and permitting us to overfly Russia on the same basis. There was the usual handshaking and, I suspect, a vodka toast or two. Then, just before the deal was signed, Russia's deputy minister for transport burst into the room and announced that Russia was demanding "unlimited fifth freedom rights," giving Aeroflot the right to fly from Canada to anywhere in the world. This would have turned Aeroflot, for all practical purposes, into a Canadian international airline, a totally unacceptable concession. When the deputy minister indicated he was serious about this cockamamie idea, the Canadian representatives stood up and left.

The tactic worked. The federal government dug in its heels for a change, and for a few weeks we took an extra hour or two to fly Toronto/Delhi/Toronto without crossing Russian air space, and Aeroflot wasted up to nine hours, including refuelling delays, flying around Canada on its way to the United States. The arrangement was costing the Russians much more than it was costing us. Eventually, saner heads prevailed in Russia. They suggested that a fully reciprocal agreement might be the best choice after all. Today both countries are free to overfly the other's territory without paying a fee.

After this victory over the Russians, I enjoyed getting feedback from Ottawa politicians about how they had stood up for us and won. Clearly they liked the taste of victory, and I wish they would stand in and fight for not only Air Canada but Canada more often. Reciprocal treatment works.

ANOTHER BATTLE is being fought with our competitor WestJet. I admire the WestJet people for building their carrier into a serious competitor within ten years. They didn't break any new ground, and airline start-ups are not as difficult these days as people outside the industry believe, as shown by the proliferation of profitable low-cost carriers the world over. But no one can deny their success.

My problem is not with what Clive Beddoe and his people have achieved, but with the ways they have achieved it, one of them involving the illegal use of confidential Air Canada data.

In early 2004, Steve Smith and Montie Brewer alerted me to some strange goings-on at WestJet. We had known for some time that the company seemed especially knowledgable about our passenger loads on specific flights. This kind of competitive information is sought in every industry. Imagine if you knew exactly how much of its inventory your competitor has sold for the next year—precise figures, in real time. That kind of information would be invaluable in helping you set your production schedule, determine pricing levels, and develop marketing plans. You could undercut the competition and dominate its market sectors with no research or development risk.

Passenger load information is valuable to airlines, which try to access it—legally—by assigning someone now and then to count the number of passengers leaving a competitor's flight upon arrival at its destination. The results are conducted on a hit-or-miss basis and are inaccurate at best. Airlines also buy what is called MIDT (Marketing Information Data Tape), information generated as a result of travel agency sales, which, again, give an accurate picture of the market.

Steve and Montie had been forwarded copies of e-mails distributed by a WestJet founder and vice-president, Mark Hill, detailing Air Canada passenger loads with uncanny accuracy. The e-mails boasted that, for example, "Air Canada had only forty-seven passengers on their flight x out of city y yesterday." When we checked our records, we might discover that only forty-four passengers had been on board because there were three no-shows, yet the figure had been correct— forty-seven seats had been booked. What was going on here?

Obviously WestJet was quoting booked loads, which is confidential information. Was WestJet accessing our corporate computer data and using it to establish its schedules, pricing, and marketing strategy? Our relations with WestJet were as frosty as ever, but we never suspected the other guys of corporate espionage.

One day Steve received a telephone call from a WestJet employee who had quite a tale to tell. A day or so earlier, the employee had visited WestJet's marketing department and commented on how valuable it would be to know Jetsgo's passenger loads. The marketing person laughed and said, "Forget about Jetsgo. Look at this." With a couple of keystrokes on his computer, he apparently brought up our flight schedule for the day and was able to display every seat sold on every Air Canada flight. Twice daily for at least ten months WestJet had down- loaded reservations records for thousands of Air Canada flights, com- piling all the details they needed to adjust their schedules and pricing in direct competition with our own.

Although twice-daily access may not sound dramatic, it was not the number of times WestJet entered our site that was most damaging but the number of files accessed each time. Our records revealed that West-Jet made over 243,000 hits, or about eight hundred per day, during this period. Using real-time 100 per cent accurate information on our flight loads, WestJet personnel could create "booking curves," allowing them to plan and rearrange their capacity, determine fare levels, and target our most profitable flights.

In at least one documented instance, WestJet personnel used this confidential data to consistently affect our prices out of Abbotsford, B.C. When we withdrew from that market, they hiked the fares by a reported 300 per cent; the entire strategy was made possible by the confidential data obtained from our website.

Although I don't know if they used the information for this purpose, one possible consequence that I find is potentially most troubling was their ability to behave in an anti-consumer and anti-competition fashion. Although the Abbotsford example is insightful, consider the following picture: WestJet and Air Canada have two similarly sized aircraft travelling from city A to city B at 9:00 AM two weeks from today. Obviously WestJet knows how many unsold seats it has—let's say fifty—but in this picture, it also knows exactly how many Air Canada has unsold—let's say ten. What would, or could, you do having this information? How about dramatically lowering prices to wildly stimulate demand? Air Canada would naturally match, and then you could watch as Air Canada's ten seats sold one by one until they were all gone. Assuming WestJet also sold ten seats in the same time period, it would still have forty seats left to sell. Now, with perfect, real-time, information, what could you do? Dramatically raise prices! The result: dramatically lower revenues for Air Canada, as passengers who book at the last minute are normally the highest yielding, and much higher revenues for WestJet.

In court documents filed on our behalf, we charged that WestJet was able to open the site thanks to the actions of Jeffrey Lafond, a former Canadian Airlines employee. Lafond had been given four years of employee pass privileges, part of our normal severance arrangements, when he left Air Canada. Using an honour system, we made it easy for qualifying employees to check the availability of seats for their use on employee passes by providing access to our load data through the employee website. It's a system built on trust, offered by most major airlines around the world. In light of this experience with WestJet we now restrict information on this website to an evaluation of the employee's chances of obtaining a pass, describing them as Poor, Medium, or Good, according to the passenger load.

When Lafond joined WestJet, he provided his Air Canada employee ID and private PIN to Mark Hill at Hill's request. WestJet claimed innocence, but in early testimony at discovery proceedings Lafond and WestJet appeared to shoot each other in the foot. WestJet's initial defence was to claim it had done nothing wrong by pulling information from our employee website because the data contained in it was public information, ignoring the fact that you needed both a personal Air Canada employee number and a private PIN to gain access. In cross-examination conducted during the discovery stage of the suit, however, Lafond testified that within an hour of providing WestJet with the access information, he asked for and received indemnification from WestJet protecting him from potential legal action that we might take against Lafond for his actions; this indemnification was personally signed by Mark Hill. Hill has since resigned as a direct result of our claims. Lafond also admitted, under oath, that WestJet had granted him full financial support in the event of a lawsuit.

The issue was clear to us: on one hand WestJet claimed Lafond had done nothing illegal by providing access to confidential information, and on the other hand the airline granted him protection against legal proceedings that might result from it.

We charge that this was an institutionalized program directed by top-level executives, a claim given new credence by Clive Beddoe's offer to resign when news of our lawsuit broke. I cannot imagine anyone in Beddoe's position offering to resign if he were innocent. The matter is before the courts as I write this. We are seeking hundreds of millions of dollars in damages as well as the revelation of certain management tactics employed at WestJet. If nothing else, our actions will correct any impression that Beddoe and his WestJet people are always the good guys wearing white hats. As an editor of one of the airline industry's leading publications said to me at one point regarding derogatory comments Beddoe made about Air Canada: "He needs to be more careful about how he treats people on the way up, because he'll be seeing the same ones on the way down."

Since losing access to our computer reservations system, WestJet has experienced decelerating traffic, revenue, and profitability. At the same time, ours have been improving, as seemingly have Jetsgo's. Jetsgo has added an interesting new dimension to the industry's composition. After the failure of Canada 3000, WestJet had the low-cost carrier field essentially to itself, growing its network methodically and at will. Jetsgo has really thrown a wrench into the works for WestJet, though.

When Jetsgo established a hub at Pearson, WestJet was thrown off its game plan and on short notice all but shut down its Hamilton operation, mothballing a new, multimillion-dollar hangar there and shifting to the higher-cost environment of Pearson. Not only was WestJet reacting to Jetsgo, an even lower-cost operation than it was, but it was now moving into the heart of our traditional stronghold: Toronto.

As our Executive Vice President—Commercial, Montie Brewer, has said: "Why did WestJet move its operation to Toronto? For the same reason bank robbers rob banks. Because that's where the money is!"

Despite WestJet's condemnation of high-cost hub operations, the company was now getting into the same game itself. Over the last two years, WestJet has shifted wildly from its origins, and more important, the Southwest model, one that for a long time it sought to emulate. In the last year, WestJet's deviations from the Southwest model, the only sustainably proven one, have included:

1. Flying into expensive hub airports
2. Getting into the frequent flier and affinity card program games
3. Selling food on board
4. Introducing live TV
5. Expanding into international/transborder markets

It will be interesting to watch WestJet in the coming years, as it has essentially run out of room to grow in the domestic market with its large 737s and is now starting routes into key U.S. airports like Los

Angeles and New York's LaGuardia. Competing against the U.S. gorillas will be a whole new game for it.

As for Jetsgo, who knows? Thus far, the company has proven resilient, and I tip my hat to it. Jetsgo timed its start-up perfectly, got old MD-80s at the depths of the market, made its pilots pay for their jobs, and produced a rock-bottom cost structure. The company out-manoeuvred WestJet at Pearson and has grown remarkably quickly on limited capital. I can't believe it is profitable, but Michel LeBlanc, president and CEO of Jetsgo, is proving himself once again to be a gritty entrepreneur who knows the business, and we'll just have to see what the future brings for the company. The key to Jetsgo's future will be its capitalization and just how good it is.

I AM NOT having as much fun as when I was vice-president of marketing or COO. For me the fun really ended when I arrived at the realization that profitability could no longer be achieved simply by designing the best schedules for the best networks, using the right aircraft. Labour costs had simply grown too much in relation to those at the low-cost carriers and a correction was sorely needed. But I am still here, running one of the largest and most respected airlines in the world. Some assume I remain because I'm stubborn, which may be true to an extent. Others believe I am here strictly for the money, which is not true at all. I'm here because I believe in this company and its people, and because I am optimistic about its future. I am by nature positive, but in this case my feelings are rooted in facts that few people outside the industry seem to understand and appreciate.

Incredibly, I am now the longest-serving CEO of a North American airline, the most senior in service on the Star Alliance board and probably on the IATA board as well. I look forward to moving on to a more enjoyable and slower-paced, lower-pressure job, but at this stage I'm obsessed with seeing Air Canada successfully through CCAA and toward the successful redefined future I know it has.

I want everyone at Air Canada to enjoy careers that are satisfying, rewarding, and as stable as they can be in this industry. I also want the company to remain competitive over the long haul, instead of lurching

245

from one cost-based crisis to another, and for some people these two messages may seem difficult to connect. I have no desire, for example, to see employees' salaries reduced or their shifts altered or their work styles negatively affected. These changes do not help me do my job, and I know that they are not welcomed by employees either. Some of the key decisions in running this company, especially those relating to income and work shifts, are the most difficult and painful to make, and I accept that I have to be prepared to make those decisions and take the heat for it.

Essentially, my assignment has been to fix a great carrier that is part of a broken industry. I smile whenever I reflect on the fact that Air Canada has been leading the change in this industry and that others have been following us in our efforts to deal with challenges that every airline of our size and scope faces or will face. So much of our work involves structural change and dealing with banks and government that sometimes weeks will go by when I'm not dealing directly with decisions about aircraft beyond commenting on a dirty plane or questioning why a flight was delayed. Some innovations are still being made, however, and watching them succeed at Air Canada before being copied by airlines around the world is one of the gratifying aspects of what I do. The new ideas range from significant structural modifications, such as multibranding, to lesser moves, such as repainting one of our aircraft in retro colours as part of the company's sixtieth anniversary celebration. This move proved so successful that Delta, Mexicana, Avianca, American, and other airlines did the same thing to commemorate their corporate anniversaries. It didn't revolutionize the industry, but it proved to the world that fresh thinking was coming out of Air Canada.

One of the great benefits that came my way with the job was an invitation to join Conquistadores del Cielo, a small group of people engaged at the highest levels of the aviation and aerospace industry. The members have included aviation legends such as Donald Douglas and Juan Trippe and currently include the CEOs of most great companies in these arenas. Limited to only about 150 members, Conquistadores del Cielo is an absolute who's who of aviation. We get together

246

twice a year for shooting competitions, horseback riding, and a variety of boys' games, in between some great camaraderie.

I recall one meeting in the Bahamas when I was a guest and not yet a full-fledged member, walking through an outdoor barbecue setting with Mike Graff, another invited guest and president of Bombardier Aerospace at the time. Mike is about my age, perhaps a few years older, and as we meandered towards a table he was grumbling about all the old, boring guys who made up the Conquistadores del Cielo. I disagreed with him—I found the members, especially the most senior ones, fascinating, so many with the most amazing stories to tell. And they were such good, polite, and gracious gentlemen.

Mike was still complaining about spending a weekend with a bunch of old bores when we reached a table where a couple of members wearing baseball caps were already seated. The waiter asked if we would like to sit with them. Not even Mike could say no, of course, and risk offending them. As I sat down one of the guys looked up, reached out a hand, and said, "Hi, I'm Neil Armstrong." Whenever I see Mike, I ask if he has met any more old guys with boring tales to tell, like being the first man to walk on the moon.

I learned very early in the business that although operating an airline has its unique aspects, it remains in one dimension exactly like any other industry: good people make good companies, and despite differences that may arise between us, Air Canada employees continue to impress me with their talents, abilities, and compassion.

It was Air Canada employees who launched Dreams Take Flight to provide trips of a lifetime for physically, mentally, and socially challenged children. The company supplies the aircraft to carry the kids to Disneyland or Disney World, but it's the employees themselves who volunteer their time and effort to earn money from bake sales, dances, car washes, T-shirt sales, corporate sponsors, or anyone who can help make a dream come true for these kids.

Since the program was launched in 1989, nearly four thousand children with special needs have enjoyed the magic of Disney thanks to the efforts of Air Canada employee volunteers. In the early days, records were kept in a shoebox; today teams in eight Canadian cities and two

U.S. cities support the program and make it work. Their efforts involve much more than booking and filling flights; these youngsters have medical problems and physical or emotional challenges that require doctors to be on board the flight and available throughout the day. Making Dreams Take Flight such a success over the fifteen years of its operation has required a tremendous amount of hard work and commitment by the Air Canada volunteers who assist in looking after the health and physical needs of the children.

I am always proud of Air Canada employees, but never more than when I see them operating a Dreams Take Flight trip. On a trip from Calgary to Disneyland, I travelled with an amazing little guy named Ryan, who suffers from MS. Our chat during the flight and the smile that shone from his face as the two of us covered what seemed like every inch of the Magic Kingdom were worth all of the challenges that have come with running Canada's national airline.

Anyone who has the ability to assist others while being able to fulfil personal obligations is morally obligated to use it. It's a simple measure of humanity. When I was vice-president of marketing I pushed the company to assist the Starlight Foundation, the group dedicated to making wishes come true for children suffering from serious illnesses. Fulfilling many of these wishes requires an airline ticket, and our support of the organization meant that people could connect with Air Canada to provide thousands of tickets to these kids and their parents each year.

We might not have a lot of cash to donate to charity, but we sure can provide a lot of free travel for children and their families in need; and we do.

Who cannot get satisfaction out of helping children? In 2003, I served as the chairman for the corporate fund-raising drive on behalf of Montreal Children's Hospital (I'm also on its board of directors). I was proud to note that it was the best year in the hospital's history for generating corporate donations but disappointed to realize that our success was not really a victory because the better we got at generating money to buy new hospital equipment, the more we relieved pressure on the government to do the job of providing adequate funding. I know I'm repeating myself, but government alone won't solve the health care crisis in

Canada, no matter how much money it keeps throwing at the problem. More money is needed, but only with a role for private enterprise working alongside the national health program will Canadians enjoy the quality of care that I know they want and that they have a right to expect.

Many corporate activities go unacknowledged. That's fine, but I'm proud enough of those at Air Canada, and of the spirit they represent, to add a couple here. During the summer and early fall of 2003, when the interior of British Columbia was hit with forest fires around Kelowna, the photos and stories of people returning to their homes and discovering only a heap of ashes were heartbreaking. We could not replace the homes or erase the pain of their loss, but it occurred to us that we could provide an opportunity for these families to escape their sorrows for a few days by visiting friends or relatives elsewhere. So we offered free return air fare anywhere in Canada to families in the Kelowna area who had lost their homes so that they could visit their loved ones or friends away from the devastation.

And when Kobe, Japan, was almost destroyed by an earthquake, we made excess cargo capacity on our Boeing 747 service available without charge to carry prefab buildings and shelters for the Japanese people. Japanese officials and citizens of Kobe wrote hundreds of letters of gratitude, but no one in Canada took note of this gesture. When an earthquake struck Nicaragua in July 2000, we sent a Boeing 747 loaded with supplies and volunteers to help rebuild the affected areas. It feels good to be able to offer such assistance to people in need, and although I refuse to hype doing some good deeds, I would feel even better if this kind of activity were recognized here in Canada.

Throughout this book, I have tried to illustrate the manner in which I deal with people, especially those employed at Air Canada. I have always been dedicated to this company's ultimate success and to the long-term benefit of its employees. To that end, I have made fair treatment of employees a top priority even when—especially when—I needed sacrifices from them.

I don't believe in glass ceilings or quotas or any standard of judgement beyond an individual's capability. Not only is operating a corporation on any other basis wrong, it's stupid: how can you justify appointing anyone except the best-qualified person to a position in your company? Why would you penalize your organization by rejecting the best candidate based on gender, race, or sexual orientation?

I have sometimes been described as being "too Japanese," for I believe that, if possible, a company should look after its employees and their families for life. I also believe that people with the ability and dedication to do a good job on behalf of their employer deserve a rewarding work environment and an opportunity to advance. I have been told that I was the first Air Canada CEO to appoint an openly gay person to executive management, and I will not tolerate the exclusion of anyone, male or female, gay or heterosexual, from promotion based on anything except proven qualifications.

Whenever I have to authorize a reduction in the Air Canada employment list, it makes me almost physically ill, because I feel personal responsibility for it. Layoffs are, in one respect or another, a reflection of failed management, and anyone who authorizes layoffs should admit this. I become annoyed whenever the share price of a company rises at news of a massive layoff. It does not take brilliant management to cut employment rosters, and it does not help a company's prospects when a large portion of its assets—that is, its experienced and motivated employees—are no longer available to the firm. It may be absolutely necessary at times, but it is also tragic.

Unfortunately, I cannot do this job without making some strategic decisions that affect our employees in negative ways, specifically in relation to their salaries and wages. There is no other way to run a company in the face of radically altered competition in the post–September 11 world. Legacy airlines such as Air Canada cannot survive in the face of competitors who pay half the wages we do, or less. Nor can we maintain the cycle of endless wage and salary increases that marked much of the 1990s. Since assuming the CEO position, I have managed to retain control over these increases, keeping them within the consumer price index for the first time in years, and without a single disruptive strike. This performance, though far better than that of our North American peers, was obviously still not enough.

I have zero patience with anyone who harasses either me or the people around me. I will not tolerate bullying, unfairness, or discrimination, and I refuse to accept any excuse for that kind of behaviour. I can laugh at a good joke, but I cannot find humour in stories that mock disabled people, are racist, or deal with disasters. I abide by the corny old Golden Rule, with the added commandment of "Live and let live."

In spite of this, I have been painted in a different hue by some media coverage. One business magazine even chose me as one of Canada's ten toughest bosses. I like to think that the toughness related to my ability to make difficult decisions as CEO, but it undoubtedly added to an already high volume of criticism I receive in this job, something I have learned to handle over the years.

In some cases, the most brutal criticism has been the result of my insistence on maintaining a reasonable standard of behaviour. I will always stand behind my employees when they are doing their job, even if I have to take the flak for doing it, as I did a few years ago.

One of our customers, employed by a major Canadian manufacturer, achieved Super Elite status on the basis of all the miles he flew performing his business duties. When he left his employer to launch his own company, the customer flew with us less often and bought cheaper tickets. As a result, he risked losing his Super Elite status, which meant he no longer qualified for perks such as concierge service and check-ins at the Super Elite desk. That's when he started buying flowers and perfume for female employees and befriended two women on our staff, including one in sales and another at check-in. He was also using some unacceptable ticketing tricks, all to work the system and keep the benefits he had grown accustomed to but no longer qualified for.

When our Aeroplan staff discovered what he was up to, they correctly cancelled his Super Elite card. He appealed first to Rupert Duchesne, who told him that rules were rules and refused to restore his Super Elite privileges. That's when the customer appealed to me. I gave him the same answer as Rupert had, because the Aeroplan people were right and he was wrong.

251

He didn't give up. The appeals kept coming, we kept saying no, and the customer grew more and more belligerent. Things became so outrageous that, unbeknownst to me, our lawyers cut off his Aeroplan account. When that happened, the customer went complaining to the press as a beleaguered victim of our unfair policy and my nasty personality, I suppose. The press ate it up, and the next day there was a picture of this forlorn-looking victim of corporate wrath set in the middle of a newspaper article taking up almost a full page. The crux of the article was "Don't complain to Robert Milton because you might get your Aeroplan account cut off." The real story, of course, was that this guy had been caught abusing the system, and I was supporting the decisions of those who had caught him. But it was never told in that fashion, and for months after the article appeared I received letters from Aeroplan members who had legitimate questions or concerns begging me not to cut off their Aeroplan account just because they were raising an issue or two.

Sometimes my notoriety resulted in more amusing and heartwarming situations, like the time I took my family to New York. We were picked up at the airport and I had a short conversation with someone from the ground transportation company. When I finished chatting with him Lizanne asked me, "Do you know that man?" From the back of the limousine, Emily said in a tiny voice, "Everybody knows my daddy."

The "how" of handling unfair criticism is easy. I reduce my profile, do my job as best I can, and take immense comfort in the support of my family, especially my children, who never fail to delight and surprise me with their personalities.

The "why" is a little more complex. I do not stay on the job because of the money. If my motives were strictly mercenary I could have left in response to several offers over the years, such as the one that arose in late 2002, when I was asked to participate in the start-up of a new airline in the United States.

The deal would have guaranteed me US$20 million, and it was so tempting that I told the board I planned to pursue it. The timing was good; unlike the rest of the industry, still shaken by the events of September 11, we were profitable again, which would permit me to depart on a high note. I didn't really want to leave Air Canada, but launching a new airline would be exciting and stimulating.

Accepting the offer meant relocating to Connecticut, and while I was in Japan on business Lizanne and my mother drove down from Montreal with the kids to check out houses there. Upon returning from Japan I met the family in Connecticut, inspected some great homes, and drove back with them to Montreal. In my absence, the board had on its own initiative prepared and approved an incentive package for me to remain at Air Canada, consisting of a five-year contract worth a guaranteed $28 million. Now I was really torn. Did I stay at Air Canada, where I felt at home, or jump into the adventure of a start-up airline?

I chose to stay, primarily in response to the board's expression of confidence in me, and left shortly afterwards on a Christmas vacation. I returned in January to a totally changed situation. Our bookings, which had been strong and growing just a few weeks earlier, were weak and shrinking in response to concerns about Iraq, and I sensed a malaise spreading throughout the international airline industry.

Clearly, we were drifting towards a crisis mode, and I informed the board that everyone in the company would have to agree to pay cuts in order to make us profitable again. In those circumstances I told them that I would stay but that I could not accept the $28 million package, including $3 million that was due immediately.

And so we remained in Montreal. Only when I agreed to stay at Air Canada did my mother reveal that Lizanne had cried all the way from Montreal to Connecticut during that journey to search for a new home, on the assumption that I would be joining the start-up venture. Lizanne simply did not want to leave Montreal and all the roots we had put down there. It's a cliché, but true; some things really are more important than money.

A year later, as the media and unions bashed me for taking $20 million (though I had received nothing), I felt a deep "sticks and stones may break my bones" sort of satisfaction for having taken a big financial hit, although I did not speak of it publicly, to stand with our employees, who I knew would soon also have to take such a hit.

LIZANNE AND I have grown to love Montreal, in spite of the winters. It is a unique and constantly exciting city, with rewards for us and our children that are unavailable anywhere else in North America. Emily and Nicholas are increasingly bilingual, and we have made many friends whose company we enjoy.

It will take a great opportunity to get Lizanne to consider leaving. One such opportunity arose during the CCAA process. One of the world's largest shipping companies, based in London, offered me the CEO position. The pay and benefits were tremendous. This time Lizanne was willing to give up Montreal, but now I couldn't. I couldn't desert Air Canada during the middle of the CCAA process. I had to see Air Canada successfully out of CCAA—then, who knows?

SO WHERE do we go from here?

One facet of our business that I trust will improve is our relations with the federal government. Paul Martin has caught the proverbial hot potato—or perhaps stink bomb is a more appropriate term—left from a decade of abuse and arrogance by the federal Liberals who governed this country. Having absorbed details of Paxport (the mishandled plan to redevelop Terminal 2 at Pearson International Airport), the gun registry fiasco, Shawinigate, the sponsorship mess, and various other scandals, including over a decade of indecision about the Sea King helicopter replacements, Canadians have finally seen what much of the Chrétien government was: a bunch of bullies who wasted money on things like a privacy commissioner who blasted Air Canada before he himself went down in flames. Abusive and unencumbered by strong parliamentary opposition, the Liberals had the country by the throat, and I hope Canadians can now see what we were trying to deal with over all those years.

Instead of a spirit of co-operation, whenever dealings with some people in the federal government arose, we encountered contempt for business and our business in particular. The federal Liberals operated with absolute disdain and an unbelievable degree of arrogance for anyone except their own. Once they lost control, the skeletons started coming out of the closets, and today they are there for all to see.

During a discussion with Prime Minister Paul Martin a few months before he moved into Sussex Drive, he indicated that I could expect a constructive dialogue between his government and Air Canada. "You won't always like what we come up with," Martin said, "but I understand that this airline is important to Canada and its economy."

"You know what?" I responded. "I can honestly tell you that I have never heard a high-level elected member of government in this country say that before, either in public or to me privately." He seemed astonished, but it is true. Thus far Martin has absolutely lived up to his commitment to constructive dialogue and support where appropriate.

THE REALITIES of post–September 11 for the airlines must be dealt with in a hard-nosed fashion. Those who fail to take the necessary measures will not survive. Some of those measures are as basic as eliminating free meal service on short flights and offering quality meals at fair prices for those who choose to purchase them. Others, however, are more wide-ranging and more profound. They include sizing new aircraft more closely to the needs of routes and extending the use of features such as electronic ticketing to reduce labour costs. These and other steps are being implemented widely, and they will have a significant effect on the bottom line.

We need to exploit our international advantage, because it represents our best profit potential for future growth and success. Even when we held 80 per cent of the domestic market, the revenues from those flights represented only about a third of our mainline receipts. It doesn't take a chartered accountant to calculate that our long-term financial health depends on flying people into and out of Canada rather than between Canadian airports.

The idea of depending on international service as a prime source of income is not new in the airline industry. Consider Emirates and Singapore Airlines, two operations that consistently score well with travellers around the world and are always among the most profitable airlines. Their domestic service is non-existent, so they rely on international flights for their survival. The international market, plus transborder flights to the United States, are both the lifeblood and the future of Air Canada. We have 300 million people to serve in North America, another 300 million in Europe, and billions in Asia. When any of these people wish to travel to North America, we want to be the top airline on their list. Once they arrive in Canada, we'll provide seamless connections within the country and across the border to the United States with schedules closely tied to international inbound and outbound flights. I see a successful Air Canada of the future recognized as one of the half-dozen best international airlines, connecting regions everywhere in the world, with domestic service still representing an important but smaller share of total revenue.

We must also expand our cross-border market presence, which has always brought us substantial income. The United States is not only the world's largest international market but also one of the world's most competitive markets. When I arrived at Air Canada in 1992, we had about one third of the Canada–U.S. traffic, which was considered respectable. Our share has since doubled; about 60 per cent of all passengers flying across the U.S. border travel with Air Canada.

As part of our plan to meet changing market realities, we evaluated both the Brazilian Embraer 190 and the Canadian Bombardier CRJ-705 in late 2003. The CRJ-705 is essentially a seventy-four-seat configuration in a fuselage designed for ninety passengers, so it provides exceptional roominess for passengers. It is also a light aircraft, making it more economical to fly, and since we have been using Bombardier equipment for many years now, there is a commonality between it and older models that makes its operation simpler for pilots and mechanics.

The Embraer product, however, is an exceedingly comfortable aircraft in its ninety-three-seat layout. I expect that it will also be a game-changer.

While people marvel at WestJet's low cost per available seat mile relative to ours, they are ignoring a few key issues. The first is our revenue premium, which is currently greater than their cost advantage. I do not believe our revenue advantage will be sustainable at its present level, but with smaller jets and less pressure to fill the aircraft (they have to fill 136 seats on a 737-700 and we'll only have to fill 93 on a regional jet), their ability to generate sufficient revenues, even with their lower cost structure, will be challenged. In the meantime, with lower trip costs, our regional jets will be able to offer more frequencies on more routes, bypassing hubs like Toronto. Eventually WestJet may get its own small jets. That's fine, but I like our prospects with the combination of the CRJs plus our newly agreed upon labour contracts.

Thanks to the restructuring process and a radically reduced cost base, we will be able to explore expansion into new international markets. We can do it. We will do it.

THIRTY YEARS AGO I was a kid leaning against the rusty wire fence encircling Singapore's airport, watching the 707s, DC-8s, and other aircraft passing through. I knew the equipment, I knew the airlines, and I knew the destinations. I learned how airlines operated complex schedules and how the schedules meshed, making the journey comfortable for the passengers, ensuring that cargo reached its destination on time, and enabling the airline to earn a profit for shareholders.

Much has changed since then, and much has not. Aircraft are safer, quieter, more comfortable, and more efficient. Passengers still hate delays, flight attendants still must remember to smile, and weather still is an uncontrollable factor, whether the plane is soaring across the Atlantic in June or waiting to be de-iced on a February morning in Edmonton.

I suppose if I needed assurance that I had achieved my boyhood dream, it came during a June 2004 IATA Board of Governors meeting in Singapore, when it was announced that I had been selected to serve as the organization's chairman for 2005–2006, an honour made all the more gratifying when I was told the vote had been unanimous. The achievement was as satisfying to me as a speech to the entire IATA assembly I had given two years earlier as a member of the IATA board, when I glanced down and noticed Fred Smith, the founder of FedEx, listening to what I was saying. Fred invented an entire industry based on aviation service. He saw an opportunity and made things happen in a remarkable way, and the college kid who had written papers on Fred's management philosophy was now talking about another aspect of aviation, and there was Fred Smith absorbing his words.

Every single night during my years at Air Canada, the kid from Singapore has gone to bed thinking about the thousands of people in dozens of aluminum vessels bearing the Air Canada logo and soaring high above oceans, mountains, and cities. He wants them to arrive at their destinations on time. He wants their flight to be comfortable, whether they are travelling on vacation, on business, or on a mission to comfort themselves or others. But more than anything else, he wants those aircraft to fly safely. And despite the difficult challenges and other attractive opportunities, he doesn't want to be doing anything else.

257

NOTES

Numbers at left refer to pages where the quotations or discussions occur.

CHAPTER 2

15   "I learned more about people..." "PrimeTimers," *thecitizennews.com*, September 1, 1999.

20   re Air Canada's privatization agreement: Calin Rovinescu, "The Critical Path to Airline Privatization," paper delivered to IATA in October 1998.

21   re Air Canada being subject to the Official Languages Act: "Air Canada," in Allan Tupper and G. Bruce Doern, eds., *Privatization, Public Policy and Public Corporations in Canada* (Ottawa: Institute for Research on Public Policy, 1988).

CHAPTER 4

43   "If you get your passengers to their destinations..." UTPB *News*, August 13, 2001.

CHAPTER 5

65   re the continuing meltdown at Canadian Airlines: *Financial Post*, June 30, 1999, pp. C1, C6.

68   re Benson "raising a white flag": *Financial Post*, June 30, 1999, pp. C1, C6.

68 re Benson's speech to shareholders in Calgary: *Globe and Mail*, June 30, 1999, pp. A1, A6.

69 re the Competition Bureau's investigation of Air Canada and Canadian Airlines: *Globe and Mail*, July 1, 1999, pp. A1, A5.

CHAPTER 6

71 re Collenette considering changing the foreign-ownership rules: *Globe and Mail*, August 16, 1999, pp. A1, A5.

71 re rise in the share prices of both airlines: *Financial Post*, August 18, 1999, p. D1.

72 "to provide the government with political cover…" *Globe and Mail*, August 16, 1999, p. A4.

74 re Collenette knowing of Schwartz's proposal before the suspension of the Competition Act: *Globe and Mail*, August 24, 1999, p. B1.

75 "the military would find it difficult…" *National Post*, September 13, 1999, p. A1.

76 "aware of Onex's interest…" *Globe and Mail*, September 9, 1999, p. B1.

80 re Onex press releases suggesting half the CAW members would be unemployed after the merger: *Canadian News Digest*, The Canadian Press, August 30, 1999.

80 re false accusation withdrawn by Hargrove: CBC, "The National," November 4, 1999.

82 "He [Schwartz] is crashing into…" *Airwise News*, September 11, 1999.

84 re Schwartz's purchase of Air Canada shares: *National Post*, September 9, 1999, p. C1.

85 re Canadian Airlines being obligated to pay an "escape fee" to AMR: September 24, 1999, p. B1.

85 re outlandish promises in Onex ads: *Globe and Mail*, October 9, 1999, p. A3.

chapter 7

87 re five-point rejection of the Onex proposal: *National Post*, September 22, 1999, pp. A1, C6.

88 re Air Canada's ten-year commitment to Star Alliance: *Globe and Mail*, October 20, 1999, pp. A1, A19, B6.

93 "listening carefully to what Canadians have told us…" *Globe and Mail*, October 20, 1999, pp. A1, A2, A19.

95 re Air Canada's offer to shareholders for up to 68.7 million common and non-voting shares: *Airwise News*, November 3, 1999.

97 "Naturally we will respect that decision…" "Judge Hands Air Canada Takeover Victory," *Airwise News*, November 6, 1999.

CHAPTER 8

103 "The notion that the government forced Air Canada to merge…" "Turbulent Times," *Canadian Business*, October 29, 2001, pp. 72–77.

CHAPTER 10

136 re Beddoes' statement that Air Canada was privatized with billions of dollars
     in taxpayers' money: John Langford and Ken Huffman, "Air Canada," in Allan
     Tupper and G. Bruce Doern, eds., *Privatization, Public Policy and Public
     Corporations in Canada* (Ottawa: Institute for Research on Public Policy, 1988).
136 re Beddoes' statement that Air Canada's hub system creates airport crowding:
     National Post, August 5, 2003.
138 re United's pilots signing the most expensive contract in airline history:
     ChronWatch/Wall Street Journal, October 21, 2002.

CHAPTER 11

149 re the effects of September 11 on airlines such as Swissair: Tom McFeat, CBC
     News Online, November 12, 2001.

CHAPTER 14

186 "Air Canada's attempt to deflect criticism…"
     www.travelpress.com/newsarchive/1999-01-January/99
189 re Turpen's development of San Francisco International airport: "Point-
     Counterpoint: Two Views on SFO's Runway Plan," *Palo Alto Daily News*,
     August 30, 2001.
191 re projected increases in fees at Pearson International airport: Giovanni
     Bisignani, letter to Lou Turpen, November 18, 2003.
191 "We believe Robert Milton…" *Globe and Mail*, October 22, 2003, p. B1.
192 "I think we really should…" *Globe and Mail*, October 25, 2003, p. B2.
193 "and now [Air Canada] faces higher landing charges…" *Globe and Mail Report
     On Business*, September 10, 2003, pp. B1, B6.
193 re the GTAA's promise to increase landing fees 25 per cent in 2004:
     Globe and Mail, October 22, 2003, p. A6.

CHAPTER 16

219 "We [Mizuho] have reviewed the [Cerberus and Trinity] proposals…" Quoted
     by Justice J.M. Farley, Ontario Superior Court of Justice, December 8, 2003,
     court file no. 03-CL-4932.
220 "It appears that some stakeholders had their appetites whetted…" Ibid.

CHAPTER 17

226 "I listened to my members…" Toronto Star, April 1, 2004, p. 1.

INDEX